So Wrong for So Long

So Wrong for So Long

How the Press, the Pundits—
and the President—
Failed on Iraq

GREG MITCHELL

EDITOR OF *EDITOR & PUBLISHER*

FOREWORD BY JOSEPH L. GALLOWAY
AUTHOR OF *We Were Soldiers Once . . . and Young*

PREFACE BY BRUCE SPRINGSTEEN

UNION SQUARE PRESS
An imprint of Sterling Publishing Co., Inc.

New York / London
www.sterlingpublishing.com

STERLING and the distinctive Sterling logo are registered trademarks of
Sterling Publishing Co., Inc.

Library of Congress Cataloging-in-Publication Data

Mitchell, Greg, 1947-
  So wrong for so long : how the press, the pundits—and the president—failed on Iraq / Greg Mitchell;
foreword by Joseph L. Galloway ; preface by Bruce Springsteen.
    p. cm.
  Includes bibliographical references and index.
  ISBN-13: 978-1-4027-5657-3
  ISBN-10: 1-4027-5657-7
  1. Iraq War, 2003—Press coverage—United States. 2. Iraq War, 2003—Mass media and the war. 3.
Iraq War, 2003—Journalism, Military. 4. Freedom of speech—United States. 5. United States—
Politics and government—2001- I. Title.

DS79.76.M5575 2008
956.7044'31--dc22

2007045258

10 9 8 7 6 5 4 3 2 1

Published by Sterling Publishing Co., Inc.
387 Park Avenue South, New York, NY 10016
© 2008 by Greg Mitchell
Foreword © 2008 by Joseph L. Galloway
Preface © 2008 by Bruce Springsteen
Significant portions of these articles have been previously published by *Editor & Publisher* a division of
Nielsen Business Media, Inc. © Printed with permission
The name "Editor & Publisher" and its accompanying logo, are exclusive trademarks of Nielsen Business
Media, Inc. All Rights Reserved
Distributed in Canada by Sterling Publishing
c/o Canadian Manda Group, 165 Dufferin Street
Toronto, Ontario, Canada M6K 3H6
Distributed in the United Kingdom by GMC Distribution Services
Castle Place, 166 High Street, Lewes, East Sussex, England BN7 1XU
Distributed in Australia by Capricorn Link (Australia) Pty. Ltd.
P.O. Box 704, Windsor, NSW 2756, Australia

Manufactured in the United States of America
All rights reserved

Sterling ISBN-13: 978-1-4027-5657-3
    ISBN-10: 1-4027-5657-7

For information about custom editions, special sales, premium and
corporate purchases, please contact Sterling Special Sales
Department at 800-805-5489 or specialsales@sterlingpublishing.com

In memory of John Bedway, proud veteran

We are inevitably the mouthpiece for whatever administration is in power.
—Karen DeYoung, reporter, *The Washington Post*, 2004

Let's review the rules. The president makes decisions, he's the decider. The press secretary announces those decisions, and you people of the press type those decisions down. Make, announce, type. Put them through a spellcheck and go home.
—Stephen Colbert, 2006

ACKNOWLEDGMENTS

I would like to thank staff members at Editor & Publisher, *especially Mark Fitzgerald, Shawn Moynihan, and Joe Strupp; my agent, Sarah Lazin; and the Nielsen Company for permission to reprint columns. At Union Square Press, a nod to my editor, Philip Turner, and to Hannah Reich for her fine detail work. I'm grateful for the contributions of Joe Galloway and Bruce Springsteen—here and well beyond this book. Special thanks to Barbara Bedway for column ideas, commentary, and the catching of errors and typos in the original pieces too numerous to count. Although in this book there is much criticism of the media's performance, I want to emphasize my deep respect for the many journalists who have spent months or years in the war zone (some of them draw raves in the columns that follow, some do not), often risking life and limb.*

—GM

CONTENTS

PREFACE

Telling the Truth from Lies

We live in a time when it's never been more difficult to tell the truth from lies and lies from the truth. As a result, it has never been more important to have a free press that presents the truth without fear or favor.

Unfortunately, while our press may still be free, it has not been fully informing "we the people." Greg Mitchell's *So Wrong for So Long* goes a long way toward correcting some of the misconceptions that the media haven't been ready to deal with and, just as importantly, the kinds of obstructions that have kept the media from fully doing their job.

The total effect of Greg's excellent book is to remind us all that we need to be more questioning, skeptical, and savvy than ever in assessing information that's presented to us. And we need to teach our children to do the same.

Bruce Springsteen
New Jersey
November 2007

FOREWORD

The First Casualty

In war, truth is too often the first casualty, and it is not just a president or a secretary of defense or assorted official spokesmen who do the killing. Our brothers and sisters in the media also participate in the execution. Greg Mitchell has taken that as his lesson in *So Wrong for So Long: How the Press, the Pundits—and the President—Failed on Iraq* and, in so doing, has done a service for future generations of reporters, and I believe, for readers of the news.

Looking back to that fall of 2002 when war drums were beating loudly, and the president and his closest advisors spoke with certainty—and deceit—about Saddam Hussein's possession of weapons of mass destruction and the danger he ostensibly posed to our country and our friends and allies, most in the media either swallowed it whole or timidly refused to do their jobs and question the official rationale for war.

The great gray lady, *The New York Times*, and the voice inside the Beltway, *The Washington Post*, put dozens of unquestioning reports on the Bush administration's claims about Saddam's quest for a nuclear weapon on their front pages. The few reports that even suggested that some experts were questioning those claims were buried deep inside, among the Viagra ads.

The *Times* front-paged reporter Judith Miller's breathless stories about Iraq's quest for WMD that came straight out of the mouths of a series of bogus Iraqi "defectors." After the invasion, the paper of record ignored for too long the fact that Ms. Miller virtually became the ex-officio commander of a U.S. task force charged with searching Iraq for proof of nuclear ambitions and possession of vast quantities of WMD.

Did the national outburst of patriotism and an epidemic of American flag decals and flag lapel pins on the expensive suits of television anchors frighten those who had long believed that their newspapers set the nation's agenda?

How could those agenda-setters and so many others in the media abandon their first duty to challenge and question the assertions of the politicians holding high office?

To his credit, Greg Mitchell was writing columns and putting out a pre-war cover article in *Editor & Publisher* that raised those and other important questions before the first American soldier ever planted a boot inside Iraq. Also doing critical reporting on the administration's claims were a few good people working in the Washington, D.C., bureau of Knight Ridder Newspapers: bureau chief John Walcott and reporters Jonathan Landay and Warren Strobel. I worked there with them and made my own contributions to some of the critical stories before the war began, and afterward. But it would be several years before the work of these Knight Ridder reporters was widely acknowledged.

During the years the war has dragged on, I made two reporting trips to Iraq—one in the fall of 2003, and again in 2005–2006. The soldiers and Marines I lived with and went on operations and convoys with were like the same fine young Americans I wrote about in earlier wars. In fact, many of their commanders, from colonels to four-star generals, were officers I had marched or ridden with when they were captains and majors earlier on. All were doing their best with a bad hand dealt them by their civilian overlords—too few troops to do the job assigned, struggling against faulty decisions by people like Ambassador L. Paul Bremer of the Coalition Provisional Authority (CPA) that only fueled the insurgency, and laboring under the micromanagement of Defense Secretary Donald H. Rumsfeld, whose ears were closed against any advice contrary to his own thinking.

I was an early and harsh critic of the administration's conduct of the war. In the interest of full disclosure, I must say that I had worked for a year in 2001–2002 as a special consultant to Gen. Colin Powell, then secretary of state, and had sources very close to the debates and infighting going on over the conduct of the war at the highest levels. It was clear that Vice President Dick Cheney and Secretary Rumsfeld were riding roughshod over anyone who urged caution and careful thought. By 2005 I was writing columns suggesting that Rumsfeld, and his deputies Paul Wolfowitz and Douglas Feith, should be fired for their mistakes, along with the then-Chairman of the Joint Chiefs, Air Force Gen. Richard Myers. None of this endeared me to either the White House or the Pentagon bosses.

Not until the 2007 perjury trial of Vice President Cheney's hatchet man, I. Lewis "Scooter" Libby, would the overly cozy relationship that too many Washington pundits and reporters maintained with Libby and George W. Bush's spinmeister Karl Rove be exposed to the open air.

Not until after Judy Miller went to jail for refusing to identify Libby as her source inside the administration, briefly becoming an unlikely heroine of the free press, would *The Times* sever its relationship with her and publish an apology of sorts for the groundless page one stories of hers they'd edited and published.

Those of us old enough to remember the Vietnam War, and to carry visible and invisible scars from our work there, felt uneasy about Iraq and the stated reasons for pre-emptively invading that country. Those feelings only grew stronger in the months after March and April of 2003 when the president and his men were doing premature victory laps around the press rooms at the White House and the Pentagon.

Mitchell lays it all out in this book. Read it and weep. If you are a consumer of the news, I urge that you reserve judgment when reading reports quoting the calculated rhetoric of government officials.

And, if you are a reporter, take a solemn vow not to believe everything you hear, and barely half of what you see.

Joseph L. Galloway
Bayside, Texas
October 2007

INTRODUCTION

If only this were merely a book of history. Sadly, the war in Iraq is still very much with us, which makes this a current affairs volume as well. More than anything, however, I hope it serves as a warning for the future. Next time, forget "Shoot first, ask questions later," and instead recall Machiavelli's warning: "Wars begin where you will, but they do not end where you please."

When I first proposed this collection, editors at several major publishing houses suggested that by the time the book came out, surely the conflict would be winding down and the U.S. would be out of Iraq. That was in 2004. Several thousand deaths and tens of thousands of injuries later (and that's just counting the American forces), we are still there, and unfortunately, I have produced a much longer, sadder, and angrier volume. This book explores how the media helped get us into Iraq and then for many years did not do enough to point the way out. Its aim, however, is not to cast blame, but rather to provide vital lessons so that this type of catastrophe will not happen again.

Perhaps, as Stephen Colbert, when he was still on *The Daily Show,* observed, it's all Saddam Hussein's fault—for not having those weapons of mass destruction. Surely, if we'd found them, public opinion about the U.S. invasion would have remained at favorable levels far longer. Yet the fact that we did not find WMD did not inspire much of the media to quickly look more deeply, and with more skepticism, at how we got into the war. Nor did it seem to shred the authority most commentators continued to grant the president, Pentagon officials, and others involved in planning and running the war. Not even the disgraceful propaganda campaigns surrounding the capture of Jessica Lynch and the killing of Pat Tillman accomplished that.

The press, in its daily reporting, became more dogged as years passed, but by then it was too late. Editorial pages and TV pundits, meanwhile, lagged far behind the public—and even behind some conservative Republicans in Congress—in crying "Enough!" Victory, or at least a decisive turning point, was always just around the next IED-blasted corner. In early 2007, TV commentators punted at the most crucial moment since the invasion of Iraq—and not a single major newspaper came out against Bush's "surge" until after it was announced.

As events unfolded in Iraq over many months, and then years, some of us old-timers—David Halberstam, to name another—who had lived through the Vietnam era knew that the longer we stayed, the longer we'd have to stay, to justify the invasion and all the killing and maiming that followed. At least this would be the mindset of those directing the war, editorial writers at *The Washington Post*, and various hosts and guests on cable news channels. If you see Vietnam turn up a fair amount in this book, it's not so much to look back as to look ahead.

Much of what journalists need to know about public officials can be summed up in two words: as the muckraker I. F. Stone once advised, "Governments lie." Early in my training as a reporter in the late 1960s—in journalism school and on a daily newspaper—I was taught to be skeptical of any statement by those in authority that just might be self-serving. (At the time, I only got a chance to put that into practice in interviewing the local mayor or housing department chief.) A few years later, the lies of President Nixon—on the war, on Watergate, on not being a crook—promoted a period of aggressive probing throughout the news business.

Sure, some in the media went overboard, trying to be the next Woodward or Bernstein; but better to be overly skeptical than overly credulous. We saw the result of the latter, three decades later, during the run-up to the Iraq adventure. Who can forget the days when simply questioning the evidence of WMD in Iraq made you appear weak-kneed or even "French"?

Thomas Ricks, the military reporter for *The Washington Post* (and author of a fine book about the war, titled *Fiasco*), spoke volumes when he explained his paper's failures in the run-up to the war by saying, "There was an attitude among editors: Look, we're going to war, why do we even worry about all the contrary stuff?" His colleague Karen DeYoung put it in even more appalling terms: "We are inevitably the mouthpiece for whatever administration is in power." Walter Isaacson, who headed CNN when the war began, later informed Bill Moyers that "big people in corporations were calling up" when the network showed civilian casualties, declaring, "You're being anti-American here." Bob Simon, the CBS correspondent, told Moyers that covering the marketing of the war was so "explosive" that he felt he should "keep it, in a way, almost light—if that doesn't seem ridiculous."

While most of the reporters in Iraq recovered from their early rah-rah "*we are taking Baghdad*" coverage to produce years of tough-minded and valuable work (to the extent that it was possible amid the horrid violence), their counterparts on the home front often fell down on the job. At times, it seemed that they, not their colleagues traveling with our armed forces in Iraq, were the "embedded" reporters operating under fear of censorship or sanctions for stepping out of line. Declarations from the White House or the military about "progress" in Iraq, or assertions that Iran or al-Qaeda were the true villains there, were reported widely, with contrasting evidence often buried.

Few journalists were brave enough to nakedly declare, at any of the many apt opportunities, that a scheme is not a vision (to borrow the Leonard Cohen lyric). When Chris Matthews, after the U.S. took Baghdad, declared on MSNBC that "We're all neo-cons now," he acted as if that "all" included the press and that this was somehow a good thing. Blindfolding our democracy rarely strengthens us on the battlefield. No lesson for the future could be more clear than the need to take with a huge grain of salt every statement by any official who just might be pushing a cause or covering his ass. Even an emperor—or a Colin Powell—sometimes wears no clothes.

Then there was the failure to visually reveal the true horror of what was transpiring in the war. It was bad enough that the Pentagon banned photos of returning coffins; but then TV producers and newspaper editors on their own chose to display few images of the carnage, sanitizing a bloody landscape. Some photographers complained, and Pim Van Hemmen, assistant managing editor for photography at *The Star-Ledger* in Newark, N.J., said in 2005, "We in the news business are not doing a very good job of showing our readers what has really happened over there."

As a column much later in this book makes clear, Stephen Colbert's routine at the White House Correspondents' Dinner in 2006 was celebrated or lamented for his pointed barbs at the president while Bush sat just a few feet away. What many may forget, however, is that his critique of the *press* was just as biting—and widely resented by many of the journalists in attendance. Some of the same guests had attended a similar dinner two years earlier and roared with laughter when the president aired a goofy video that showed him looking around the White House for those darn missing WMDs (as dozens of American kids were dying in Iraq that month).

One of Colbert's passages could serve as an epitaph for the early coverage of the war. Addressing the reporters in the hall, Colbert, in his faux rightwing blowhard persona, said, "Let's review the rules. Here's how it works. The president makes decisions, he's the decider. The press secretary announces those decisions, and you people of the press type those decisions down. Make, announce, type. Put them through a spell-check and go home. Get to know your family again. Make love to your wife. Write that novel you got kicking around in your head. You know, the one about the intrepid Washington reporter with the courage to stand up to the administration. You know—fiction."

By the time of Gen. David Petraeus's report in September 2007—giving a thumbs-up to Gen. David Petraeus's handling of the "surge"—media commentary had grown more critical. Still, *The Washington Post* editorial page and legions of pundits continued to back the war, despite their promises, months earlier, to withdraw support if "benchmarks" were not met. Glenn Greenwald, the popular Salon blogger, described the formula this way: "1) If X does not happen, there is no justification for staying; 2) X has not happened; 3) we must stay."

It's not as if we weren't warned. Looking back at the news reports and television punditry from the autumn of 2002, I'm struck by how confidently, even avidly, so many assumed that the U.S. would, indeed, attack Iraq. Exactly when was uncertain, although it was expected to be sooner rather than later. Some felt that there was reason enough to do it; others believed that Bush was crazy enough to do it. Either way, it seemed almost a fait accompli.

Of course, "almost" is the key word here. It was the media's job to test that "almost" to the hilt, and they failed—or refused—to do so. They would carry more stories about preparations for war than ones that probed the ostensible reasons for it. News organizations may not have savored an invasion, but clearly most of them did not do much to throw roadblocks in the way. By *The Washington Post*'s own count—after the damage was done—that newspaper had carried more than 140 stories on its front page focusing on arguments for the war while contrary information "got lost," as one *Post* staffer told Howard Kurtz.

If the aftermath of our attack has been a slow-motion train wreck, the run-up was a swaggering parade, with stops at nearly every street corner for applause. Just to review one month in 2002:

• September 8: *The New York Times* publishes its infamous front-page "aluminum" tubes story by Judith Miller and Michael Gordon. Vice President Cheney then cites the article on Sunday TV talk shows, saying, "We do know, with absolute certainty" that Saddam is attempting "to build a nuclear weapon." National security chief Condoleezza Rice comments, "We don't want the smoking gun to be a mushroom cloud."

• September 12: President Bush makes the case for war at the United Nations, highlighting Iraq's supposed nuclear push.

• September 16: Iraq accepts the unconditional return of U.N. inspectors.

• September 24: CIA director George Tenet briefs the Senate Foreign Relations Committee, citing what he claims are Iraq's attempts to get aluminum tubes and uranium from Niger as evidence of its advanced nuclear program.

• September 26: Condoleezza Rice charges that al-Qaeda operatives have found refuge in Baghdad, and she accuses Saddam of helping Osama bin Laden's followers to develop chemical weapons.

No wonder that, as early as October 7, 2002, *Editor & Publisher*, the magazine I edit (it has covered the newspaper industry since 1884), was opening one story with "As the United States prepares to invade Iraq . . ." Three days later, President Bush got the fateful resolution from Congress that enabled him to go to war any time he wanted. Few expected him to actually wait until the following March.

The day after the congressional vote, *The Washington Post* recorded that 126 House Democrats came out against the final resolution; but, as Walter Pincus, one of the few reporters at the paper who pushed for more skeptical coverage of WMD, later observed, "None was quoted giving a reason for his or her vote except for Rep. Joe Baca (Calif.), who said a military briefing had disclosed that

U.S. soldiers did not have adequate protection against biological weapons." Pincus noted that no other reason given to oppose the resolution offered by any others "was reported in the two *Post* stories about passage of the resolution that day."

Few editorials expressed alarm about the consequences of the vote, a kind of modern-day Gulf of Tonkin resolution produced by artful manipulation of intelligence. *The Washington Post* was typical in backing the decision by Congress to give Bush "broad authority to move against Iraq." The *Chicago Tribune* went so far as to praise "the willingness of Congress to place its faith in Bush." *The Wall Street Journal* praised Senate Democrats for backing the measure "at crunch time."

A month later, *E&P* warned, in a cover story, "People Get Ready: There's a War A-coming." The feature referred to it as "a likely U.S. invasion of Iraq." One veteran correspondent at *The Atlanta Journal-Constitution* said he looked forward to covering it. "It's what I do," he said. "It's covering the story, and it's still exciting." By that time, news organizations were sending reporters to England to undergo hazardous-duty training (including how to prepare for chemical and biological attacks).

On November 8, the U.N. Security Council unanimously approved Resolution 1441, imposing tough new arms inspections, and warned that Iraq would face "serious consequences" if it ignored them. Five days later, Iraq accepted the terms, and U.N. inspectors returned within days, after a four-year absence. Soon they conducted a surprise inspection at one of Saddam's Baghdad palaces, and found nothing suspicious.

Peace marches began in the fall, and in some cases the media didn't take them as seriously as they did reports of Iraqi WMD. Most glaringly, *The New York Times* carried only a short piece following a huge rally in Washington, D.C., on October 26, noting that the number of protesters amounted to fewer than organizers expected. The report was so at odds with reality that the paper had to run a rare "make-up" piece three days later, admitting that the mass turnout had actually "startled even organizers."

In an editorial published in the November 11 issue, *E&P* stated: "Simply put, newspapers must take steps now to ensure that the First Amendment is not the first casualty of war. The most important step is to sustain citizen involvement in all decisions about the prospect and conduct of an Iraqi war through fair news coverage and fearless opinion-page debate. Yes, the president has his congressional resolution, and at the end of last week he looked likely to get something similar from the United Nations. This White House, always uncomfortable under public scrutiny, would like to think that ends all discussion. Newspapers, whatever their position, must reinforce the principle that Americans deserve an informed voice whenever government considers sending their sons and daughters into harm's way. Finally, newspapers must prepare themselves to rebut with forcefulness and facts all the falsehoods that emerge in the confusion of war."

Three days later, in an online article, we quoted Helen Thomas, that voice in the wilderness still covering the White House, in a college speech denouncing Bush's "bullying drumbeat . . . I have never covered a president who actually wanted to go to war." Reporters in Knight Ridder's Washington office were among the few regularly raising tough questions about WMD. On December 7, Iraqi officials presented the U.N. a 12,000-page dossier on their government's weapons programs, old and new, proving, it said, that their country was "empty of weapons of mass destruction." This was met with widespread skepticism in London and Washington—and in the media—and on December 19 the U.S. accused the Iraqis of being in "material breach" of the U.N. resolution.

In early January 2003, a Knight Ridder/Princeton Research poll revealed that 44 percent of Americans thought "most" or "some" of the September 11, 2001, hijackers had come from Iraq. Only 17 percent of those polled offered the correct answer: None. Is it fair to say that the media had failed to give this little detail appropriate attention from the start? In the same sample, 41 percent said that Iraq already possessed nuclear weapons, which not even the Bush administration claimed. Despite being far off base in these utterly crucial areas, 66 percent of respondents claimed to have a "good understanding" of the arguments for and against going to war with Iraq.

Meanwhile, weapons inspectors, despite wide access, continued to find no evidence of WMD in Iraq. United Nations officials said they still needed a few more months to complete their mission.

Three weeks later, alarmed by this nearly mindless march to war, I assembled a special issue of *E&P*. The cover featured a photo of President Bush in an Army jacket, with troops behind him, under the blurb: "Unanswered Questions: In Grip of War Fever, Has the Press Missed the Mark on Bush and Iraq?" The answer then was clear, even if few in the media appeared troubled by it. Our editorial observed that "while news organizations so far have been remarkably effective lobbying a reluctant White House and Pentagon in advance for meaningful access to U.S. military operations in Iraq, the press has been almost entirely silent about its own wartime responsibilities. Considering its sordid history when reporting war, this lack of introspection is not reassuring. . . .

"War," we continued, "bewitchingly combines two fatal attractions for even the best reporters: an especially hysterical brand of pack journalism that substitutes groupthink for reason—and a cornucopia of dramatic stories that are too good to check and, anyway, may well be impossible to check. Add to these age-old temptations a passel of White House and Pentagon briefers pitching a white noise of fact-free sound bites, and it's a wonder any truth ever emerges from the battlefield. There may be some marginal improvement in journalists' working conditions this time around. But the one last preparation the press must make is to confront its own ongoing legacy of war reporting stained by the journalistic sins of omission and commission. Unless the press engages in that self-examination, it will be taking into combat an arrogance that may again sabotage the brave work of its best practitioners."

Contributing editor Jim Moscou—who had undergone that hazardous-duty training in England—observed in the same January 27, 2003, issue that reporters "not only will write from the front lines but arrive more ready for war than their predecessors. Maybe too ready. Preparation should neither taint journalistic skepticism nor, as disturbingly evident in recent months, spark what appears to be dangerous newsroom momentum and groupthink. 'When a news organization puts so much preparation into something, a lot of people have a lot at stake to see it happen,' a veteran reporter (who asked not to be named) at one of America's largest papers told me. With daily meetings at the highest levels, the expenses, the foreign assignments, 'the whole thing is just whipping people into a tizzy. People ultimately want to see it happen. We want to participate in it.'

"As the cream of America's newsrooms clamor to do push-ups, I wonder if the time would have been better spent asking questions. We'll probably get our war. And it may be the war we deserve. A young reporter for a Denver newspaper said to me that he thought war reporting was 'the highest calling' for a journalist. He's preparing for Iraq. He's a nice guy, enthusiastic about his job. But the comment gnawed at me. Weeks later, I realized he was dead wrong. The highest calling in journalism is not war reporting. It's finding the story that would help prevent a war. Along the road to Baghdad, we seem to have lost that idea."

Then there was this disturbing paradox: Many felt that we needed to go to war because Saddam had WMD; but if he did have them and we attacked his country, surely he would use them against us, inflicting massive (and particularly gruesome) casualties. Why would he make the weapons to use in a "worst-case" scenario and not deploy them when the absolute worst-case scenario arrived? So perhaps these hawks never *really* thought he had them and just used the possibility to promote—I would use the word "sell"—an overthrow. Paul Wolfowitz admitted in *Vanity Fair* that the alleged WMD threat was not the best reason to go to war, just the most exploitable.

This book reveals some of the consequences of the media failure to ask more questions, while accepting weak or misleading answers—and how the press, despite the heroic efforts of many reporters and photographers in the war zone, too often continued to miss the mark in the five years that have followed.

The more than seventy-five columns written for *E&P* and adapted for *So Wrong for So Long* are arranged chronologically. They follow most of the major twists and turns in White House strategy and media response (or lack of it), from the 2003 "run-up" to the 2007 "surge" and beyond. It's all here: Mission Accomplished, Abu Ghraib, the "Friedman Unit," Judith Miller as martyr and goat, suicidal soldiers and dead civilians, Rumsfeld and the armor we "went to war with," Pat Tillman, Valerie Plame, Jill Carroll, Jon Stewart, the cult of Petraeus. Serious stuff, but Neil Young and Bruce Springsteen also appear, as do Oprah and the Ghost of Baghdad Bob.

Will the lessons be heeded? Certainly, few of those who promoted the war based on false information have lost any standing in the media, even if they did lose respect from some in the audience. *The Washington Post*, for example, not only continued to carry columns by several regulars who had repeatedly misfired on the war—and mocked anti-war critics—but it even went out and hired Michael Gerson, President Bush's main speechwriter during the run-up to the invasion. William Kristol, one of the war's intellectual architects, kept his *Time* magazine column, contributed op-eds to the *Post*, and didn't seem to lose any face time on TV. The *Post*'s editorial page, meanwhile, remained hawkish on the war through thick and thin, often contrary to virtually everything emerging in the paper's own news pages.

Will Rogers once said that the first thing you do when you find yourself in a hole is quit digging. In regard to the Iraq catastrophe, the media not only helped create the hole, it did not do nearly enough to help America dig out.

New York City
October 2007

2003

JANUARY

The near-inevitability of a U.S. attack on Iraq did not seem to trouble most editorial writers or TV pundits as a final showdown approached in early 2003, even though United Nations weapons inspectors had failed to find any trace of WMD after nearly two months of intensive detective work. On January 24, a story penned by Judith Miller appeared in The New York Times *under the headline: "Defectors Bolster U.S. Case Against Iraq, Officials Say." An E&P survey of editorials concluded on January 26: "Despite rising doubts . . . there doesn't seem to be one U.S. newspaper among the top 50 dailies by circulation that is strongly 'anti-war.' The papers appear united in their desire for Saddam Hussein's disarmament, if not overthrow, and disagree only on the means, or at least the urgency." Not surprisingly,* The Wall Street Journal *led the formation of hawks. Under the headline "To Pyongyang via Baghdad," it argued on January 13 that only by swiftly ousting Hussein from power could we then confront North Korea. The Washington Post wrote of Hans Blix, the United Nations' chief WMD hunter, "He would like to head off U.S. military action at any cost, even though such action clearly has been justified by Iraq's failure to comply." In the following piece, from E&P's special "Unanswered Questions" issue, an array of well-known editors and reporters expressed some worries, many of which had received scant attention in the national media.*

On the War Path

JANUARY 27, 2003

Smooth ramp-up to war, or slippery slope? Now that the Super Bowl and Golden Globes are over, Americans finally seem ready to debate an attack on Iraq. Yet, as Michael Getler, *The Washington Post*'s ombudsman, observed recently, "Whatever was proper, there now seems, to me at least, a sense of unreality about this moment" and, worse, "as a citizen, and a consumer of news, I don't feel prepared." Much of the fault for this rests with the officials planning the war, who have not fully explained the reasons for it, but no small measure also resides with U.S. media.

Now, with polls showing rising doubts about the wisdom of a war at this moment, we examine some of the issues the press should—indeed, must—confront before the bombs start falling.

Nearly everyone we talked to last week, on all sides of the issue, agrees the prelude to war has been exceedingly difficult to cover. "It is much tougher these days because the desire to control is greater," observes David Halberstam, who first came to fame covering the Vietnam War for *The New York Times*. "I think the press has done well asking questions. But most people who have Vietnam in their bones are uneasy about this war."

Phil Bronstein, who covered the Persian Gulf War for the *San Francisco Examiner* and now edits the *San Francisco Chronicle*, says: "News is managed more than ever by very smart and shrewd people. A lot of questions are being asked, but they are not being answered."

Still, press coverage overall has been "as aggressive as you can be on a subject that is complicated and closely held," says Bill Keller, columnist for *The New York Times*. "I think newspapers have learned their lesson from the Gulf War: not to let yourself be too dependent on the military handlers." Howell Raines, executive editor of the *Times*, explains, "We approach this story with the full knowledge that the military is not always forthcoming."

As with so many press issues, where you sit depends on where you stand, politically. Those who favor a pre-emptive strike on Saddam Hussein tend to feel coverage so far has been fine (with a few caveats), while opponents of a quick war find fault. The one thing that "can be laid at the doorstep of all papers is a tendency to take the leaks at face value," says Keller. "It would be nice to see a little more awareness in those stories of how much stagecraft is involved."

David Shaw, media writer for the *Los Angeles Times*, says simply: "It seems the outstanding question is, Why Iraq and not North Korea?" Columnist Richard Reeves feels there should be more focus on how President Bush is personalizing his anger at Saddam Hussein into a need for war.

"There has been very little coverage of the worldview," observes journalist and educator Orville Schell. "We have been pretty hermetically sealed. It revolves too much around Washington as the sun. Other arguments are hardly equal."

For Mark Jurkowitz, media critic for *The Boston Globe*, "the story that has been missed is the mood of the country. I don't get a sense of how it is playing in Peoria. How does the average guy sitting around the dinner table feel about it? I think Americans are very ambivalent about this war. It is not an easy story to tell. The level of response to the war is so nuanced, it can't be summed up in a sound bite, and a lot of people have not worked out in their own minds how they feel."

The Washington Post's Howard Kurtz comments: "Some papers by their own admission haven't devoted as much attention as they should to the anti-war voices out there that are forming a significant minority against invading Iraq. Journalists are sometimes lulled by political consensus when both the White House and Congress have signed on to a potential war. It is harder to judge the anti-war movement than in the Vietnam days when it cut such a wide swath across society, but that isn't much of an excuse. The press needs to be careful about reflecting all sides."

Columnist Arianna Huffington cites "the lack of reporting on potential casualties. Sitting on a desk somewhere in the Pentagon is a computer printout listing projected American casualties for a range of Iraq invasion scenarios. Unfortunately, these vital figures are the only numbers that haven't been part of the war debate—or the press coverage. The fact is, the number of Americans in favor of going to war with Iraq plummets when the prospect of thousands of American casualties is added to the question."

No matter what their views on the wisdom of war at this time, nearly all the observers have concerns about what coverage will be like if and when it breaks out. For U.S. correspondents in Iraq, "it wouldn't be like Ernie Pyle in a Jeep right behind the troops," George Will says, noting that, with "precision weapons" and other tools of modern warfare, it can be "hard to know where the front line is."

If there is a war, Reeves is pessimistic about how the media will perform. "We'll cover only what they let us see," he says, adding that the U.S. government will put a positive spin on everything. If the truth eventually comes out, Reeves adds, it will be "too late," as when it was learned the Patriot missiles that supposedly performed so well in the Gulf War didn't intercept many Scud missiles after all.

To illustrate this blinkered military mind-set, he cites what he calls "Kelly's Law"—first postulated when Reeves was in Honduras during the Iran-Contra era of the 1980s. Coming upon a roadblock set up by Honduran soldiers, Reeves observed a U.S. Army truck driven by a Sgt. Kelly. Two C-47 planes came flying over the mountains, and 20 paratroopers dropped from each plane. "What's that about?" Reeves asked Kelly. "What's what about?" Kelly replied. "The paratroopers!" Reeves said. "What paratroopers?" Kelly answered.

If a war occurs, columnist Leonard Pitts sees "battles between military censors and newspapers." He also feels newspapers, like society in general, tend to "rally around the government in times of war. There's a sensitivity toward not writing anything that jeopardizes the government's aims or, especially, the safety of the troops. But while that's important, newspapers can't abdicate their responsibility to be the askers of skeptical questions—especially when there's so much doubt internationally and in this country about whether this war is necessary."

Ruben Navarrette of *The Dallas Morning News* and the Washington Post Writers Group, on the other hand, says the United States "has a duty to disarm Saddam, preferably with the help of others, but alone if we must," and so he's concerned about "boomer" coverage of the war: "With boomers in charge, the tendency is to assume the government is lying and go from there." But Norman Solomon, another syndicated columnist, sees this quite differently. "Experience tells us that once the Pentagon's missiles start to fly, the space for critical assessments and dissent in U.S. news media quickly contracts," says Solomon. "Journalists get caught up in the war fever—their careers may benefit, but journalism suffers."

And many journalists will pull their punches, Solomon adds. "In contrast to state censorship, which is usually easy to recognize, self-censorship by journalists is rarely out in the open," he says. "In the highly competitive media environment, you don't need to be a rocket scientist or a social scientist to know that dissent does not boost careers. This is especially true in times of war. The rewards of going along to get along are clear. So are the hazards of failure to toe the line."

It's hard to say how experiencing 9/11 in New York City shaped my personal response to the run-up to war against the Iraqis, who had not attacked us. My story was little different from thousands of others in the region, who were in the city that day, felt some of the horror and panic, and lost a friend or relative or neighbor in the collapse of the Twin Towers. By some logic, this should make most of us more likely to lust for revenge than someone in, say, Peoria. But polls would later reveal that, in fact, New Yorkers were more opposed to an attack on Iraq than others nearly anywhere else. Why? Perhaps, because we were so deeply hurt, we studied and pondered what had actually happened that day instead of merely listening to talk radio or TV gasbags, and, unlike so many others, we knew that no Iraqis had been among the hijackers. So any feelings of revenge could be limited to al-Qaeda and the Taliban. Or maybe some of us just rejected any revenge, knowing that it would not bring back any loved ones. Perhaps the residue of 9/11 simply made me, and many others, feel all the more angry that the deaths that day were being used to emotionally manipulate Americans into backing an attack on Iraq. Despite the column that follows, I still received dozens of letters charging that I simply did not recognize or respect the terrorist threat.

My 9/11 Story—and Iraq's

JANUARY 29, 2003

Like others in the VNU editorial edifice, we work closer to Ground Zero than nearly any other magazine staffers in New York, and perhaps that's why we brought a special passion to our post-9/11 coverage. But I had another, even more personal, reason. It also helps explain why the use of the September 11, 2001, terrorist attacks to justify an invasion of a country that had nothing to do with them disturbs me so much.

Every weekday morning, when I finish my commute by exiting the subway at Astor Place, nothing but empty sky greets me looking south down Lafayette Street. Until a little more than a year ago, I saw something quite different filling much of the same sky: the twin totems of the World Trade Center, welcoming me above ground in Manhattan.

Compared with the stories of some New Yorkers, my own 9/11 story pales, but it informs everything I write and feel about the tragedy. That morning, I was midway to Grand Central Terminal on a train speeding along the Hudson when the conductor came on the public-address system and said, "A plane has just hit the World Trade Center." And, sure enough, straight down the river, there was one of the Twin Towers smoking. Then, a few minutes later, pulling into Grand Central, came another announcement: "You're not going to believe this, folks, but a plane has just hit the other tower."

My first thought was: "What floor does Jon Albert work on?" I recalled it as being horrendously high. I had just talked with my friend the previous night. He was on the board of the local Little League, and I was a manager. I had coached his son Stephen for several years, and wrote about Jon and his boy in my recent book, *Joy in Mudville*. That month, I was coaching his son on my "fall ball" team.

Only much later, when I learned the flight paths of the two jetliners, did I realize that as I was riding a train along the river, at least one of the hijacked planes flew directly overhead. Nearing the city, I might have even heard one of them.

After arriving, I spent the next three hours trying to reach our office, more than 30 blocks south. I took a cab for a few blocks, then traffic stopped. I walked back to Grand Central thinking the subways might be running again. They weren't, and Grand Central had been evacuated. Like other New Yorkers, I staggered around in a daze for an hour. Catching bits of news off TV sets in bars and cafes, we learned that another hijacked airliner might be heading our way.

Then I trudged to the office. As I got below 14th Street, I could see the mountain of deadly smoke covering that patch of blue sky that once embraced the towers. I was a veteran of ground zeroes, having spent some time in Hiroshima and Nagasaki, but this was here, this was now. Swirls of acrid dust blew in my face—pulverized steel or (I imagined) human residue.

Well, I reached the office, somehow got some stories up on our Web site, and when the trains started running again, I headed for home in the evening. When I got there, I found out that Jon Albert had not yet returned, and everyone feared the worst.

None of us could reach our office the next day, as everything south of 14th Street was sealed off, but many of us dodged the police lines on Thursday to help get the issue out on time: a small miracle. To do it, we had to ignore the disturbing smells from outside that often filtered through our ventilation system. Our first cover was all black with "September 11, 2001" in white type. My friend Jon Albert still hadn't come home.

Two weeks later, I took my son, along with one of Jon's two boys, to a Mets game. Stephen still thought Dad was coming home. He never did, and the paperback edition of *Joy in Mudville* is now dedicated to him.

At present, President Bush seems intent on attacking Iraq, at least partly because of Saddam's alleged—but wholly unproven—links to al-Qaeda and the September 11 attacks. I can't imagine a worse tribute to Jon Albert and the others who died on 9/11: more death from the air, and in the air.

———————————————————————

FEBRUARY

In his State of the Union address on January 28, President Bush famously called Iraq part of an "axis of evil" (along with Iran and North Korea), with each pursuing nuclear weapons. He vowed that the U.S. "will not permit the world's most dangerous regimes to threaten us with the world's most destructive weapons." Bush also uttered what would become known as "the 16 words" (later retracted): "The British Government has learned that Saddam Hussein recently sought significant quantities of uranium from Africa."

Daniel Ellsberg wasn't buying any of it. I had first met Ellsberg in the mid-1980s when I was editor of Nuclear Times *magazine and he was morphing from "the man who leaked the Pentagon Papers" to a tireless (and oft-arrested) antinuclear activist. Years later, I always enjoyed chatting with him at conferences and picking his nimble brain on national security issues. Once, at such a gathering on Cape Cod, I saw him strip to his shorts on a beach and dive into the frigid October waters without fear—it seemed to be some kind of metaphor. While undeniably brilliant, he was viewed as an unreliable source by many in the media, but often, like Seymour Hersh, he seemed to possess some sort of mind-boggling inside info that just might be true. As years passed, perhaps his most positive contribution came in urging latter-day insiders to do what he had done in the 1970s: leak—or at least talk to the media about—nefarious plans that might harm America. When I interviewed him for E&P, he was about to re-emerge, if briefly, in the cultural mainstream thanks to a new biography, his autobiography, and a TV bio-pic. Ellsberg's commentary would prove remarkably prescient.*

Ellsberg: Have the Media Learned the Lessons of Vietnam?
FEBRUARY 1, 2003

Daniel Ellsberg has never been a journalist, but he is one of the most important figures in the history of American journalism. His release of the Pentagon

Papers in 1971 not only sparked a landmark freedom-of-the-press case, it changed journalism forever, inspiring an era of "leaks," whistleblowers, and wider skepticism about official statements.

His book, *Secrets: A Memoir of Vietnam and the Pentagon Papers*, was published to much acclaim last fall. Ellsberg is uniquely qualified to address the issue of the media and war: as a former Marine, a Rand Corp. analyst, and an advisor to Robert McNamara, Clark Clifford, and Henry Kissinger on Vietnam— not to mention as one of the most famous newspaper sources in history. I interviewed Ellsberg, who has long lived near San Francisco, last week.

MITCHELL: What do you think of press coverage of the run-up to the war?

ELLSBERG: People used to ask me, at the time of the Pentagon Papers, how the press was covering Vietnam, and I would respond that I could put it two ways: they were doing badly, but better than any other institution in society—or they were doing better than any other institution in society, but badly.

Back then, the press only looked good compared to the administration's account of itself, which was awful from beginning to end, and compared to Congress, which only once held a real hearing on the war. Dissenters within the administration behaved badly, too. They understood the war was heading for disaster, and, without exception, including me, did not break ranks.

With Vietnam, the press accepted the government's view until very late in the game, [to a] large extent until the Pentagon Papers came out. The public felt, "Why are we learning this stuff only now?" Many of those documents were with officials, and they knew the story. The public wondered, "Why is the story of actual government decision-making still a secret?"

I'm not sure if the press learned from Vietnam how to do better. In any case, the press as a whole is not doing it better now.

MITCHELL: What exactly do they need to do better?

ELLSBERG: They are not doing the job that should be done on informing themselves, Congress, and the public on the decision-making process, the dissenting positions within the government, and the real considerations in the decision. Without that, Congress and the public cannot bring pressure to bear—before the bombs drop.

Still, they are getting more leaks. Many in the Pentagon, CIA, and State Department see this may be a reckless war and that many may die needlessly. We do know much more than we did at a comparable time with Vietnam. And, as in past, the foreign press is reporting much more adequately than the U.S. press—and the U.S. press, as before, is largely ignoring that.

Do editors and publishers feel, individually, that they understand the reasons we are going to war, and the consequences? And if they are basing their own understanding on what is being put out by the government, then they, and their readers, don't understand it very well at all. I suggest that, just as in Vietnam, when the bombs start dropping, the American public will be entering this war with a very limited understanding of why we are at war and what the consequences will be in both the short and long terms.

Thirty years later, Americans are still asking why we went to war in Vietnam and stayed at war. Of course, the American presidents gave answers at that time—and we are still looking for better answers.

MITCHELL: What differences do you see between today's Iraqi crisis and Vietnam?

ELLSBERG: One difference with Vietnam in '64 is: we now know we are headed to a big war with a lot of troops. But, still, the public feels it will be short and cheap, like the Gulf War, Kosovo, and Afghanistan. They expect that model. Why? Has the press failed to pursue other scenarios? The administration has mainly conveyed what its top civilian leaders seem to believe—or want us to believe—that this war can be as quick and cheap as those examples. There seems to be no military leader who has that same confidence.

It could go like that, but, as I saw in Vietnam, in war the uncertainties are extreme. To be confident of any outcome is naive or foolish. The press could step into this breach by aggressively probing for, and reporting, the views of dissenters who clearly abound in the Pentagon, CIA, and State Department.

MITCHELL: But aren't revealing stories now appearing? And how does the average editor take advantage of that?

ELLSBERG: Thanks to the Internet and links to skeptical or analytical pieces all over the U.S. and world, it is possible, with some work, to actually get a pretty clear picture of the real reasons for the war and the deceptiveness of the official reasons and the costs and risks of the war. They are out there, but scattered.

MITCHELL: Why has the press had such a hard time getting at the truth, as you see it?

ELLSBERG: There is as much lying going on as in Vietnam, as in Iran-Contra, as in the Catholic Church sex scandal, as in Enron—you can't have more lying than that, and that's how much we have. Are American officials peculiar in this? No, worldwide, all government officials lie, as I. F. Stone said, and everything needs to be checked from other sources of information. And anything they say may be a big lie. That was true in Vietnam, and the Pentagon Papers proved that, if nothing else.

So it is irresponsible for anyone in the press to take your understanding exclusively from government accounts, from the president or secretary of defense or lower-level officials. That definitely includes backgrounders that purport to be the "real" inside story. Just as press conferences are a vehicle for lying to the public, backgrounders are a vehicle for lying to the press, convincing the press they are getting the inside story when all they are getting is a story that is sellable to the press. That doesn't mean that everything they say is false, but that nothing is to be relied on as the actual or whole truth.

MITCHELL: So what exactly are the lies you say the press should be examining more deeply?

ELLSBERG: The first lie is: Saddam represents the Number One danger to U.S. security in the world. To allow the president and Rumsfeld to make that statement over and over is akin to them saying without challenge from the press that they accept the flat-earth theory. To say Saddam is the Number One danger is being made without real challenge from the press, with few exceptions. More dangerous than al-Qaeda? North Korea? Russian nukes loose in the world? An India-Pakistan nuclear war?

I'm impressed by the testimony of Gen. Anthony Zinni, Bush's mediator in the Middle East, who said he'd place Saddam sixth or seventh on any list of dangers we face. The question is, are we helping our cause against threats one through five by going after number six or seven?

Two: That we are reducing the threat of the use of weapons of mass destruction by attacking Iraq. This is one of the most dangerous assertions, since all evidence is that we are *increasing* the threat of such terrorism by the attack, as CIA Director [George] Tenet said in his letter to Congress. Tenet said the danger is very low that Saddam will use weapons if not attacked and fairly high if he is attacked.

Three: The reason we are singling Saddam out is that he cannot be contained or deterred, unlike other leaders in the world, and again this is largely unchallenged by the mainstream press. No one brings out the following point: This is a man who had weapons of mass destruction, including nerve gas, and missiles capable of hitting Israel and ready to go in the 1991 war—which he does not now have—and he kept his finger off the button. So how unreliable is he if not on the brink of being deposed or killed?

MITCHELL: What specific questions are not being asked or not asked often enough by the press?

ELLSBERG: One question the press is not asking: Is there a single high military man who believes this war should happen now, that it is appropriate and [the] risks worthwhile? Every indication leaking out is that most feel that it is far from certain, even unlikely, that the war will be as short and successful as the civilian bosses say. What are we gaining that is worth the chance of a disastrous outcome? The military chiefs do not agree with civilians in the Pentagon, as far as we can tell. And does anyone in State or the CIA strongly favor war? Another question, about how the oil reserves play out in this—has that issue been fully explored for the American public, and have they weighed it adequately?

MITCHELL: What about the possible loss of Iraqi lives?

ELLSBERG: The lesson the government learned from Vietnam is to rely on bombing rather than troops, no matter what the cost to civilian life, and at high altitudes. Second, keep the American public in the dark as to how many foreigners we are actually killing.

Have editors ever asked how many we killed in the Gulf War? Have you ever seen a number on that? We never really even got good figures in Vietnam.

In Vietnam, early on, I was pressing for estimates of civilian casualties of bombing. Over and over, I was asking the embassy consul in Vietnam, and later [Henry] Kissinger in 1969, to undertake that: What is the range of estimates? The Bush administration does not want to answer that question now, but the press has got to get that out.

This government, like in Vietnam, is lying us into a war. Like Vietnam, it's a reckless, unnecessary war, where the risks greatly outweigh any possible benefits. I'd make this argument to insiders: Don't do what I did. Don't keep your mouth shut when you know people are being lied to. Tell the truth before the bombs are falling, while there's still a chance to do something about it.

On February 3, a New York Times *story was topped with: "All Aboard: America's War Train Is Leaving the Station." Naturally, the world—and the media commentators—anxiously awaited Secretary of State Colin Powell's appearance at the United Nations on February 5, when he was expected to make the administration's case for war before a skeptical body. While most pundits were already sold on the invasion, polls showed that the public was divided—or simply misinformed or confused. So the performance of the much-respected and moderate Powell could go a long way to greasing the skids for war. Afterward, few pundits felt that they needed to fact-check before declaring that Powell had made his case.*

Powell Conquers the Media

FEBRUARY 7, 2003

The day after Secretary of State Colin Powell's speech before the U.N. Security Council, TV commentators and newspaper editorials, and even many liberal pundits, declared their support for the Bush administration's hard-line stance on Iraq. CNN's Bill Schneider said that "no one" disputed Powell's findings. Bob Woodward, asked by Larry King on CNN what happens if we go to war and don't find any WMD, answered: "I think the chance of that happening is about zero. There's just too much there." George Will suggested that Powell's speech would "change all minds open to evidence."

As recently as a week ago—following weapons inspector Hans Blix's report to the United Nations and the president's State of the Union address—more than two-thirds of the nation's leading editorial pages, we found, called for the release of more detailed evidence and increased diplomatic maneuvering. The 80-minute presentation by Powell seems to have silenced most of the critics.

Consider the following day-after editorial endorsements, all from sources not always on the side of the White House. As media writer Mark Jurkowitz put it in *The Boston Globe*, Powell's speech may not have convinced France of the need to topple Saddam, but "it seemed to work wonders on opinion makers and editorial shakers in the media universe."

The *San Francisco Chronicle* called the speech "impressive in its breadth and eloquence." *The Denver Post* likened Powell to "Marshal Dillon facing down a gunslinger in Dodge City," adding that he had presented "not just one 'smoking gun' but a battery of them." *The Tampa Tribune* called Powell's case "overwhelming," while *The Oregonian* in Portland found it "devastating." To *The Hartford Courant* it was "masterful."

The *San Jose Mercury News* asserted that Powell made his case "without resorting to exaggeration, a rhetorical tool he didn't need." The *San Antonio Express-News* called the speech "irrefutable," adding, "only those ready to believe Iraq and assume that the United States would manufacture false evidence against Saddam would not be persuaded by Powell's case."

And what of the two giants of the East? *The Washington Post* echoed others who found Powell's evidence irrefutable. An editorial in the paper judged that "it is hard to imagine how anyone could doubt that Iraq possesses weapons of mass destruction. . . . Mr. Powell's evidence, including satellite photographs, audio recordings and reports from detainees and other informants, was overwhelming."

Here's the *Post*'s Jim Hoagland: "Colin Powell did more than present the world with a convincing and detailed X-ray of Iraq's secret weapons and terrorism programs yesterday. He also exposed the enduring bad faith of several key members of the U.N. Security Council when it comes to Iraq and its 'web of lies,' in Powell's phrase. . . . To continue to say that the Bush administration has not made its case, you must now believe that Colin Powell lied in the most serious statement he will ever make, or was taken in by manufactured evidence. I don't believe that. Today, neither should you."

That paper's liberal columnist, Mary McGrory, wrote that Powell "persuaded me, and I was as tough as France to convince." She even likened the Powell report to the day John Dean "unloaded" on Nixon in the Watergate hearings. Another liberal at that paper, Richard Cohen, declared that Powell's testimony "had to prove to anyone that Iraq not only hasn't accounted for its weapons of mass destruction but without a doubt still retains them. Only a fool—or possibly a Frenchman—could conclude otherwise."

The New York Times, meanwhile, hailed Powell's "powerful" and "sober, factual case." Like many other papers, the *Times*, on its news pages—in separate stories by Steven Weisman, Michael Gordon, and Adam Clymer—also bent over backward to give Powell the benefit of nearly every doubt. Apparently in thrall to Powell's moderate reputation, no one even mentioned that he was essentially acting as lead prosecutor with every reason to shape, or even create, facts to fit his brief.

Weisman called Powell's evidence "a nearly encyclopedic catalog that reached further than many had expected." He and Clymer both recalled Adlai Stevenson's speech to the U.N. in 1962 exposing Soviet missiles in Cuba. Gordon closed his piece by asserting that "it will be difficult for skeptics to argue that Washington's case against Iraq is based on groundless suspicions and not intelligence information."

While newspapers unanimously praised Powell and criticized Saddam Hussein, they still disagreed over how to act, and when. A once-tiny hawkish faction has grown to include 15 major newspapers. *The Dallas Morning News* reflected the sentiment behind calls for quick force: "The U.S. Secretary of State did everything but perform cornea transplants on the countries that still claim to see no reason for forcibly disarming Iraq."

Those in the more cautious, but still pro-war, camp generally advocate the forceful overthrow of Hussein while contending that broad international support still should be a prerequisite for any invasion. "The go-it-alone ultimatum is one the U.S. and the international community would do well to avoid—and one that Powell's much-needed presentation should help head off," *USA Today* wrote. Others called for a second U.N. resolution to authorize the use of force.

Even the shrinking number of war skeptics seemed unsure of how to bring about a peaceful solution to the conflict. *The Boston Globe* still hoped for either a coup or Hussein's exile. *The New York Times* and *San Francisco Chronicle* urged the president to let diplomacy work. Others echoed France's proposal—calling for the return of a beefed-up weapons-inspection team.

———————————————

The Washington Post published a story on February 13 headlined "Bin Laden–Hussein Link Hazy"—but buried it on page A20. Hans Blix delivered a report that questioned some of Colin Powell's evidence. It received only momentary coverage in the U.S. media. The following day, February 15, huge anti-war protests were staged around the world. In the U.S., the Pentagon made plans to provide the media with surprising access to combat zones in Iraq but with one major condition: reporters and cameramen had to agree to strict prohibitions. The contract banned "embedded" reporters (more than 500 were expected) from releasing a wide range of material on operations and forces, and even the results of missions, without approval of commanders. The document warned, "Violation of the ground rules may result in the immediate termination of the embed."

Some feared that journalists would provide excessively positive coverage to their protectors and tent-mates. In addition, the lure (and relative safety) of traveling with the troops discouraged others from trying to cover the conflict independently. New York Times *war reporter Chris Hedges (who had just published his book* War Is a Force That Gives Us Meaning*) told E&P, "I don't get on press buses." He warned that the embedding would not result in an "accurate picture," pointing out that when "you rely on the military for transportation," you just know they are "not going to drive the press vehicle to sites if things go terribly wrong." He added: "Most reporters at war are part of the problem. You always go out and look for that narrative, like the hometown hero, to give the war a kind of coherency that it doesn't have." At this point, I couldn't think of a better person to talk to about all this than Sydney Schanberg.*

Schanberg Hits the Ground Rules Running

FEBRUARY 24, 2003

"Em-bed-ded," said Sydney H. Schanberg, savoring the word's many ambiguities and connotations. "Embedded means, 'You're there.' It also means, 'You're stuck.'" Schanberg is one of the media's leading authorities on hazardous duty. As a correspondent for *The New York Times*, his adventures in Vietnam and Cambodia during the 1970s—and the plight of his former aide, Dith Pran—were dramatized in the Oscar-winning 1984 film *The Killing Fields*. An Army veteran himself, Schanberg, 68, left the *Times* in 1986 and now writes for *The Village Voice* in New York.

Last week, after *E&P* received a copy of the "ground rules" for embedded reporters, we forwarded a copy to Schanberg. His reaction? He's impressed by the Pentagon's promise of media access and long list of what will be "releasable." It appears to be a "big leap forward" from the military's shutting off (or jerking around) reporters in the country's most recent armed conflicts. And, in any case, "anything's better than covering the war from a briefing room, where you are always the stupidest person in the room."

But, on closer inspection, doubts grew. "If I were an editor and I received this document," he said, "I'd be on the phone to the Pentagon for clarification within 10 minutes. I'd be saying, 'What do you mean by *that?*'" This is critical because the embedding concept is clearly aimed at getting "good P.R." for the military, he added. "It's hard for any reporter to be aggressively critical of someone you're bonding with," Schanberg pointed out. Perhaps that's why he has "never been embedded" and in Vietnam insisted on being "self-governed." In fact, he urged editors now to request fewer embedded slots or at least allow their best reporters to roam freely.

"You'd rather not be hampered at all," he admitted, "but as a journalist, and a realist, I don't expect to walk into the military's shop and break all the china. You're a fool if you believe that. But the military, on the other hand, must recognize you are a professional." Indeed, he found in Vietnam that only one in a thousand reporters would ever knowingly jeopardize a military operation, and no doubt that remains true today.

Many of the new ground rules Schanberg finds sensible or benign. The rule forbidding journalists from carrying firearms seems like a good one, although a few gonzos did pack pistols in Vietnam, he recalled. "Anything that makes you look like a combatant," he said, "is bad." That's also why he (unlike Chris Hedges) is against reporters speeding off in jeeps. The new rules, in fact, ban breaking away in any vehicle.

Schanberg is also impressed that the rules seem to carry no requirement for submitting copy to authorities—i.e., no opportunity for censorship. That doesn't mean self-censorship will not arise. And the more he studied the rules, the more he found vague language, restrictions, and situations where copy can be held, if not sanitized. For example, Rule 4F7 says that the date, time, or location of completed missions and actions, as well as results, are "releasable"—but "only if described in general terms."

He's also concerned about Rule 4A: "All interviews with service members will be on the record." Sounds fine, right? The problem is, if soldiers fear their names may be in papers, it "has the possibility of shutting people up," Schanberg declared. If they say anything negative about an operation or living conditions, their superior "may have their ass." In Vietnam, he recalled, "most things guys really wanted to tell you were not on the record." Also, will reporters always have a military escort—or "baby-sitter," as he put it—to listen in as they interview troops or visit local hospitals?

Even what he initially saw as a big plus—not having to submit stories for approval—came to look like a double-edged sword when he considered the strongly worded language about expelling "embeds" who get out of line. "You might be able to file what you want," he explained, "but you will always have to worry about the penalty if you are on the edge of the rules. That's certainly designed to make you pull your punches if you have any doubts. They're saying, 'Here are the rules: If you don't follow them, you get thrown out.'"

This made him reflect on a war reporter's higher calling. "Civil disobedience," he said, "is needed sometimes, and you just have to accept the possible consequences." He offered the example of rushing off on your own, against orders, to the scene of a rumored massacre of civilians (a scene, one recalls, from *The Killing Fields*). "The only way we will know anything for sure," Schanberg advised, "is when the rules go into practice. That's the test, and until then we need to say—we'll believe it when we see it."

MARCH

On March 5, the foreign ministers of France, Russia, and Germany declared that they would "not allow" a new resolution authorizing military action to pass the U.N. security council. No matter. By all accounts, the U.S. government was ready to press ahead. Editorial pages remained divided between those who felt that the U.S. had waited long enough to take action and others who were not quite ready to give up on diplomacy. Few questioned that the Iraq WMD threat was real, however.

President Bush conducted a televised press conference on March 6, stating in his intro, "We will not wait to see what terrorists or terrorist states could do with weapons of mass destruction." Some of the questions from the press were sharp, but one asking about his religious strength gave him an opportunity to say, "My faith sustains me because I pray daily. I pray for guidance and wisdom and strength.... But it's a humbling experience to think that people I will never have met have lifted me and my family up in prayer. And for that I'm grateful."

It was the mood of the affair that was most disquieting. Bush smiled and made his usual quips, and many of the reporters played the game and did not press him hard. This was how these press gatherings had gone throughout the run-up to war. But this meeting was heavily scripted, with Bush looking at a slip of paper and calling on reporters in a pre-arranged order. When it was over, I felt that the press had blown its last best chance to really put his feet to the fire, and along with Ari Berman, then our intern, came up with a few questions we wished reporters had asked.

Eleven Questions We Wish They'd Asked
MARCH 7, 2003

Considering that we seem to be on the verge of a major war, with little firm evidence of the Iraqi WMD driving it, the questions for President Bush at his final press conference before the war seems likely to start were relatively tame. Here are a few we wish they'd asked.

1. Why is the U.S. threatening an optional war if 59 percent of Americans do not support a U.S. invasion without the approval of the U.N. Security Council, according to a Feb. 24–26 *USA Today*/CNN/Gallup poll?

2. If our allies have the same information on WMD—and the Iraqi threat is so real—why do some of our friends refuse to take part in your coalition?

3. You praise the Iraqi people, say we have no quarrel with them, pledge to save them from the dictator and give them democracy. Would you tell us how many of them are likely to die in this war?

4. You say one major reason for taking this action is to protect Americans from terrorism. How do you respond to the warnings of CIA Director George Tenet and others that invading Iraq would in fact likely increase terrorism?

5. Rather than make us wait for a supplemental budget request—after the war has been launched—to tell us what it (and its aftermath) will cost, don't you think the American people, who will pay the bill, deserve to know the latest long-term estimates before the fact?

6. You say Saddam Hussein has weapons of mass destruction and is evil enough to use them. If not during an American invasion of his country, then when? How many deaths on our side do you expect?

7. Why, if North Korea has the capability to produce six nuclear warheads by mid-summer, are you letting their very reluctant neighbors take the lead in deterring them while demanding that the U.S. take charge in confronting Saddam?

8. With the economy shaken and deficits climbing, how do you respond to critics who say you're ignoring domestic issues and the long-term economic security of this country by focusing so much of your time and resources on Iraq?

9. Why did the U.S. edit the 12,000-page Iraqi weapons report (as recently revealed) to the U.N. Security Council, removing all names of U.S. companies that sold weapons materials to the Iraqis in the past?

10. You claimed tonight that Iraq has started producing new missiles—but are these nothing more than less-capable versions (fully permitted by the U.N.) of the missiles being destroyed now?

11. How do you respond to radio commentator Daniel Schorr's statement that the "coalition of the willing" is actually a "coalition of the billing"?

———————————————

A few days later, some in the media expressed regrets about that scripted Bush press conference. ABC's Terry Moran said the president was not "sufficiently challenged" and that reporters ended up "looking like zombies." Elisabeth Bumiller of The New York Times *said, "We were very deferential" because "it's very intense, it's frightening to stand up there . . . on prime-time live TV asking the president of the United States a question when the country's about to go to war." She admitted that "no one wanted to get into an argument with the president at this very serious time." A* Newsweek *cover story was titled "Saddam's War." Bill O'Reilly, appearing on ABC, vowed: "If the Americans go in and overthrow Saddam Hussein and it's clean, he has nothing, I will apologize to the nation, and I will not trust the Bush administration again, all right?"*

On Meet the Press *on March 16, Vice President Cheney said of Saddam Hussein: "We believe he has, in fact, reconstituted nuclear weapons." The next day, Bush gave Saddam 48 hours to leave the country, with his two sons. When that didn't happen, Shock and Awe began (amazingly, I was sitting in the Green Room at Fox News at about the moment the first jets took off). The invasion moved quickly at first, with embedded journalists supplying breathless accounts and video of the jets taking off from aircraft carriers and jeeps racing across the desert toward Baghdad. In a sign of things to come, the U.S. media provided few images of the human cost of war—their choice or the Pentagon's?—while news outlets in Europe did show photos of dead or wounded.*

Then sandstorms struck and resistance from shadowy Iraqis grew (even as Saddam's army seemed to melt away). This raised concerns about an occupation, though there was no question that the U.S. would win the battle phase in short order. Anthony Shadid in The Washington Post *revealed that "In public and private conversations, many Baghdad residents volunteer that they see U.S. forces as an invading, rather than liberating, army."* The Post *also reported that broadcast news consultants in the U.S. were "advising news and talk stations across the nation to wave the flag and downplay protest against the war."*

Rummy Meets McNamara

MARCH 31, 2003

Coming when it did, the photograph seemed like a cruel joke, or a Photoshop prank, just as nearly everyone in America (except perhaps a few Fox News commentators) was awakening to the bone-chilling reality of a quick war that was threatening to turn into a longer slog. And there, splashed across a spread in *The New York Times*, was a picture of a smiling Donald Rumsfeld bending over to shake the hand of an equally buoyant Robert S. McNamara.

Unfortunately, it did not look like McNamara was whispering, "What part of the word 'Vietnam' don't you understand?"

It was a Pentagon luncheon for former defense secretaries hosted by Rumsfeld to discuss the war in Iraq, which seemed to be undergoing more "Vietnamization" by the hour. We had seen it all before: the apparently false claims that we had won the "hearts and minds" of the people; the charges that the enemy was not fighting fair; and a rising toll of dead, wounded, or missing military personnel—and journalists. And that's even before the postwar occupation begins.

Of course, it is absurd to compare a war of less than two weeks with one that lasted more than a decade. But still, many hear echoes, faint or strong, of Vietnam. Only a few days have passed since CNN's Walter Rodgers, in Iraq in the early moments of the war, told anchor Aaron Brown, "It's great fun," but that seems like a year ago now.

With the conflict under way—and getting nastier—we thought we'd check back with some well-known reporters we had visited during the long run-up to war.

As with Vietnam, too many in the press follow the Pentagon line, says Joseph L. Galloway, the Bronze Star winner and author who is now military-affairs correspondent for Knight Ridder. "One thing not lacking," he adds, dryly, "is optimism for the game plan, but if it hasn't been cleared with the enemy, it tends not to work." He called the press briefings "bullshit."

Tom Wicker, columnist for *The New York Times* from 1966 to 1991, tells us that he wonders why more didn't question earlier Rumsfeld's plan for a lighter and quicker force in Iraq when many generals were predicting the war would have to be won with more boots on the ground. "Journalists," he says, "share the common perception that technology will triumph."

Even so, Sydney H. Schanberg, who won a Pulitzer Prize for his reporting in Cambodia, cautions against embracing the Vietnam analogy too tightly. But like Galloway, he feels the press briefings are useless ("editors should send robots with tape recorders"), but reporters should stop "grumbling" about them, because "generals are doing what they do, and what you would do in their position." While the embedding process offers reporters only a slice of the war, not the whole of it, at least "we know very quickly the misjudgments at the top, so we're way ahead of Vietnam in that," Schanberg said.

But John R. MacArthur, publisher of *Harper's Magazine* and author of an important book about media coverage of the first Gulf War, warns that if the war goes on for months, you "could see a breakdown in the discipline of the Pentagon's control of coverage. The soldiers may start to become paranoid about the reporters, and the reporters angry they're getting lied to by officers. Maybe more embedded reporters will be emboldened to report what they see, and then there might be reprisals from the military, revoking privileges."

Another troubling reminder of past conflicts is the relatively little concern for civilian casualties. "We pay more attention to American deaths," says Anthony Marro, editor of *Newsday* in Melville, N.Y., whose paper publishes few photos of dead bodies, even fewer if they are Iraqi. "It is easier to report on people we know, we put more faces on the Americans, we know who they are."

Geneva Overholser, a professor at the University of Missouri School of Journalism, says that strong civilian coverage had been lacking at newspapers. "I wish they were showing us more of that reality of war," she adds. "We have more than 600 reporters embedded, and we have better access, but we are not seeing much in the way of civilian casualties."

The Boston Globe received complaints after playing up a photo of an Iraqi civilian killed by a stray bullet. Paula Nelson, *Globe* deputy director of photography in charge of page one, reveals that the photo department debated using the image. "You got a lot from that photo," she explains. "It showed a casualty, but it also showed the urban fighting involved. It was the first dead body we printed." Nelson says the paper has declined to run other photos of the dead if they showed identifiable faces.

―――――――――――――――――――――――――

APRIL

On April 2, the press highlighted the story of Pvt. Jessica Lynch, 19, who had been taken prisoner by the enemy and then—according to military propaganda—fought heroically in assisting her own rescue. The media, caught up in war fever, bought it. The Washington Post *headline read: "She Was Fighting to the Death." Katie Couric on NBC advised a military official, "I think the Special Forces rock!" Chris Hedges told* E&P *that the U.S. military's use of embedded reporters in Iraq had made the war easier to see and harder to understand: "The broadcast media display all these retired generals and charts and graphs, it looks like a giant game of Risk. I find it nauseating." But even the print embeds had little choice but to "look at Iraq totally through the eyes of the U.S. military," he pointed out. "That's a very distorted and self-serving view."*

To Hedges, this instantaneous "slice of war" reporting was bereft of context. Reporters have a difficult time interviewing Iraqi civilians, and many don't even try: "We don't know what the Iraqis think." The reporters are "talking about a country and culture they know nothing about. . . . My suspicion is that the Iraqis view it as an invasion and occupation, not a liberation. This resistance we are seeing may in fact just be the beginning of organized resistance, not the death throes of Saddam's fedayeen. I've witnessed how insurgencies build in other conflicts. . . . It reminds me of what happened to the Israelis after taking over Gaza, moving among hostile populations." Looking ahead to a long occupation, he expressed the prescient line: "It's 1967, and we've just become Israel." The next day, U.S. forces surrounded Baghdad Airport. On the evening of April 4, I appeared with Bill Moyers on his weekly PBS program, NOW.

Moyers: Beginning of the End—or Just the Beginning?

APRIL 4, 2003

It was apparent that in just a few days the American forces would enter Baghdad, with a victory in the invasion phase of the attack on Iraq at hand. But then what? Indeed, the PBS interview would conclude with Bill Moyers asking me, "Do you have a sense that when the battle is over, this story's only begun?" Here is a partial transcript.

MOYERS: Do you think the public knows that the reporters who are embedded had to sign a contract with the Pentagon in order to be accepted for this role? That they had to agree to play by the rules?

MITCHELL: Well, it's a good question whether they know, but also whether they care. I think, as we found in polls over the years, that the American people . . . believe that there should be all sorts of restrictions. And, of course, everyone agrees that in wartime there should be more restrictions. But the question is, to what degree? And we've seen in our interviews in the past couple weeks, many cases of editors getting a lot of mail from readers who are upset about their coverage. And it shows that the people have a really different view about what the rights and the responsibilities of the press are.

MOYERS: I saw your story about *USA Today* the other day . . . the editor of *USA Today* got in trouble for this photograph, didn't he?

MITCHELL: Well, they ran a photograph of some dead Iraqi soldiers on the front page. And a large number of readers, they told us, complained because on the same day they ran a photo inside of a U.S. soldier surrounded by happy Iraqi children. And so these people were saying, "Why wasn't that photo on the front page instead of the dead Iraqi soldiers?"

And the executive editor of *USA Today* told us that, yeah, the reason was simple. It was a day of great bloodshed. One of those days of great pessimism. And he thought it would have been inappropriate and misleading to show this happy photo on the front page. So he went with the more grim photo.

Another example I'll give you, *The Dallas Morning News* editor told us that they've gotten a lot of complaints for showing a photo of dead civilians or damaged civilians on the front page. And he says that it's viewed by the readers as an anti-war statement . . . showing the casualties on the other side is an anti-war statement. And that really goes against all the principles of press coverage that we believe in, which is, you know, showing what is happening. And letting the people deal with it as they can.

MOYERS: Do you think that journalists can be objective about what they're reporting when they are alongside the troops who are protecting them as they move forward?

MITCHELL: Well, I think that's one of the problems. These reporters have been living with these troops. Reporting with them, getting to know them. And, of course, that's all terrific. You know, no one could really be against that.

But in practice it could modify or adjust what they report about the actions. . . . One of the problems in this whole campaign has been that originally we were told that the embedded reporters would only make up maybe half the reporters who would be covering the conflict. The rest would be independent. But what's happened is because of the dangers over there— almost all the reporters are the embedded reporters. So there's very few free-roaming reporters who can report without any restrictions whatsoever.

But the problem is that the commentators on TV have almost from the beginning adopted a "we" attitude. They now are reporting, "We are advancing. We are taking fire. We are taking prisoners."

So all objectivity has been dropped. And, as human beings, I think we could agree it's understandable in this situation. But, as journalists, it's not the best situation where commentators, anchormen—reporters in the field—are talking about this as a "we" rather than a U.S. mission or the U.S. soldiers.

MOYERS: Fox News has become the cheerleader for the government. What does it do to other news organizations when Fox proves that jingoism is more popular than journalism?

MITCHELL: I think the problem with that is that a lot of the other—particularly the cable news networks have—felt that they have to keep up with that. I think there's a certain competition to show that they're not soft on the war, that they don't have any less patriotism than Fox. And we've seen it just this morning. I saw an interview on CNN with an Australian woman who had been in Baghdad and had just left. And the woman kept saying that, you know, she was amazed how much the Iraqi people, although they may not like Saddam Hussein, were very angry about the bombings.

Many of their children had been injured or killed. . . . And the person who was the interviewer back in the U.S. asked her one aggressive question after another. After he finished talking to her, he then sort of editorialized on the air, saying—"Well, we've talked to countless people who say that the Iraqi civilians will welcome with open arms the American soldiers." Now, that may or may not be true. But the point is that even after one of the rare kind of dissenting or contrary opinions was expressed, the anchor felt he had to then jump in and editorialize, saying, "You can disregard what this woman said. You know, we have other information."

The press should report straight down the line. You know, let the people see all sides. Let the people get all the information as quickly as they can. And let the chips fall where they may.

MOYERS: What concerns you about what's not being covered?

MITCHELL: My complaint is with the cable news networks that are on 24/7 and yet have found virtually no time to interview psychologists and theologians and other observers who could talk about what this is doing to us as a country.

MOYERS: Do you see as much cheerleading in the print press as you do on television?

MITCHELL: No, I think the print press has played it more straight down the line. They've had a—more variety of stories. They have had reports from Baghdad itself. More reports on what people are saying around the world. More reports on protests pro and con about the war. More range of editorial opinions. So I think the print press and newspapers have done a much better job, a more reflective job.

MOYERS: What do you think is at stake for democracy and how we journalists cover this war?

MITCHELL: Edward R. Murrow had a quote on his wall in his office from Thoreau in which he said something like, "To speak the truth, you need two people. One to speak it and one to hear it."

And I think that sums up the relationship not only between the military and the press, but the press and the American people. You know, the press often is reporting factual matters. And the public sometimes turns away from it. We entered this war with upwards of half the people in the country believing that Saddam Hussein was behind the 9/11 attack.

Now, how did that happen? Was that the media's fault? Was it the government's fault for putting out the stories? Or is the public sometimes not receptive, and the public wants to believe what the public wants to believe?

MOYERS: Last question. Do you have a sense that when the battle is over, this story's only begun?

MITCHELL: I don't think most Americans understand that this is going to be something that's with us for years and decades, and I'm not sure we get a sense of that from the coverage which seems to be oriented toward next week or next month, when the battle will be over. The boys will start to come home, and it will be a "glorious episode" in our past rather than something that's just the beginning of this story.

We're really at the beginning of the story of the U.S. and Iraq in the twenty-first century.

MAY

On April 9, U.S. forces took central Baghdad and millions watched on TV as locals toppled a giant statue of Saddam Hussein (it was later revealed that U.S. Marines played a large role). Chris Matthews on MSNBC said, "We're all neo-cons now." Joe Scarborough, also on MSNBC, declared: "I'm waiting to hear the words 'I was wrong' from some of the world's most elite journalists, politicians, and Hollywood types." Extensive looting soon began in Baghdad and many other large cities, with prizes ranging from household items to deadly weapons and bomb-making equipment. Donald Rumsfeld explained that "Stuff happens.... Freedom's untidy." Mobs were greeting Americans as something less than liberators. E&P noted "the inconsistencies in the American media's coverage of violence against civilians in Iraq, which often seems to accept the military's word first and ask questions later." With combat over, about two-thirds of the embeds quickly exited. But Judith Miller arrived to claim that WMD had existed in Iraq on the eve of war—but then were buried, somewhere.

On April 18, tens of thousands of Iraqis in Baghdad demonstrated against a U.S. occupation. Jay Garner arrived to serve as postwar administrator. In late April, in Baghdad and Fallujah, U.S. troops fired on demonstrators, killing more than a dozen and inspiring grenade attacks on Americans. Thomas Friedman wrote in The New York Times, "As far as I'm concerned, we do not need to find any weapons of mass destruction to justify this war ... Mr. Bush doesn't owe the world any explanation for missing chemical weapons." David Ignatius of The Washington Post wrote a column along the same lines. Richard Perle on May 1 advised, in a USA Today op-ed, "Relax, Celebrate Victory." The same day, President Bush, dressed in a flight suit, landed on the deck of the U.S.S. Abraham Lincoln and declared an end to major military operations in

Iraq—with the now-notorious "Mission Accomplished" banner arrayed behind him in the war's greatest photo op. Chris Matthews called Bush a "hero" and PBS's Gwen Ifill said he was "part Tom Cruise, part Ronald Reagan."

Back in the Daze of Mission Accomplished

MAY 1–6, 2003

After President Bush's jet landed on an aircraft carrier and his speech declaring major fighting in Iraq was over, all in front of a giant "Mission Accomplished" banner, MSNBC's Chris Matthews boomed, "He won the war. He was an effective commander. Everybody recognizes that, I believe, except a few critics." As Bush spoke, American casualties stood at 139 killed and 542 wounded.

Here are excerpts revealing how one newspaper, *The New York Times*, covered the event and aftermath. One snippet: "The Bush administration is planning to withdraw most United States combat forces from Iraq over the next several months and wants to shrink the American military presence to less than two divisions by the fall, senior allied officials said today."

By Elisabeth Bumiller

WASHINGTON, May 1—President Bush's made-for-television address tonight on the carrier *Abraham Lincoln* was a powerful, Reaganesque finale to a six-week war. But beneath the golden images of a president steaming home with his troops toward the California coast lay the cold political and military realities that drove Mr. Bush's advisors to create the moment.

The president declared an end to major combat operations, White House, Pentagon and State Department officials said, for three crucial reasons: to signify the shift of American soldiers from the role of conquerors to police, to open the way for aid from countries that refused to help militarily, and—above all—to signal to voters that Mr. Bush is shifting his focus from Baghdad to concerns at home. "This is the formalization that tells everybody we're not engaged in combat anymore, we're prepared for getting out," a senior administration official said.

By Michael R. Gordon and Eric Schmitt

BAGHDAD, May 2—The Bush administration is planning to withdraw most United States combat forces from Iraq over the next several months and wants to shrink the American military presence to less than two divisions by the fall, senior allied officials said today.

The United States currently has more than five divisions in Iraq, troops that fought their way into the country and units that were added in an attempt to stabilize it. But the Bush administration is trying to establish a new military structure in which American troops would continue to secure Baghdad while the majority of the forces in Iraq would be from other nations.

By Dexter Filkins and Ian Fisher

BAGHDAD, May 2—The war in Iraq has officially ended, but the momentous task of re-creating a new Iraqi nation seems hardly to have begun. Three weeks after Saddam Hussein fell from power, American troops are straining to manage the forces this war has unleashed: the anger, frustration, and competing ambitions of a nation suppressed for three decades.

In a virtual power vacuum, with the relationship between American military and civilian authority seeming ill defined, new political parties, Kurds, and Shiite religious groups are asserting virtual governmental authority in cities and villages across the country, sometimes right under the noses of American soldiers.

There is a growing sense among educated Iraqis eager for the American-led transformation of Iraq to work that the Americans may be losing the initiative, that the single-mindedness that won the war is slackening under the delicate task of transforming a military victory into political success.

By David E. Sanger

WASHINGTON, May 2—In his speech, Mr. Bush argued that the invasion and liberation of Iraq were part of the American response to the attacks of Sept. 11. He called the tumultuous period since those attacks "19 months that changed the world," and said Mr. Hussein's defeat was a defeat for al-Qaeda and other terrorists as well.

Politically more complex for the administration is the continuing search for chemical and biological weapons, a search that so far has turned up next to nothing. One member of Mr. Bush's war cabinet said that he suspected that Mr. Hussein had not mounted his chemical stockpiles on weapons, but suggested that sooner or later they would be found. Mr. Bush himself said tonight that the United States knew of "hundreds of sites that will be investigated."

Editorial, May 2

As presidential spectacles go, it would be hard to surpass George Bush's triumphant "Top Gun" visit to the U.S.S. *Abraham Lincoln* yesterday off the California coast. President Bush flew out to the giant aircraft carrier dressed in full fighter-pilot regalia as the "co-pilot" of a Navy warplane. After a dramatic landing on the compact deck—a new standard for high-risk presidential travel—Mr. Bush mingled with the ship's crew, then later welcomed home thousands of cheering sailors and aviators on the flight deck in a nationally televised address.

The scene will undoubtedly make for a potent campaign commercial next year. For now, though, the point was to declare an end to the combat phase of the war in Iraq and to commit the nation to the reconstruction of that shattered country.

From the moment that Mr. Bush made his intention of invading Iraq clear, the question was never whether American troops would succeed, or whether the regime they toppled would be exposed to the world as a despicable one. The question was, and still is, whether the administration has the patience to rebuild Iraq and set it on a course toward stable, enlightened governance. The chaotic situation in Afghanistan is no billboard for American talent at nation-building. The American administration of postwar Iraq has so far failed to match the efficiency and effectiveness of the military invasion. But as the United States came to the end of one phase of the Iraqi engagement last night, there was still time to do better.

Letter to the Editor, May 3

Some unanswered questions remain: Where are the weapons of mass destruction? What evidence makes Iraq "an ally of al-Qaeda"? Where is Saddam Hussein? Where is Osama bin Laden? Who is next?

Martin Deppe
Chicago

By David E. Sanger

WASHINGTON, May 4—With his administration under growing international pressure to find evidence that Saddam Hussein possessed banned weapons, President Bush told reporters today that "we'll find them," but cautioned that it would take some time because, he said, Mr. Hussein spent so many years hiding his stockpiles.

Mr. Bush's comments came after his senior aides, in interviews in recent days, had begun to back away from their pre-war claims that Mr. Hussein had an arsenal that was loaded and ready to fire.

They now contend that he developed what they call a "just in time" production strategy for his weapons, hiding chemical precursors that could be quickly loaded into empty artillery shells or short-range missiles.

Maureen Dowd, column, May 4

The tail hook caught the last cable, jerking the fighter jet from 150 m.p.h. to zero in two seconds. Out bounded the cocky, rule-breaking, daredevil flyboy, a man navigating the Highway to the Danger Zone, out along the edges where he was born to be, the further on the edge, the hotter the intensity.

He flashed that famous all-American grin as he swaggered around the deck of the aircraft carrier in his olive flight suit, ejection harness between his legs, helmet tucked under his arm, awestruck crew crowding around. Maverick was back, cooler and hotter than ever, throttling to the max with joystick politics. Compared to Karl Rove's "revvin' up your engine" myth-making cinematic style, Jerry Bruckheimer's movies look like *Lizzie McGuire*.

This time Maverick didn't just nail a few bogeys and do a 4G inverted dive with a MiG-28 at a range of two meters. This time the Top Gun wasted a couple of nasty regimes, and promised this was just the beginning.

Thomas Friedman, column, May 4

President Bush may have declared the war in Iraq effectively over. But, judging from my own e-mail box—where conservative readers are bombing me for not applauding enough the liberation of Iraq, and liberals for selling out to George Bush—the war over the war still burns on here.

Conservatives now want to use the victory in Iraq to defeat all liberal ideas at home, and to make this war a model for America's relations with the world, while liberals—fearing all that—are still quietly rooting for Mr. Bush to fail.

New American Deaths in Iraq, May 6
The Department of Defense has confirmed the deaths of the following Americans in the Iraq war:

GIVENS, Jesse A., 34, Pfc., Army; Springfield, Mo.; Third Armored Cavalry.

REYNOLDS, Sean C., 25, Sgt., Army; East Lansing, Mich.; 173rd Airborne Brigade.

JULY

Resistance to the occupation continued to grow, but most Americans, and many members of the press, still took it lightly—more as an annoyance than anything to worry about in the long term. But Chris Hedges had a different view. "We don't have a sense of what we have waded into here," Hedges told E&P. "Now that the feel-good, flag-waving part of war is over, the real culprits, the commercial-broadcast media, are going to pack up and leave. What they've done is a huge disservice to the nation. They have no sense of responsibility to continue reporting as the story gets more complicated and difficult to report. . . . Public TV tries, but they have no budget. It takes a gigantic investment. Profit-driven media organizations realize these stories take work on the part of the readers, and they just don't see the point." The result, he feared, was that "we'll see Iraq in terms of flare-ups and incidents, without any context or sense of what's happening or why. That makes it difficult for us to have informed judgments. Without providing this sort of context, the print and broadcast media cannot perform their essential role in a democracy: to keep the public informed."

On June 6, with U.S. casualties growing, Donald Rumsfeld blamed Iraq's problems on "pockets of dead-enders." The search for Saddam's WMD proved fruitless. The Associated Press, meanwhile, took the first close look at civilian casualties and found thousands. But how much more of this type of reporting would ensue? Only about two dozen embedded reporters remained in Iraq. On July 2, President Bush uttered his much-lamented "bring them on" invitation to the insurgents. Four days later, former Ambassador Joseph Wilson wrote his fateful Op-Ed for The New York Times *about his trip to Niger, disputing the administration's claim about the Iraqis having sought yellowcake there. This sparked Vice President Cheney and his top aide, I. Lewis "Scooter" Libby, to secretly seek retribution.*

Media Downplay U.S. Death Toll

JULY 17, 2003

Any way you look at it, the news is bad enough. According to Thursday's press and television reports, 33 U.S. soldiers have now died in combat since President Bush declared, in his "Mission Accomplished" speech, an end to the major fighting on May 2. This, of course, is a tragedy for the men killed and their families, and a problem for the White House. But actually the numbers are much worse—and rarely reported by the media.

According to official military records, the number of U.S. soldiers who have died in Iraq since May 2 is actually 85. This includes a staggering number of non-combat deaths. Even if killed in a non-hostile action, these soldiers are no less dead, their families no less aggrieved. And it's safe to say that nearly all of these people would still be alive if they were still back in the States. Nevertheless, the media continue to report the much lower figure of 33 as if those are the only deaths that count.

Looking at the entire war, there was much fanfare Thursday over the fact that the latest U.S. combat death this week pushed the official total to 148—finally topping the 147 figure for Gulf War 1. However, according to the Iraq Coalition Casualty Count, the total number of all U.S. deaths, combat and otherwise, in Iraq is actually 224 so far.

This Web site not only counts deaths, it describes each one in whatever detail (often sketchy) the military provides, along with the name and age and home town of each fatality. An analysis of the 85 postwar deaths by *E&P* reveals that nearly as many U.S. military personnel have died in vehicle accidents (17) as from gunshot wounds (19). Ten have died after grenade attacks and seven from accidental explosions, another seven in helicopter crashes. Six were killed by what is described as "non-hostile" gunshots, and three have drowned.

The vast majority of those killed—at least 70 percent—were age 18 to 30, but several soldiers in their 40s or 50s have also perished. Pentagon officials also disclosed that there have been about five deaths among troops assigned to the Iraq mission that commanders say might have been suicides.

The most recent non-combat death was Cory Ryan Geurin, age 18, a Marine lance corporal from Santee, Calif. "He was standing post on a palace roof in Babylon when he fell approximately 60 feet," the site said. On July 13, Jaror Puello-Coronado, 36, an Army sergeant, died while "manning a traffic point when the operator of a dump truck lost control of the vehicle." Another soldier, still officially listed as "Unknown," died on July 13 "from a non-hostile gunshot incident," according to the site. Before that, on July 9, another Marine lance corporal, age 20, died in Kuwait "in a vehicle accident."

Many other deaths are only vaguely described as the "result of non-combat injuries." One recent death occurred in a mine-clearing accident. Others "drowned" or "died of natural causes," and still others lost their lives in a "vehicle accident." What sort of accident? The Pentagon won't say, but likely a large number occurred in attempting to escape an insurgent attack. Sounds pretty "hostile" to me.

Then there's this, in a letter to me today from a reader: "My 25-year-old son is an officer in the hostilities in Iraq. He would not be there if he wasn't sent there. He emphasizes in letters and e-mails that the 'war is not over.' His convoys are attacked every day and sometimes three times a day. Why do *The New York Times* and other newspapers keep labeling their war coverage 'After the War'?"

Another reader asks about "the dearth of reporting on the deaths of Iraqi citizens (soldier or civilian) since the 'end' of the war. Since the Iraqis are a supposedly free people now, and their country is under occupation by U.S. and other foreign entities, it would seem that death and injury to these people might warrant some coverage. Iraq Body Count now reports between 6,000 and 7,800 civilian deaths in Iraq. But not a whisper of this in the mainstream news, and not much in the alternative press either."

And this: "What is a 'non-hostile gunshot wound?' I would have thought that getting a bullet through the body is always a pretty hostile affair. Or is this something which is somehow unique and can only be properly understood by people who have the unique ability to see nuclear, biological, and chemical weapons where none exist? Seems a little like the insane logic of *Catch-22*. But wasn't that just a book?"

Provocative comments and queries by other readers follow:

• "It has been widely reported by troops in the field that the reason there have been so many vehicle accidents is that, in an effort to avoid being ambushed, the soldiers drive too fast. In fact, I heard a report that in at least two incidents, soldiers killed in car accidents were actually fleeing hostile fire. These are clearly combat deaths, not accidents."

• "Why aren't the national newspapers doing obits on all of these soldiers? *The New York Times* printed entire special sections on the World Trade Center dead, and won a Pulitzer for it—are these dead any less deserving?"

• "The lack of curiosity in our press is very annoying. We don't even get the names of the dead now. Always, it is 'one was killed and four injured today.' Not only that, there is seldom any description of how they died. I learned in the British press that one soldier was on fire and ran through the streets, his face in flames, screaming before collapsing. He died, but not one newspaper in America said he burned to death. Another had his arm blown off, and as he cried, clutching at it, dying, the Iraqis cheered because they want us to leave. This was hidden from us too. Finally, just this week, our press showed a photo of a dead soldier—only he was completely covered."

• "One thing I have noticed about the mounting toll in Iraq is that we are always told that 'such and such' number of soldiers have died and so many were wounded. The wounded almost seem to be an afterthought. The extent of the wounds is rarely, if ever described. Some of these wounded must be soldiers who have lost legs or arms or eyesight— burned, broken, and suffering people who are barely recognized as a part of the ongoing carnage. Although I have never seen any figures on the total number of wounded, it must be significantly into the hundreds by now. This is a cost of war, along with the psychological damage done to these soldiers, which is rarely addressed."

• "If Bush wants any respect, he should go out on patrol with the grunts on the streets of Baghdad instead of grandstanding on an aircraft carrier. Then let him tell the soldiers that the war is over."

SEPTEMBER

On July 22, Saddam's two sons were killed in a U.S. raid in Mosul, and some in the media declared the first of what would be numerous "turning points" in quieting the insurgency. Just days later, five U.S. soldiers were killed in a 24-hour period, a shocking number at the time. On August 17, a Reuters TV cameraman was shot dead by U.S. troops after they purportedly mistook his camera for a grenade launcher, a hint of many more journalist deaths to come. E&P commented: "The notion that embedding American journalists with U.S. forces would transform relations between the military and the media is foundering in the tense and often violent reality of the occupation." The same day, insurgents blew up a key oil pipeline in the north—for the second time.

Less than a month later, a bomb ripped through the U.N. headquarters in Baghdad, killing at least 23 and leading to the organization's exit from the country. More than ever, Americans were wondering if all this really had to happen. Charley Hanley, a longtime foreign correspondent for The Associated Press—and a Pulitzer winner for his 1999 report on the No Gun Ri massacre, which happened in Korea more than half a century ago—was the first mainstream journalist to really put together a full and biting review of Colin Powell's crucial presentation to the United Nations back in February.

Why We Are in Iraq

SEPTEMBER 1, 2003

One of the most important stories of 2003 appeared recently and got significant play—but not nearly enough. There's still time for the rest of the media to catch up and, in most cases, honestly admit that they promoted one of the most lethal rush-to-judgments of the modern era. The report was written by Charles J. Hanley, special correspondent for The Associated Press, who shared a Pulitzer

Prize in 2000. It utterly demolishes Secretary of State Colin Powell's much-lauded Feb. 5 presentation to the United Nations on Iraq's weapons of mass destruction and the need to go to war to destroy them.

Still, at this late date, why is this so significant, since the damage (lives lost, billions spent and billions more committed, anti-U.S. hatred inflamed in the region) is done?

Simply put, the Powell charade was the turning point in the march to war, and the media, in almost universally declaring that he had "made the case," fell for it, hook, line, and sinker, thereby making the invasion (which some of the same newspapers now question) inevitable. It's a depressing case study of journalistic shirking of responsibility. The press essentially acted like a jury that is ready, willing, and (in this case) able to deliver a verdict—after the prosecution has spoken and before anyone else is heard or the evidence studied. A hanging jury, in a sense.

Why does any of this matter? It's fashionable to suggest that the White House was bent on war and nothing could have stopped them. But until the Powell speech, public opinion, editorial sentiment (as chronicled by *E&P* at the time), and street protests were all building against the war. The Powell speech, and the media's swallowing of it, changed all that.

After Hanley's story appeared in the *St. Petersburg* (Fla.) *Times*, a reader named William C. Wilbur wrote to the editor, "I am surprised that the *Times* has not yet commented editorially on this further evidence of how the Bush administration has misled Congress, the American public, and the world in order to justify war." It's time for many papers to admit they were hood-winked—and to vow to be more skeptical of official presentations in the future. Here are brief, edited excerpts from the Hanley article:

ALUMINUM TUBES: Powell said "most United States experts" believed aluminum tubes sought by Iraq were intended for use as centrifuge cylinders for enriching uranium for nuclear bombs. But Energy Department experts and Powell's own State Department intelligence bureau had already dissented from this CIA view. . . . No centrifuge program has been reported found.

REVIVED NUCLEAR PROGRAM: "We have no indication that Saddam Hussein has ever abandoned his nuclear weapons program," Powell said. But on July 24,

Foreign Minister Ana Palacio of Spain, a U.S. ally on Iraq, said there was "no evidence, no proof" of a nuclear bomb program before the war. No such evidence has been found since the invasion.

DECONTAMINATION VEHICLES: At two sites, Powell said trucks were "decontamination vehicles" associated with chemical weapons. But nothing has been reported found since. Norwegian inspector Jorn Siljeholm told the AP on March 19 that "decontamination vehicles" U.N. teams were led to by U.S. information invariably turned out to be water or fire trucks.

BIOWEAPONS TRAILERS: Powell said defectors had told of "biological weapons factories" on trucks and in train cars. He displayed artists' conceptions of such vehicles. After the invasion, U.S. authorities said they found two such truck trailers in Iraq, and the CIA concluded they were part of a bioweapons production line. But no trace of biological agents was found on them, Iraqis said the equipment made hydrogen for weather balloons.

DESERT WEAPONS: According to Powell, unidentified sources said the Iraqis dispersed rocket launchers and warheads holding biological weapons to the western desert, hiding them in palm groves and moving them every one to four weeks. But nothing has been reported found, after months of searching by U.S. and Australian troops in the nearly empty desert.

ANTHRAX: Powell noted Iraq had declared it produced 8,500 liters of the biological agent anthrax before 1991. None has been "verifiably accounted for," he said. But no anthrax has been reported found, post-invasion.

UNMANNED AIRCRAFT: Powell showed video of an Iraqi F-1 Mirage jet spraying "simulated anthrax." He said four such spray tanks were unaccounted for, and Iraq was building small unmanned aircraft "well suited for dispensing chemical and biological weapons." But according to U.N. inspectors' reports, the video predated the 1991 Gulf War, when the Mirage was said to have been destroyed, and three of the four spray tanks were destroyed in the 1990s. No small drones or other planes with chemical-biological capability have been reported found in Iraq since the invasion.

FOUR TONS OF VX: Powell said Iraq produced four tons of the nerve agent VX. But Powell didn't note that most of that was destroyed in the 1990s under U.N. supervision. No VX has been reported found since the invasion.

"EMBEDDED" CAPABILITY: "We know that Iraq has embedded key portions of its illicit chemical weapons infrastructure within its legitimate civilian industry," Powell said. But no "chemical weapons infrastructure" has been reported found.

CHEMICAL AGENTS: "Our conservative estimate is that Iraq today has a stockpile of between 100 and 500 tons of chemical-weapons agent," Powell said. Powell gave no basis for the assertion, and no such agents have been reported found.

CHEMICAL WARHEADS: Powell said 122-mm "chemical" warheads found by U.N. inspectors in January might be the "tip of an iceberg." But the warheads were empty, a fact Powell didn't note. No others have been reported found since the invasion.

SCUDS, NEW MISSILES: Powell said "intelligence sources" indicated Iraq had a secret force of up to a few dozen prohibited Scud-type missiles. He said it also had a program to build newer, 600-mile-range missiles. But no Scud-type missiles have been reported found. No program for long-range missiles has been reported.

Back in 2002, when the run-up to the war began, pollsters started asking how much Americans knew about who planned and carried out the 9/11 terrorist attacks. The administration, without quite saying that Saddam was involved, took every opportunity to link him to al-Qaeda and other terrorists and thereby suggest that, who knows, perhaps he had something to do with the hijackers on the planes. Since everyone knew that none of those hijackers were Iraqis, and that most hailed from the land of our ally, Saudi Arabia, the White House could not claim a direct link.

But did everyone know that? Far from it. Early polls showed that a clear majority of Americans actually thought that there were some Iraqi hijackers and that Saddam, indeed, was directly involved, contrary to all evidence. This, of course, might explain why President Bush was able to sell the war so successfully. But how did this misinformation or disinformation take root? Every few months, I returned to this subject, along with a separate myth—that the U.S. had found WMD when we invaded Iraq.

On the Second Anniversary of 9/11

SEPTEMBER 11, 2003

On this second anniversary of the Sept. 11, 2001, terror attacks, there is much to think about, especially in New York City under pure blue skies so cruelly reminiscent of that day. One of many things for the media to think about today is a simple fact: More than two-thirds of all Americans, two years after the tragedy, continue to think that Saddam Hussein was personally involved in the attack, despite the fact that no credible evidence has surfaced that links him to the crime.

Now, how much can we blame the media for this woeful misinformation? It's not a minor question, since surveys also show that avenging the 9/11 attacks proved to be the single most important reason Americans backed President Bush in his war on Iraq earlier this year—and continue to support our presence in that country.

Surely, the media are at least partly to blame, but how much? We all know that this link has also been forged by the White House and its allies. And let us not forget, polls have always shown that a sizeable number of Americans will believe anything—that Elvis is alive, for example, or that racial prejudice is dead. Still, this does not get the media off the hook.

The latest survey was released by *The Washington Post* a few days ago. It showed that 69 percent of its sample said they believe it is likely the Iraqi leader was personally involved in the 9/11 attacks. A majority of Democrats, Republicans, and Independents believe this. An Associated Press account on this finding dryly noted, "The belief in the connection persists even though there has been no proof of a link between the two."

In follow-up interviews, *Washington Post* poll respondents were generally unsure why they believed Hussein was behind the Sept. 11 attacks, often describing it as stemming from news reports or their long-standing views of Saddam. For example, Peter Bankers, 59, a New York film publicist, said his belief that Hussein was behind the attacks "has probably been fed to me in some PR way," but he doesn't know how. "I think that the whole group of people, those with anti-American feelings, they all kind of cooperated with each other," he said.

Similarly, Kim Morrison, 32, a teacher from Plymouth, Ind., described her belief in Hussein's guilt as a "gut feeling" shaped by television. "From what we've heard from the media, it seems like what they feel is that Saddam and the whole al-Qaeda thing are connected," she said. Somehow the public doesn't have its facts down yet, perhaps because many get most—or perhaps all—of their news from talk radio and gasbag TV shows that do little to promote the actual facts in this matter.

Polls also show that most Americans still believe Saddam had WMD—perhaps because most think we actually found them after we invaded the country.

Without blaming the media for everything, it is still worth pondering that surely it has done an inadequate job of illumination and education, a sentiment that *E&P* has been expressing since early spring. I saw a survey a few years ago that showed that 30 percent of Americans thought that it was the Russians who dropped the atomic bomb on Japan and another 20 percent thought the Japanese were the first to use the weapon. But that was a historical episode from more than half a century—not merely two years—ago.

2004

FEBRUARY

About a week after my column on poll numbers appeared, President Bush admitted that there was no hard evidence of a link between Saddam and the 9/11 plot—but this got little play in the media, so its impact on popular beliefs seemed doubtful. At the same time, his approval ratings had sunk to pre-9/11 levels. In early November, with claims that new oil revenue would pay for Iraq's rebuilding looking shaky, Bush easily won Senate approval for an $87 billion supplemental appropriation. The media, while focusing on the growing U.S. death toll, were practically ignoring the soaring numbers of the wounded. E&P also charted another syndrome: the undercount of the U.S. death toll by the military and media. The alarming number of deaths in the combat zone due to accidents, illness, or suicide were still not part of the official toll. A week later, several leading news outlets changed their statistics to reflect the real toll, and we felt that we had had something to do with this.

On December 14, 2003, Saddam was finally captured, and another "turning point" was likely at hand, much of the media suggested. At the end of the month, a federal prosecutor named Patrick Fitzgerald was named to head the Valerie Plame/CIA leak investigation. By mid-January 2004, the U.S. death toll had topped 500.

How We Treat the Injured
FEBRUARY 27, 2004

My vote for Iraq reporter of the year goes to a low-profile journalist who did not cover the war itself and has never even been to Baghdad. His name is Mark Benjamin, 33, and he serves as investigations editor for United Press International out of Washington, D.C. We have documented his work since last autumn, and now the heavy hitters—*The New York Times* and *The Washington Post*—are following his lead, taking a long look at the forgotten American victims of the war: the injured, the traumatized, and the suicides.

It was quite a February for Benjamin. Early in the month he was awarded second prize in the annual Raymond Clapper Memorial Awards for Outstanding Washington Reporting. The judges cited, in particular, his work last October in revealing that hundreds of soldiers at Fort Stewart, Ga., were being kept in hot cement barracks without running water while they waited, for as long as months, for medical care. (Twelve days later he exposed ghastly conditions at Fort Knox in Kentucky.)

This was one of those rare stories that produced quick and measurable results rather than mere promises. Army Secretary Les Brownlee flew to Fort Stewart, new doctors were dispatched, and within a month the barracks had been closed. Pentagon officials later declared they would spend $77 million this year to help returning troops get better treatment. And the media started paying more attention to the injured. Until then, the 2,000 non-fatal casualties were rarely mentioned.

Benjamin also was one of the first reporters to link U.S. illnesses and deaths in Iraq (and elsewhere) to possible side effects of various vaccines. And he was first to closely analyze non-combat injuries and ailments in Iraq—a step *E&P* advocated as long ago as last July. Benjamin showed that one in five medical evacuations from Iraq were for neurological or psychiatric reasons. He followed that with a probe of the unnervingly high suicide rate among soldiers in Iraq, and also revealed that two returning soldiers had killed themselves at Walter Reed Medical Center in Washington (a fact the military had kept hidden).

Now these issues are finally gaining a wider airing. In a Feb. 15 cover story for *The New York Times Magazine*, Sara Corbett profiled several badly damaged veterans of the 101st Airborne Division, now back home and coping with "sleepless nights, restless days, fractured relationships, and vials of pills that help with the pain—but not enough." The number of injured in Iraq now tops 3,000 (counting accidents), with more than 550 qualifying as psychiatric casualties. Due to body armor, fewer die in Iraq; they get to live another day, but without arms or legs, or working stomachs, or fully functioning brains.

More than 100,000 troops will return to the U.S. this year, and many are likely to display the same symptoms of post-traumatic stress found in Vietnam vets. "There will be problems," one soldier, who came home without his right arm, told Corbett. "There'll be a lot of short fuses, a lot of intolerance. People are going to have to be patient with these guys."

Four days later, Theola Labbe in *The Washington Post*, in a front-page report, explored another one of Benjamin's pet issues. There have been at least 21 suicides among our troops in Iraq—well above normal rates for the Army—and this number does not include many others still under investigation, nor the two cases at Walter Reed and others on the home front. An Iraq vet recently killed himself at a Shoney's Inn in Tennessee, possibly by drinking antifreeze and Drain Pro, the Baltimore *Sun* reported last month.

Labbe added to these facts the wrenching testimony of the soldiers' families, who reported difficulties getting details on the deaths from the military. "We call them, we have questions, we want to know, and they don't have anything to tell us," one widow said. "They don't have nothing to say, and that's not right." The mother of another suicide drove around a nearby town for three hours on a tip that a sergeant who knew her dead son was home on leave (she didn't find him).

Why the high suicide rate? Trish Wood, a researcher for the Vietnam Veterans of America Foundation, told me recently, "The spike happened after Bush declared 'major combat operations' over. The troops found themselves in a very dangerous place, with no firm date that they would return home, surrounded by Iraqis who, if not hostile, were indifferent—certainly not bestowing the 'sweets and flowers' the Iraqi exiles and the administration had predicted."

And Mark Benjamin told me last week that he fears a "large cluster" of suicides in the coming months as tens of thousands of troops rotate home.

MARCH

For years, presidents had been attending the annual dinners of media correspondents in Washington, accepting some good-natured ribbing (to show they were human) and dishing out some of their own. Usually it's not highly charged, but then again, they had rarely taken place during wartime, and charges against the media of excessive cronyism were muted. This began to change in March 2004 (and, as we will see, would approach critical mass two years later with Stephen Colbert's controversial performance at such a dinner).

Did You Hear the One About the Missing WMD?

MARCH 28, 2004

It was a classic Washington moment, or, perhaps more accurately, a Washington monument, as it represents one of the most shameful episodes in the recent history of the American media. The date: March 24. The setting: the 60th annual black-tie dinner of the Radio and Television Correspondents Association (with many print journalists there as guests) at the Hilton. On the menu: surf and turf. Attendance: 1,500. The main speaker: President Bush, one year into the Iraq war, with 500 Americans already dead. Bush, as usual at such gatherings of journalists, poked fun at himself.

Great leeway is granted to presidents (and their spouses) at such events, allowing them to offer somewhat tasteless or even off-color barbs. Audiences love to laugh along with, rather than at, a president, for a change. It's all in good fun, except when it's bad fun, such as on this night. Because in the middle of his stand-up routine before the (perhaps tipsy) journos, Bush showed on a screen behind him some candid on-the-job photos of himself. One featured him gazing out a window, as Bush narrated, smiling: "Those weapons of mass destruction have got to be somewhere." According to the transcript, this was greeted with "laughter and applause."

A few seconds later, he was shown looking under papers, behind drapes, and even under his desk, with this narration: "Nope, no weapons over there" (met with more laughter and applause), and then "Maybe under here?" (just laughter this time). Still searching, he settled for finding a photo revealing the Skull and Bones secret signal.

The Washington Post seemed to find this something of a howl. Jennifer Frey's report, carried on the front page of the Style section—under the headline "George Bush, Entertainer in Chief"—led with Donald Trump's appearance, and mentioned without comment Bush's "recurring joke" of searching for the WMD. The Associated Press review was equally jovial: "President Bush poked fun at his staff, his Democratic challenger, and himself Wednesday night at a black-tie dinner where he hobnobbed with the news media." In fact, it is hard to find any immediate account of the affair that raised questions about the president's slide show. Many noted that the WMD jokes were met with general and loud laughter.

The reporters covering the gala were apparently as swept away with laughter as the guests. One of the few attendees to criticize the president's gag, David Corn of *The Nation*, tells me he heard not a single complaint from his colleagues at the after-dinner party. Corn wondered if they would have laughed if President Reagan, following the truck bombing of our Marine barracks in Beirut, which killed 241, had said at a similar dinner: "Guess we forgot to put in a stop light."

The backlash, such as it is, that has emerged since has come not from many in the media, but from Democrats—and some Iraq veterans. But don't expect any public second thoughts from most attendees. After all, many of them also sold the public a bill of goods on WMD. No kidding.

APRIL

As noted earlier, I was raising the Vietnam analogy as early as my interview with Daniel Ellsberg two months before the war started. What those who belittled the Vietnam comparisons—they don't do it so much anymore—didn't understand, or chose not to confront, was that the link was never meant to suggest that casualties or overall impact in American society (without a draft) would be equal, but that the U.S. engagement would likely last for many, many years, because once an occupation starts, any president is reluctant to admit failure or that lives were needlessly lost. Several times, in coming years, I would compare similar optimistic statements by President Johnson and President Bush.

Good Morning, Vietnam

APRIL 8, 2004

Over a very pleasant breakfast in Illinois last fall, a distinguished military officer/journalist chided me, quite pleasantly, for warning, on more than one occasion, that the current conflict in Iraq could turn into a Vietnam-like quagmire. He wasn't the first to do that and, I have to admit, at the time it crossed my mind that he could be right.

Five months later, even Bill O'Reilly is making the connection. On Monday he compared the Iraqis to the South Vietnamese in their lack of devotion to the United States and our values. "If these people won't help us, we need to get out in an orderly manner," he said. Patrick Buchanan, who had opposed the war but then backed U.S. efforts once the fighting began, said this week, "We have gotten ourselves bogged down in what is clearly a quagmire." And in a newspaper column on Wednesday, he wrote, "What Fallujah and the Shiite attacks Sunday tell us is that failure is now an option."

But then, like me, they are old enough to have lived through the Vietnam era. So for the benefit of those who did not, or who did but don't see the link, allow me—on this day when banner headlines across the country suggest that Iraq this week is experiencing its own mini-version of a "Tet Offensive"—to make the following arguments.

Of course, Iraq is not precisely Vietnam, even beyond the desert vs. jungle terrain. We've been there for one year, not a decade. And there are, of course, many other dissimilarities.

But anyone who lived through Vietnam, even halfway aware, has to be haunted by the current frustration with the failure to truly win the "hearts and minds" of the Iraqi people; with dropping bombs on certain cities to save them; with the charges that critics of the war and its aftermath here at home are aiding and abetting the enemy; with no exit strategy in place—no light at the end of the tunnel.

Then there's the matter of the bogus "Gulf of Tonkin incident" in spades: no weapons of mass destruction.

On top of that, this week, we witness spiraling U.S. casualties, and hear calls to send more U.S. troops to Iraq, which will (surely) win the peace. U.S. officers on the scene lament that going after the bad guys necessitates killing civilians, which they recognize inspires even greater anger and opposition against us. Our soldiers do not know who is on our side—who they should save and who they should shoot. Sound familiar?

"You're going to have good days and bad days," Secretary of Defense McNamara said this week. I mean, Secretary of Defense Rumsfeld.

It's said that we are making progress in Iraq because polls show that the majority of Iraqis are with us—just as it was said that most of the South Vietnamese were on our side. Free elections are a panacea. Look what that got us in Vietnam.

And, most chillingly, the administration, and many newspapers, in editorials, raise the very issue that kept us in Vietnam so long: we must not "bug out," as Richard Nixon memorably put it, or "cut and run." Plus: Every casualty we take means we have to stay longer—so they will have not died in vain. And we must show our "resolve" or we will be seen as "weak." There's even a new "domino theory" in reverse: we must establish democracy in Iraq (apparently at any cost) to inspire American-friendly governments throughout the region.

So it seems only right that we still have William Safire with us, as he was with Nixon then, urging all of us, last week, to turn the page on how we got into this war, as this represents the evil of being stuck in the past when there is so much in the present to address—this from a man who wrote countless columns on Whitewater for years when Bill Clinton was president.

And for those who believe John Kerry may be the answer: Even if he becomes president, he will inherit an impossible situation under tremendous pressure (as an allegedly weak-on-defense Democrat) not to "bug out"—especially since he supported the war at the start. His top national security advisor suggested this week that Kerry might be in favor of sending *more* troops now.

With that in mind, it seems proper to close with the shockingly long list of one-day American fatalities in Iraq listed in *The New York Times* today, as a reminder of the human costs of this war—and the beauty of this glorious mix of names (even a Mitchell) that reflect the true greatness of this country: Robert Arsiaga, Ahmed Cason, Yihiyh Chen, Israel Garza, Deryk Hallal, Stephen Hiller, Forest Jostes, David McKeever, Michael Mitchell, Gerardo Moreno, Christopher Ramos, Matthew Serio, Casey Sheehan, Jesse Thiry. R.I.P.

Military prohibitions kept the press from taking pictures of the coffins carrying American troops arriving back home, often via a base in Dover, Delaware. This continued a policy embraced by the Clinton administration, and the media, with scattered exceptions, did not fight the ban very strenuously. This was in keeping with the almost antiseptic coverage of the war, at least in the visual realm. The media rarely showed dead or badly wounded bodies, and at this juncture did not often visit hospitals where the most tragically damaged were housed. The father of a slain soldier featured in this column, Bill Mitchell, would become an ongoing character in my writing over the following year.

Coffin Fit

APRIL 28, 2004

The father of a U.S. Army soldier killed in Iraq earlier this month, who believes his son was in one of the caskets shown in the now-famous Tami Silicio photograph, has written a letter to *The Seattle Times* thanking the newspaper for publishing the picture that broke a Pentagon ban. "Hiding the death and destruction of this war does not make it easier on anyone except those who want to keep the truth away from the people," the father, Bill Mitchell, wrote yesterday. The letter has not yet been published.

In a postscript to the letter, he added: "I would be willing to help that poor woman in Kuwait [Silicio] who lost her job over the picture which she felt needed to be seen. Possibly even with enough press coverage, the other parents who lost children on the same day as my son would also feel that she did a service for us." Mitchell is the father of SSG Michael W. Mitchell, 25, who was killed on April 4. Mike Mitchell had served in Iraq for 11 months as part of the 1st Armored Division.

Publication of the Silicio photo in *The Seattle Times* sparked controversy, with many newspapers endorsing the move but critics upset that it was done without permission of the families. The Pentagon and White House have reaffirmed the ban on such photos, also citing concerns about the families. But the father of Mike Mitchell has stepped forward to offer his approval, believing his son's casket may be in that photo. Bill Mitchell, who lives in Atascadero, Calif., had first contacted *E&P* last week after I happened to mention Mike Mitchell by name in a list of fallen soldiers at the close of my April 8 column.

The text of his letter to Hal Bernton, the *Seattle Times* reporter who wrote the story that accompanied the Silicio photo, follows:

"Dear Hal, I read with great interest your article regarding the woman who was fired for taking the pictures of the flag-draped coffins. My son, SSG Michael W. Mitchell, was killed on 4/4/04 in the first day of the Shiite uprising in Sadr City. He was one of eight soldiers killed that day in that attack. I am quite positive that he was inside one of those coffins in the picture.

"I am happy that you ran the story and showed the picture. I would like everyone to know the devastation that this event has brought upon Mike's family and friends. In fact, Mike's grandpa at 86 says that this is the worst thing that has happened in his entire life—that says a lot right there!!!

"Hiding the death and destruction of this war does not make it easier on anyone except those who want to keep the truth away from the people. I know that the current government policy has the bodies being flown in under the cloak of darkness. I also know that photographers are barred from the area so that pictures such as the one you ran in your newspaper cannot be shown to the people. Pictures such as these alter people's perception and awareness and they have to admit the reality of the situation that young men and women are being killed.

"I do believe our government learned this lesson from the war in Vietnam and that was one of the influential factors in bringing about its end. Things are getting worse in Iraq and if there is anything that I can do so that other parents can be spared the pain that is happening in my life, I will do it. Sincerely, Bill Mitchell."

MAY

April would be the cruelest month for American troops in Iraq since the invasion, with 135 service personnel losing their lives. Suicide bombs were killing dozens in the relatively "secured" (by the British) southern city of Basra. Then, any hope that world opinion, and sentiment inside Iraq, would shift in favor of the American efforts was shattered in late April when the first images of torture at Abu Ghraib prison were revealed, in The New Yorker *and on CBS, causing rage in the Middle East and anger here at home (though Rush Limbaugh and others opined that it just seemed like a frathouse sex party, "Abu Grab Ass"). Should the media have known about the prisoner abuse much earlier? As it was, CBS held off airing the images for two weeks at the request of the U.S. military.*

May 1 marked the first anniversary of "Mission Accomplished," and Bush chose the occasion to declare that "daily life" for the Iraqis was "improving" and "a world away" from conditions during Saddam's regime. Wags in the press quickly pointed out that on the level of jobs, electricity, clean water, and violence in the streets, among other measures, things were much worse. Bush also said, despite the Abu Ghraib revelations, that "people are no longer disappearing into political prisons, torture chambers. . . ." For the following column, I chatted with a Washington Post *reporter whose new book featured as its leading character a not very well-known general named David Petraeus.*

General Petraeus: "Tell Me How This Ends"
MAY 1, 2004

When Rick Atkinson learned that he'd won the 2003 Pulitzer Prize for history for his book *An Army at Dawn*, he was in Iraq covering the 101st Airborne's push toward Baghdad for *The Washington Post*. A year later, at Pulitzer time, he was back in Washington and his acclaimed book about his embedded experience in Iraq, *In the Company of Soldiers*, was climbing the best-seller charts. One thing had not changed: He still opposed the war he had covered with such distinction.

That shouldn't come as a surprise. The most-noted quote from his new book belongs to its protagonist, Maj. Gen. David Petraeus, commander of the 101st. About a week into the war last spring, he said to Atkinson, "Tell me how this ends." Atkinson considered it a "private joke" at the time, but it soon became Petraeus's mantra.

Atkinson, 51, has unassailable credentials in this field. He has written four books related to war, with another two in the works on World War II campaigns in Sicily and in Western Europe. His father was an infantry officer. As a writer, he considers war "my theme."

With that background, he feels "some obligation to be an interlocutor between the military and the public. There aren't many of us who have spent much of our lives trying to understand military culture and what the Army does." Beyond that, he considers war a useful lens for exploring who we are, even if it sometimes "requires looking through the glass darkly."

When I interviewed Atkinson recently, I knew how he felt about the war today but not a lot about his doubts while he was traveling with the troops through the heat and dust storms last spring, "embracing the suck," as the grunts put it. His book concentrates on observing Petraeus and his division up close without commenting at great length about the run-up to the war or Atkinson's political views.

In the postwar epilogue, however, he speaks frankly. Petraeus and his soldiers had performed well, taking relatively few casualties, and showing both restraint and courage in battle. But they "were better than the cause they served." It was "vital not to conflate the warriors with the war." The *casus belli* for the war, that Iraq posed an imminent threat to America, "was inflated and perhaps fraudulent." And if "the war's predicate was phony, it cheapened the sacrifices of the dead and living alike."

So I asked Atkinson, who has captured so well the glory-filled Allied struggle in World War II, whether he felt the new book was somewhat hollow, documenting the wrong war in the wrong place at the wrong time. Did he have mixed feelings about his own effort? "There's nothing mixed about it at all," he fired back. "I was against the war before, during, and after it. I have no mixed feelings about the hundreds of dead soldiers—it was a poor use of their lives. I was certain last March that we as a nation had not done all we could to make sure lives were not lost, but I'm dogmatic about it now."

Doubting the war, and with another book due, why had he put his life on the line to cover it? "I'm as weak-kneed as the next fellow in terms of getting killed or wounded in a war," he admitted. "You have to pick and choose in putting your life on the line. I just felt it was part of my responsibility to the *Post* and as a reporter, that I will share some of the risks."

Now, as a scholar of World War II, the lesson he draws is "that if you're going to fight a global war, whether it's against the Axis in the 1940s or against terrorism today, nothing is more vital than nurturing a powerful, righteous coalition." Failing to do this has placed a tragically unfair burden on our military. "They took down a country the size of California in three weeks," he pointed out, "but there was not much thought devoted to the question of what happens next. It's astonishing how little thought was given."

But what about the argument that leaving Iraq now would dishonor the soldiers who have died so far? "It's not George Bush's military," he replied, "but the country's as a whole, and the collective proprietorship means we collectively decide if it is used properly and the cause is worth their sacrifice—and whether that cause should be truncated or we stay there forever."

So what can newspaper correspondents do now? Wars that last as long as this one inevitably become "corrupt," Atkinson said. "Even righteous wars corrupt soldiers, and documenting that is one of the responsibilities of reporters. A more concerted effort to watch this inevitable process of corruption is a hard, but an important, task."

The generally conservative Steve Chapman, in his Chicago Tribune *column, summed up the "stay the course" predicament like this: "We can't manage an increasingly turbulent Iraq with the forces we have. We don't have many extra troops to send. We can't turn over security to Iraqis because they can't be trusted. We can't get other countries to help us out. And things keep getting worse." Yet, he pointed out, "Democrats and*

Republicans agree that we have to go on squandering American lives because we don't know what else to do."

As May unfolded, each day brought fresh horrors, images, or details about the Abu Ghraib abuses. Pictures of shackled and hooded prisoners gave way to detainees on leashes, cowering before snarling dogs, or just plain beaten and bruised. On May 10, an Iraqi human rights official charged that American overseer Paul Bremer had been repeatedly informed about abuses at Abu Ghraib. The New Yorker *revealed that Donald Rumsfeld personally okayed a set of procedures that led to the abuses. Several major newspapers called for Rumsfeld to quit. At this time, I disclosed how my college pal, Charley Hanley at* The Associated Press, *had actually "broken" the Abu Ghraib story months before it came out via* The New Yorker *and other outlets—but the rest of the media had paid it little mind.*

Why Did the Press Ignore an Early Report on Abu Ghraib?

Is the press trying to make up for lost time once again? The media are now bursting with accounts of prison abuse at Abu Ghraib and other Iraqi prisons, but where were they last fall when evidence of wrongdoing started to emerge—when a public accounting might have halted what turned out to be the worst of the incidents? "It was not an officially sanctioned story that begins with a handout from an official source," Charles J. Hanley, Pulitzer Prize–winning correspondent for The Associated Press, told me this week.

Hanley started looking into accusations of abuse when he returned to Baghdad for his latest tour of press duty last September (he had earlier broken several key stories). It led to a series of pieces, culminating in a shocking report on Nov. 1, 2003, based on interviews with six released detainees.

He is still amazed that apparently no one else was looking into the allegations, and no major newspaper picked up on his reporting after it appeared. Why? "That's something you'd have to ask editors at major newspapers," he said. "But there does seem to be a very strong prejudice toward investing U.S. official statements with credibility while disregarding statements from almost any other source—and in this current situation, Iraqi sources."

The Hanley stories last fall told of detainees being attacked by dogs, humiliated by guards, and spending days with hoods over their heads, now familiar images in the American—and Arab—mind. Even after the Pentagon promised an investigation in January, and announced arrests in March, Hanley was "surprised there was not more interest and investigative reporting done. It's hard to fault my colleagues in Baghdad considering the pressure and danger they feel. Many stories are missed—that's the way it is in war. But clearly there is a mind-set in the U.S. media that slows the aggressive pursuit of stories that make the U.S. military look bad. The greatest fall-down, of course, was the uncritical and often ignorant swallowing of claims about weapons of mass destruction presented by often unidentified sources."

A partial transcript of our discussion follows.

MITCHELL: When did you get involved in the prison angle?

HANLEY: Last September I arrived in Baghdad for another tour. What sparked my interest was an obscure British Web site that cited Amnesty International saying it had gotten some information about possible abuses.

I set about trying to locate released detainees. I think my first approach was to defense lawyer–types from the Iraqi League of Lawyers. They gave me some secondhand information. While working on that, I talked to the military officer at the CPA [Coalition Provisional Authority] who was responsible for the prison program. He let out that they had just shut down Camp Cropper at Baghdad airport, which had the worst reputation for abuse at that time. They did not announce it, they just told me that in passing. I can only surmise that they did not want to draw attention to Cropper.

I did that story on Oct. 5, mainly about the closing of Cropper but also cited Amnesty's contention about physical abuse and their protests. Then on Oct. 9, I did a longer piece based mainly on the lawyers and what they were finding inside. The president of the Lawyers League was a former political prisoner under the Baathist regime. They had so many families coming to them saying husbands or sons [in prison] did nothing, they had been held for months, and couldn't even find where they were. Only a few of the lawyers had gotten inside. Of course we now know, from the Red Cross, that a large percentage of the inmates were mistakenly imprisoned.

MITCHELL: What led you to the released detainees?

HANLEY: The key was finding the right person at the Iraqi equivalent of the Red Cross, the Red Crescent Society. Then they began leading me to released detainees. In the end, with my interpreter, we spoke to six of the former detainees and they were from all three major camps—Cropper at the airport, Bucca in the south, and Abu Ghraib. One of them might have been in all three. We spent hours talking to them. Nothing like what we found had been published at that time, as I found out in a check of our database.

After writing the big piece, we held it and presented the U.S. command in Baghdad with a list of specific questions: Were certain kinds of deprivation and physical punishment used against detainees, as we were told, and why? How many deaths had occurred, and what were the circumstances? What types of weapons were used to put down disturbances? How many cases had there been of discipline or prosecution because of abuse? We learned that the MP [military police] brigade had sent responses to the Baghdad command, but they were never released to us, and there was no explanation given. Around this time, the MP general, Janis Karpinski, told an Arab TV interviewer the detainees were treated humanely. We quoted her on that.

MITCHELL: So what happened after your AP story came out on Nov. 1?

HANLEY: The play was very disappointing. A few papers ran it, like the *Tulsa World* and *Akron Beacon Journal*. It got wide use in Germany. None of the major U.S. newspapers published the story. And I was surprised to see that none of them followed up.

MITCHELL: Why do you think no one else jumped on it?

HANLEY: One reason is simple and practical—it's a difficult story to get, in a chaotic city like Baghdad. Although, in the end, simply realizing that the Red Crescent Society was the Red Cross liaison could have occurred to others. But the other thing is, there was no official structure to the story. It was not an officially sanctioned story that begins with a handout from an official source. A handout from CPA eventually happened in January, but even after that there was not much pursuit.

The story did not pop out at everybody. But there was a lot going on else-where. Clearly there is a lot of indiscriminate killing going on in Iraq in general and there's little focus on that. It's not like the only human rights story is behind the walls. But the one behind the walls is toughest to get out.

MITCHELL: Why didn't more papers just run your story, when it was handed to them, then?

HANLEY: That's something you'd have to ask editors at major newspapers. But I do think there's often disproportionate weight of credibility given to the statements of U.S. officials. There seems to be a tendency at times to discount the statements of others—people like Iraqi former detainees—if they're not some-how supported by a U.S. source, or perhaps by photographs.

MITCHELL: Rumsfeld said this week the military, not the media, reported the Abu Ghraib abuses.

HANLEY: This is strictly correct if you're talking about the specific abuses shown in some of the photos. But the AP provided specifics on other abuses through-out the system many months earlier and at the time was unable to get the U.S. military command to comment on them.

MITCHELL: What do you think will happen now?

HANLEY: My gut tells me the story will spread outward to Guantanamo and Afghanistan and to other prisons in Iraq. I guess it already is.

Starting with a column in early May, I confronted head-on the timidity of editorial pages around the country, as well as TV pundits, in failing to urge a major change in course in Iraq. Some had grown critical of Bush officials in promoting misleading evidence about WMD in the run-up to war; many others harshly criticized Rumsfeld for poor planning, and execution, in the post-invasion period. But almost none had stated that we needed to dramatically change course, perhaps by dictating "benchmarks" for the Iraqi leaders or setting a timeline for a phased withdrawal. In following years, I would write at least a dozen of these columns, which unfortunately rarely changed, as the editorial pages and pundits remained calcified on this matter, invariably expressing the belief, or at least the hope, that the outlook was about to change in our favor in Iraq. But at least Al Neuharth responded early on. He was an unlikely pioneer. A World War II hero, top executive at Gannett in its most Republican period, later founder of the very moderate USA Today *(once dubbed "McPaper"), he was far from a Michael Moore type. Now retired, but writing a weekly column for* USA Today, *he was utterly free to speak his mind, and he did.*

A Rare Call for Withdrawal

MAY 17, 2004

Al Neuharth tells me that he has written exactly 818 weekly columns for *USA Today* and his latest, on Friday, which advocated a U.S. withdrawal from Iraq—and urged President Bush not to seek re-election—has drawn "the fifth or sixth biggest reader response" of any of them. That's not to say the feedback is all positive. "It's split," he reports. "Rabid Democrats love it and rabid Republicans not at all. As usual, the independents are the most thoughtful." The heavy response, he says, "is not necessarily any testimony to my column but it shows the country is bitterly split on this subject."

So far, on this issue, among the top names in journalism, Neuharth is pretty much a Lone Ranger, but he has been in that position before. "I'm just an old fighting infantryman," Neuharth explains, "saying our troops don't have a real fighting chance." Neuharth calls the Iraq adventure "the biggest military mess mis-created by the Oval Office and miscarried by the Pentagon in my 80-year lifetime."

Over the phone, Neuharth points out that he does not speak for the *USA Today* editorial page, but, as the newspaper's founder, with a widely read column in the nation's largest circulation paper, his view surely has some impact. Still, he says he is "just another opinion writer" who is "not out to save the world." But he hopes to influence other opinion leaders. "The more authoritative folks, whether they are editors of papers or political figures, they are a little afraid to say, 'Yes, we need to get out,' because they are afraid of being accused of cutting and running," he says.

"I was a mild critic of the way we went into the war, and I've written that the [WMD] issue was bogus and I was never convinced this was worth going to war for. After the last few weeks with the prison abuses and the retaliation in Iraq, I felt that it was time for somebody to say, 'Look, it's time for us to quit justifying our position and find a responsible way to get out' . . . something I'd been thinking about a long time.

"But I have a sense that everyone is afraid to touch it. You're not supposed to be critical of a president in wartime.

"Well, I was in a war and one of the things I'm preparing for right now is the World War II Memorial celebration in Washington later this month, where I am on a panel with Mike Wallace. They are bringing a lot of us old farts back for our swan song. It made me think a lot more about how troops are supported in certain wars and ultimately abandoned in others, as happened in Vietnam—and I think will happen here. I just think it's inexcusable if a president or secretary of defense doesn't prepare well and can't give full support for troops they send into battle."

Still, Neuharth worries that "media leaders are reluctant to express" a strong view that puts them too far "out front." So he hopes that after his column, and any others that follow, "opinion leaders will look at this more critically as times goes on." He fears "it's going to keep getting worse in Iraq" and, because of that, Bush himself "may try to reduce troops . . . the call to send more troops will not be followed."

That would be good news for a large segment of readers who have responded to his column: National Guardsmen and reservists. Fighting in Iraq more than a year after the purported end of the war "is not what they signed up to do," Neuharth comments.

———————————————

My May 7 column on the lack of editorials calling for a change in policy in Iraq continued to resonate. Here's what one odd couple made of it, and my reply.

Rush Limbaugh, Abe Rosenthal, and Me

MAY 21, 2004

A. M. Rosenthal, former *New York Times* executive editor, now writing for the New York City daily *The Sun*, grossly mischaracterized something I wrote in this space two weeks ago. By yesterday, Rush Limbaugh, no surprise, was amplifying the lie.

In his *Sun* column on Tuesday, titled "Insulting the Victims," Rosenthal's views on the prison-abuse scandal in Iraq ranged widely, not to say wildly—he referred to the insurgency there as a "government"—but concluded that journalists who cover the brutalization of inmates without explicitly mentioning Saddam's mass graves "are truly embarrassing."

Let's forget for the moment the desperation of measuring our behavior on the Saddam yardstick. And the fact that most of the prisoners abused in Abu Ghraib likely had nothing to do with the mass graves, or possibly anything else very sinister (judging by the Red Cross estimate that most detainees in Iraq were wrongly seized). As Mark Twain might have put it, the man is "entattled" to his opinion. But before Rosenthal got to that final point, he chose to twist, to his own ends, something I wrote recently, introducing it this way: "The other day, an editor of *Editor & Publisher*, a trade paper, said all American journalists should come out in unity and demand the American withdrawal from Iraq."

Rosenthal went on: "The planned unity of newspapers, television, and magazines is not my idea of good journalism—or journalism at all." Now, on this point, one can only agree. The problem is, I never called for any such thing. My May 7 column was not addressed to "all American journalists" (print, TV, radio, Internet), and not even all newspaper journalists. It was aimed only at those who decide on editorials for the nation's largest newspapers—and it did not, in any case, advocate that they "all" do anything. I merely suggested that at least ONE major paper come out for a phased U.S. pullout from Iraq—as opposed to, say, sending more troops, which has been the favored position.

It seemed like a modest request, since the most recent *USA Today*/CNN/Gallup poll shows that 47 percent of the public now want us to bring home some or all of our troops. I imagine it's over 50 percent by now, the way things are going. Subsequently, appearing on CNN, I put that request in even more humble terms: I asked major newspapers to "consider advocating" a phased U.S. pullout from Iraq, or at the minimum begin a "healthy debate" on this subject.

Why did Rosenthal grossly mischaracterize what I am seeking? Perhaps he is afraid of that "healthy debate" on Iraq. And, of course, it is Rosenthal himself who ends up calling for "planned unity" by urging all editors "to present background stories about the millions killed by Saddam"—or else be branded "truly embarrassing."

Naturally, while the truth was still putting on its boots—or, to update Twain, its Adidas—this lie was traveling halfway around the world, via the Web. The rightwing Web site NewsMax quoted Rosenthal approvingly, adding its view of *E&P* as an "embarrassing" magazine. This didn't stop the site from quoting us approvingly, and at length, two days later in excerpting a column on the Plame affair—apparently because it portrayed *The New York Times* in a bad light.

Finally, if inevitably, Rush Limbaugh got around to the Rosenthal column, which he apparently came across on what he called the "watchdog" site "run by a guy named Jim Romenesko." Limbaugh then quoted the wildly inaccurate Rosenthal comments on *E&P*, pointing out that this is "a media trade paper" with a Web site that caters to the media "chatting to each other. . . . But that's what *Editor & Publisher* is, I'm not kidding."

Finally, acting aghast, he added (according to the transcript posted on his Web site): "So we've got an editor of a media trade publication, actually suggesting a coordinated, unified agenda." This led, as you knew it would, to suggestions of liberal media bias.

Still, I have to thank Rush for one thing. In the course of his attack, he mentioned *E&P* on the Web, "but, you know, I don't go there every day." Love that line. We should blaze it across the top of our home page, as an endorsement.

Several writers—Jack Shafer and Michael Massing come to mind—were early and persistent critics of Judith Miller and the failure of The New York Times *to rebuke her for her deeply destructive WMD reporting, but no publication was as persistent as E&P in this matter. One of our online columnists, William E. Jackson, Jr., produced many stinging pieces, often relying on sources inside the* Times *newsroom or Washington bureau. Finally, Bill Keller, the paper's executive editor, would order a partial confession—what Shafer memorably called a "mini-culpa." The* Times *tried to shield the guilty parties, and I was the first to identify who wrote the flawed pieces. The paper's reluctant review sparked some other papers that had carried the faulty* Times *accounts to run corrections of their own. Many of them placed their own apology in a far more prominent positions than did the* Times.

About *Times:* It Finally Accepts Blame on WMD

May 27, 2004

Battered for months by criticism of their paper's coverage of WMD in Iraq—mainly directed at star reporter Judith Miller—the editors of *The New York Times,* in an extraordinary note to readers this morning, finally tackled the subject, acknowledging it was "past time" they do so. Following the sudden fall last week of Ahmad Chalabi, Miller's most famous source, they probably had no choice.

While it does not, in some ways, go nearly far enough, and is buried on page A10, this low-key but scathing self-rebuke is nothing less than a primer on how not to do journalism, particularly if you are an enormously influential newspaper with a costly invasion of another nation at stake. Today's critique is, in its own way, as devastating as last year's front-page corrective on Jayson Blair, though not nearly as long.

Nowhere in it, however, does the name of Judith Miller appear. The editors claim that the "problematic articles varied in authorship" and point out that while critics have "focused blame on individual reporters . . . the problem was more complicated."

Yet, even in the *paper's own view,* Miller was the main culprit, though they seem reluctant, or ashamed, to say so. This is clear in analyzing today's critique. The editors single out six articles as being especially unfortunate, and (a little research reveals) Judith Miller had a hand in four of them: writing two on her own, co-authoring the other two with Michael Gordon. The only two non-Miller pieces were the earliest in the chronology, and they barely receive mention.

While refusing to name Miller, the critique in the *Times* plainly and persistently finds fault. In referring to one of the bogus Miller pieces, the editors explain, "It looks as if we, along with the administration, were taken in." Then, just as tellingly, they add: "And until now we have not reported that to our readers." The editors observe that administration officials now acknowledge "they sometimes fell for misinformation" from exile sources, mentioning Chalabi as one. So, they note, did many news organizations, adding, "in particular, this one," an amazing admission.

Then consider this: "Editors at several levels who should have been challenging reporters and pressing for more skepticism were perhaps too intent on rushing scoops into the paper. Accounts of Iraqi defectors were not always weighed against their strong desire to have Saddam Hussein ousted. Articles based on dire claims about Iraq tended to get prominent display, while follow-up articles that called the original ones into question were sometimes buried. In some cases, there was no follow-up at all."

Yet nowhere does the *Times* suggest that it is penalizing any editors or reporters in any way.

One of the false Miller and Gordon stories (touting the now-famous "aluminum tubes") did contain a few qualifiers, but they were "buried deep." When the pair followed up five days later they did report some misgivings by others, but these too "appeared deep in the article." When the *Times* finally gave "full voice" to skeptics, the challenge was reported on page A10, but "it might well have belonged on page A1."

Of course, the same could be said of their note today—it also falls on page A10.

Another Miller article, from April 21, 2003, that featured an Iraqi scientist (who later turned out to be an intelligence officer), seemed to go out of its way to provide what the *Times* calls "the justification the Americans had been seeking for the invasion." But in hindsight there was just one problem: "The *Times* never followed up on the veracity of this source or the attempts to verify his claims."

Yet the critique ends on a hopeful note: "We consider the story of Iraq's weapons, and of the pattern of misinformation, to be unfinished business. And we fully intend to continue aggressive reporting aimed at setting the record straight."

But Executive Editor Bill Keller continues to defend the editors' note, and blamed "overwrought" critics for overreacting to the WMD coverage in the *Times*. Asked why he finally published the editors' note, Keller (quoted in *The*

Washington Post) replied: "Mainly because it was a distraction. This buzz about our coverage had become a kind of conventional wisdom, much of it overwrought and misinformed."

With his managing editor, Jill Abramson, he penned a memo to staffers explaining that the critique in the paper was "not an attempt to find a scapegoat or to blame reporters for not knowing then what we know now." The problem, of course, was that certain reporters ignored, or only paid lip service to, evidence that "we know now" but was often also available then.

JUNE

As the U.S. death toll mounted, several media outlets honored the victims by giving a name to the numbers. Ted Koppel read the hundreds of names on ABC's Nightline *as their photos appeared on screen,* USA Today *and other papers printed an entire list. In each instance, those who took note of the dead were accused of doing it as an "anti-war" statement. Even before it was scheduled to appear, Garry Trudeau's plan to list the more than 700 names of U.S. military personnel killed in Iraq in an upcoming* Doonesbury *sparked controversy, with some readers bombarding newspapers with calls to pull the cartoon that day. One of the names that would appear in the May 31 comic strip: Mike Mitchell.*

From Sadr City to *Doonesbury*

JUNE 1, 2004

Bill Mitchell never expected his boy to make *Doonesbury*, let alone *Nightline*. He was happy enough that his son Mike had made a man of himself in the U.S. Army, while not losing his compassion and fun-loving nature. But now, this spring, here is the face of Michael W. Mitchell, staff sergeant in the U.S. Army, in *The Washington Post*, on *Nightline*, and on the front page of *USA Today*, his name plastered all over other newspapers and, this past Sunday, etched in a panel of Garry Trudeau's comic strip.

What this means, of course, is that Mike Mitchell is a victim of the war in Iraq, shot by a sniper on April 4, dead at the age of 25, after volunteering to take control of a tank's machine gun during an ambush in Sadr City.

What does his father, a 53-year-old Army veteran who lives in Atascadero, Calif., think of the *Doonesbury* mention and similar honors, which some pro-warriors in the press have denounced? "I like seeing the names out there," he told me last week, six days before Trudeau's tribute. "Otherwise, they are just unknown soldiers."

Surprisingly, he took it further: "I would welcome printing the name of anyone who has died due to this war. Is an American death worth more than the death of an Iraqi, an Australian, or a Spaniard? I would bet you the grieving parents of those who were killed could straighten out some people in America who only think our loved ones are important! These deaths are the real cost of war, and every single one should be given the honorable mention it deserves."

Bill didn't require the death of his son to oppose this war, however. He carried a sign during a March 20 peace protest near his home that read, "Bring my son home now." Less than three weeks later, Mike would come home, in a coffin with a flag draped over it.

I met Bill Mitchell (no relation) in an odd but apt way. Back in April, I ended a column with a tribute to the Americans lately killed in action, using a list *The New York Times* (but few others) carries every day. Among the names: Michael W. Mitchell. Someone apparently forwarded this column to Bill, who was in Germany, looking after Mike's fiancee, Bianca. Bill wrote me a note thanking me for attaching a name to the number that was his son.

We began corresponding. When Tami Silicio's now-famous photo of caskets waiting to be flown home from Kuwait appeared in *The Seattle Times*, breaking the Pentagon ban on such shots, Bill told me he was positive the body of his son was in one of them. Later, he sent me a letter he'd just mailed to *The Seattle Times*, backing what Silicio and the newspaper had done, and I wrote a column about that.

Then Bill sent me a copy of a letter he had mailed to Mike's commanding officer, full of pride, gratitude, and anger. One line jumped out at me, as Bill described the "irony" that his son "was killed by the very people that he was liberating. This is insanity!" He added: "I am having a major problem with being OK with his death under these circumstances and I really do not believe that Iraq, the world, or the lives of his family and friends are better due to his death." One can only imagine the pain between those lines.

Bill's now back in California. When Bill was out of the country, he had to refuse offers to appear on major TV shows, and he now finds that interest in Mike's story has passed. "It's as if I missed the window of opportunity," he said. Now the media focus on more sensational war news while "ignoring those who are still dying every day." But Bill also takes a longer view: "Someone needs to take a step back and analyze what has happened in Iraq over the last 14 months. We are now at war with those very people that we set out to liberate. I just keep asking people how they would be acting if Iraqi tanks were running up and down the streets of America."

JULY

The federal 9/11 commission concluded there was no substantive link between al-Qaeda and Saddam Hussein. A New York Times *editorial called on President Bush to "apologize to the American people, who were led to believe something different." Then it chastised Dick Cheney for "continuing to declare" a likely Saddam/Osama connection. Well, Cheney wasn't going to take that hunkering down. He called the* Times *coverage of the commission's findings "outrageous," sometimes "malicious," and continued to call evidence of the Iraq connection to al-Qaeda "overwhelming." Cheney also claimed, "We still don't know" if Iraq had anything to do with the 9/11 attacks. For example, he said, the claim that chief hijacker Atta met an Iraqi intelligence official in Prague in 2001—an idea strongly promoted by William Safire—has "never been refuted." This seemed odd, since the commission had just declared that meeting almost certainly did not take place. The* Times *also cited polls showing that 40 percent of the public still believed Saddam had something to do with 9/11, and suggested that misleading information coming from the administration had something to do with that. On June 28, the U.S. transferred "sovereignty" to Iraq, with Paul Bremer exiting and President Bush declaring "Let freedom ring."*

The Pluck of the Irish

JULY 1, 2004

Even those who rarely feel sorry for George W. Bush might admit to experiencing a few pangs of sympathy this week. His approval ratings hit rock bottom, Michael Moore's bushwhacking film opened big, and, to top it off, the president had to contend with a journalist who actually had the temerity to ask him tough questions.

The flap over his brief interview with Carole Coleman of RTE, Ireland's state TV network, on June 25, continued Wednesday, as news spread that, in retaliation for her sometimes rude interruptions, the White House had lodged a complaint with the Irish embassy in Washington and canceled RTE's meeting with Laura Bush. A White House aide told Coleman, "You were more vicious than any of the White House press corps."

Also Wednesday, a reporter badgered Bush spokesman Scott McClellan concerning Coleman's claim that the White House had pre-approved her tough questions three days in advance. Since when, several journalists asked, did the White House OK questions from interviewers ahead of time? McClellan denied that he had asked for her questions, saying that wasn't official policy, but could not say whether another office had seen them.

This may be nothing but a blip in America, but Ireland is still buzzing about it. It was the first Irish TV interview with an American president since Ronald Reagan occupied the White House, and it came just before Bush's heavily guarded visit to the Emerald Isle last Saturday. "Many viewed Bush's repeated chastisements of Coleman when she tried to challenge him as testy and defensive," Jim Dee of *The Irish Times* wrote for the *Boston Herald*. Writing in *The Irish Echo*, an American newspaper, Susan Falvella-Garraty observed that Bush probably now thinks that RTE stands for "Radio-Television-Evil."

Still, one could almost feel a little sorry for Bush, as he has grown so accustomed to reporters who are often stenographic, not confrontational. Since he has done so few interviews outside this feel-good bubble, he couldn't have been fully prepared for the quite different European style of aggressively holding officials accountable. Reporters there, when they get the chance, often pepper even the most admired politicians with harsh queries, sometimes butting in before a national leader has finished a sound bite.

Predictably, Coleman succeeded in getting Bush's Irish up. During the interview he must have considered repeating the F-bomb that Dick Cheney dropped on Patrick Leahy, or recalling when he told Michael Moore to get a real job. "Bono was never like this," he might have pondered. According to the Irish embassy, the White House seemed most concerned about Coleman interrupting or "talking over" the president. Indeed, impatient with stock answers, she did. Here's a little flavor, if you haven't caught any excerpts on the telly:

BUSH: Look, Saddam Hussein had used weapons of mass destruction against his own people, against the neighborhood. He was a brutal dictator who posed a threat, such a threat that the United Nations voted unanimously to say, Mr. Saddam Hussein . . .

COLEMAN: Indeed, Mr. President, but you didn't find the weapons of mass destruction.

BUSH: Let me finish. Let me finish. May I finish? . . .

COLEMAN: The world is a more dangerous place today. I don't know whether you can see that or not.

BUSH: Why do you say that? . . .

BUSH: Of course, I'm not going to put people in harm's way, our young, if I didn't think the world would be better. And . . .

COLEMAN: Why is it that others . . .

BUSH: Let me finish. . .

BUSH: Like Iraq, the Palestinian and the Israeli issue is going to require good security measures . . .

COLEMAN: And a bit more even-handedness from America?

BUSH: . . . and we're working on security measures.

Writing for the libertarian Web site Reasononline, Jesse Walker claimed Coleman "wasn't rude to Bush at all," but was "fair and professional." The president simply "seemed unfamiliar with the idea that a journalist might want some say in the direction of an interview." He noted that at one juncture, Bush "expressed his displeasure by emitting one of those deliberately audible mouth-noises that worked so well for Al Gore in 2000's first presidential debate."

Coleman herself admitted, "There were a few stages at which I had to move him along for reasons of timing and he's not used to being moved along by the American media. Perhaps they're a bit more deferential."

Well, if the American reporters don't think they go along to get along, the White House seems to think so. According to Miriam Lord in the *Irish Independent*, a White House staffer suggested to Coleman as she went into the interview that she ask him a question about the outfit that Irish prime minister Bertie Ahern wore to the recent G8 summit. Ahern, in case you missed it, wore canary-yellow trousers.

Perhaps Coleman, instead, should have asked Bush, former Texas Rangers owner, what he thinks of Michael Moore's baseball cap.

AUGUST

On July 9, a Senate committee report blamed the CIA and its outgoing director George Tenet for the White House's unfounded claims of WMD in Iraq. And speaking of unfounded claims: The federal prosecutor investigating the leak of CIA agent Valerie Plame's name to the media issued a subpoena for the testimony of Judith Miller. Meanwhile, her newspaper, The New York Times, *following its "mini-culpa" for its news coverage, now admitted "mistakes" in its editorials during the run-up to the war. But* The Washington Post, *which was even more hawkish on its editorial page and also guilty of misleading WMD reporting, had published no culpas of any kind so far. That changed suddenly.*

Post War Apology Falls Short

AUGUST 15, 2004

Like *The New York Times* with its editors' note in May, *The Washington Post* deserves credit for admitting serious mistakes in its pre-war coverage of WMD in Iraq. As with the *Times*, however, it is a day late and a holler short. At least the *Post* ran Howard Kurtz's critical Aug. 12 piece on the front page, something it inevitably failed to do with stories skeptical of the march to war. But praise for any paper should be limited when it merely acknowledges the obvious, with little corrective action promised. It should also be noted that last week's story was solely Kurtz's idea, although Executive Editor Leonard Downie, Jr., agreed to publish it.

E&P has regularly hailed the paper's postwar WMD coverage, singling out Barton Gellman, Dana Priest, Walter Pincus, and others for often beating *The New York Times*. The *Post* has no obvious Judith Miller albatross hanging around its neck. It put the Kurtz piece in a prominent position, not buried, as the *Times* did with its May editors' note. It even named a few names, also something the *Times* failed to do.

So why not give the *Post* a pass on the lax standards and disturbing attitudes revealed in the Kurtz article?

If the issue involved nothing more than a housing scandal in Montgomery County, fine. But when a newspaper helps enable a major military strike and lengthy occupation, readers may feel insulted by Downie's we-couldn't-have-stopped-the-war-anyway plea. This is especially true when a war turns out so badly, in lives lost, in money squandered, and as a net loss in the war on terrorism. Add to that the paper's notoriously hawkish editorial page rantings about the war.

By the *Post*'s own admission, in the months before the war, it ran more than 140 stories on its front page promoting the war, while contrary information "got lost," as one *Post* staffer told Kurtz. So allow me to pursue a few points. First, three quotes from *Post* staffers that speak for themselves:

• "There was an attitude among editors: Look, we're going to war, why do we even worry about all the contrary stuff?"—*Pentagon correspondent Thomas Ricks*

• "We are inevitably the mouthpiece for whatever administration is in power."—*Reporter Karen DeYoung*

• "[Bob] Woodward, for his part, said it was risky for journalists to write anything that might look silly if weapons were ultimately found in Iraq."—*Howard Kurtz*

Next, consider the highly revealing excuses, offered by *Post* editors:

• Executive Editor Downie said experts who questioned the war wouldn't go on record often enough. But his paper, and others, quoted unnamed pro-war sources willy-nilly.

• Downie also asserted that "voices raising questions about the war were lonely ones." This is simply rewriting history. On the eve of the invasion, polls showed that half the public wanted to delay the invasion to give the United Nations inspectors more time to do their duty, and millions had already marched in the streets. *E&P* surveys at the time showed that many of the editorial pages of major U.S. newspapers (though, crucially, not the *Post*) were expressing their own doubts about the need for immediate war. Many intelligence experts questioned the administration's evidence but were given little play, on or off the record, at the *Post*.

• Liz Spayd, assistant managing editor for news, offered another weak defense in explaining why a key article questioning the existence of WMD, by 32-year *Post* veteran Walter Pincus, was finally published on page A17 (and only after Woodward intervened): Pincus's stories are "difficult to edit," as she put it. But editors are paid to edit, particularly when stories pertain to the most critical issue of our time. Matthew Vita, then national security editor and now deputy assistant managing editor, offered another defense for the Pincus miscue: "We were dealing with an awful lot of stories, and that was one of the ones that slipped through the cracks."

• That rationale also applied to another sad case. In the days before the war, Dana Priest and Karen DeYoung finished a piece that said CIA officials had communicated significant doubts to the administration about evidence linking Iraq to an attempted uranium purchase. The story was held until March 22, three days *after* the war began. "Editors blamed a flood of copy about the impending invasion," Kurtz explained.

• Vita had a different excuse on another missed opportunity. One of the fresh revelations in the Kurtz piece was how, in October 2002, Tom Ricks (who has covered national security issues for 15 years) turned in a piece titled "Doubts," indicating that Pentagon officials were worried that the risks of an invasion of Iraq were being underestimated. It was killed by Vita. He told Kurtz that a problem with the piece was that many of the quotes with names attached came from "retired guys." But the *Post* (and much of the rest of the media) rarely shied away from "retired guys" who promoted the war.

• Other excuses rippled through the Kurtz piece, featuring phrases like "always easy in hindsight," "editing difficulties," "communication problems," and "there is limited space on page 1." One editor explained, "You couldn't get beyond the veneer and hurdle of what this groupthink had already established," even though the British press somehow managed to overcome that. Amid all the excuses, *Post* staffers denied that the paper was under any pressure from the White House.

• At the end of the Kurtz piece, Downie offered his ultimate defense. "People who were opposed to the war from the beginning and have been critical of the media's coverage in the period before the war have this belief that somehow the media should have crusaded against the war," Downie said. "They have the mistaken impression that somehow if the media's coverage had been different, there wouldn't have been a war."

Two responses to that final excuse come quickly to mind. For one, most of those against the war did not ask for a media "crusade" against invasion, merely that the press stick to the facts and provide a balanced assessment: in other words, that the *Post* do its minimum journalistic duty. If anything, the *Post*, and some other major news outlets, came closer to crusading *for* the war.

And does Downie honestly believe that nothing the media might have done could have possibly stopped the war? Especially when, as noted, public and editorial opinion on the eve of war was divided? Does he take issue with Walter Lippmann's notion that the press plays a vital role in "manufacturing consent"? And does he really believe his must-read newspaper lacks any clout? If so, what does that say about the state of modern newspapering?

SEPTEMBER

On August 27, Bush admitted for the first time that he had made a "miscalculation of what the conditions would be" in postwar Iraq. Three days later, he attributed most of the postwar difficulties to our "catastrophic success" in the invasion. Then, after a giant anti-war march in the New York City streets, he was nominated by his party for a second term. I was in the hall when he gave his acceptance speech, sitting about fifty feet from a female protestor who was kicked out while he was speaking. Sen. John Kerry, who had held an early lead, was now being "Swiftboated" and seemed incapable of taking a clear anti-war stand. The U.S. death toll in Iraq reached 1,000 around Sept. 7, and leading papers again ran lists of names and photos of the dead. But Bush and company remained surprisingly upbeat on progress in the war.

George W. Bush: The New "Baghdad Bob"?

SEPTEMBER 19, 2004

On his Friday night chat show on HBO, comedian Bill Maher cracked a joke about President Bush remaining relentlessly upbeat about our war effort in Iraq despite a week of seemingly serious setbacks. That made me realize that Bush sounds more like the notorious "Baghdad Bob" every day.

Baghdad Bob, of course, was Saddam Hussein's wacky minister of information, now immortalized on T-shirts, Web sites, and even a DVD for his optimistic, if fanciful, statements about Iraq's triumph over the American infidels, right up to the point we toppled his boss's statue. Baghdad Bob, real name Muhammed Saeed al-Sahaf, somehow survived and at last report was happily working as an Arab TV commentator, *sans* trademark beret.

But Bush as Bob?

Consider that in the past week violence flared at unprecedented levels across Iraq; U.S. deaths there soared past the 1,000 mark with more killed than at any time in recent weeks; a declassified National Intelligence Estimate painted a dire picture of prospects in Iraq; and reports circulated that our military plans to mobilize more troops and launch bloody attacks (post-election) on insurgent strongholds. A leading GOP senator, Chuck Hagel of Nebraska, said, "The worst thing we can do is hold ourselves hostage to some grand illusion that we're winning. Right now, we are not winning. Things are getting worse."

And yet President Bush suggested all week that Iraq was firmly on the path to stability and democracy. On Friday he told a newspaper, "The Iraqis are defying the dire predictions of a lot of people by moving toward democracy. . . . I'm pleased with the progress."

So was John Kerry right last week when he said Bush was living in "a fantasy world of spin"? Is the president really not so different from Baghdad Bob? Should he now be known as "D.C. Dubya"? Or "Baghdad Bush"?

Here are a few Baghdad Bob classics from the spring of 2003, verbatim (courtesy of one of his many Web shrines), uttered during the U.S. invasion. See if you can imagine them coming out of the mouth of our president speaking to the press today:

"I will only answer reasonable questions."

"The United Nations . . . it is all their fault."

"No, I am not scared, and neither should you be."

"Be assured: Baghdad is safe, protected."

"We are in control, they are not in control of anything, they don't even control themselves!"

"The battle is very fierce and God made us victorious."

"They mock me for how I speak. I speak better English than they do."

"I have detailed information about the situation . . . which completely proves that what they allege are illusions. . . . They lie every day."

"They are achieving nothing; they are suffering from casualties. Those casualties are increasing, not decreasing."

"They think that by killing civilians and trying to distort the feelings of the people they will win."

"I blame Al Jazeera."

"I would like to clarify a simple fact here: How can you lay siege to a whole country? Who is really under siege now?"

"We're giving them a real lesson today. 'Heavy' doesn't accurately describe the level of casualties we have inflicted."

"Those are not Iraqis at all. Where did they bring them from?"

"The American press is all about lies! All they tell is lies, lies, and more lies!"

"Even those who live on another planet, if there are such people, would condemn them."

"This is unbiased: They are retreating on all fronts. Their effort is a subject of laughter throughout the world."

"The force that was near the airport, this force was destroyed."

"Our estimates are that none of them will come out alive unless they surrender to us quickly."

"They hold no place in Iraq. This is an illusion."

"Once again, I blame Al Jazeera."

"These cowards have no morals. They have no shame about lying."

"You can go and visit those places. Everything is okay. They are not in Najaf. They are nowhere. They are on the moon."

"Rumsfeld, he needs to be hit on the head."

Bruce Springsteen, the often-political Boss, had endorsed Sen. John Kerry and said in a Rolling Stone *interview that the press had been "intimidated. . . . The job of the press is to tell the truth without fear or favor. We have to get back to that standard." One Baghdad correspondent for a top U.S. paper did speak out frankly—but not for publication. It made it to print anyway.*

What a Reporter in Iraq Really Thinks About the War

SEPTEMBER 29, 2004

Readers of any nail-biting story from Iraq in a major mainstream newspaper must often wonder what the dispassionate reporter really thinks about the chaotic situation there, and what he or she might be saying in private letters or in conversations with friends back home. Now, at least in the case of *Wall Street Journal* correspondent Farnaz Fassihi, we know. A lengthy letter from Baghdad she recently sent to friends "has rapidly become a global chain mail," Fassihi commented this week.

In her letter, she had written, "Iraqis say that thanks to America they got freedom in exchange for insecurity. Guess what? They say they'd take security over freedom any day, even if it means having a dictator ruler." And: "Despite President Bush's rosy assessments, Iraq remains a disaster. If under Saddam it was a 'potential' threat, under the Americans it has been transformed to 'imminent and active threat,' a foreign policy failure bound to haunt the United States for decades to come."

After she confirmed writing the letter on Wednesday, Paul Steiger, editor of *The Wall Street Journal*, stood up for her, telling the *New York Post* that her "private opinions have in no way distorted her coverage, which has been a model of intelligent and courageous reporting, and scrupulous accuracy and fairness." Fassihi, 32, covered the 9/11 terror attacks in New York for *The Star-Ledger* of Newark, N.J., and has also worked for *The Providence Journal*.

The reporter's letter opens with this revelation: "Being a foreign correspondent in Baghdad these days is like being under virtual house arrest. Forget about the reasons that lured me to this job: a chance to see the world, explore the exotic, meet new people in faraway lands, discover their ways and tell stories that could make a difference. Little by little, day-by-day, being based in Iraq has defied all those reasons.

"I am house-bound. . . . There has been one too many close calls, including a car bomb so near our house that it blew out all the windows. So now my most pressing concern every day is not to write a kick-ass story but to stay alive and make sure our Iraqi employees stay alive. In Baghdad I am a security personnel first, a reporter second."

Fassihi observed that the insurgency had spread "from isolated pockets in the Sunni triangle to include most of Iraq." The Iraqi government, she wrote, "doesn't control most Iraqi cities. . . . The situation, basically, means a raging barbaric guerilla war. In four days, 110 people died and over 300 got injured in Baghdad alone. The numbers are so shocking that the ministry of health—which was attempting an exercise of public transparency by releasing the numbers—has now stopped disclosing them. Insurgents now attack Americans 87 times a day.

"A friend drove thru the Shiite slum of Sadr City yesterday. He said young men were openly placing improvised explosive devices into the ground. They melt a shallow hole into the asphalt, dig the explosive, cover it with dirt and put an old tire or plastic can over it to signal to the locals this is booby-trapped. He said on the main roads of Sadr City, there were a dozen landmines per every ten yards. His car snaked and swirled to avoid driving over them. Behind the walls sits an angry Iraqi ready to detonate them as soon as an American convoy gets near. This is in Shiite land, the population that was supposed to love America for liberating Iraq."

For journalists, Fassihi wrote, "the significant turning point came with the wave of abduction and kidnappings. Only two weeks ago we felt safe around Baghdad because foreigners were being abducted on the roads and highways between towns. Then came a frantic phone call from a journalist female friend at 11 P.M. telling me two Italian women had been abducted from their homes in broad daylight. Then the two Americans, who got beheaded this week, and the Brit were abducted from their homes in a residential neighborhood. . . .

"I went to an emergency meeting for foreign correspondents with the military and embassy to discuss the kidnappings. We were somberly told our fate would largely depend on where we were in the kidnapping chain once it was determined we were missing. Here is how it goes: criminal gangs grab you and sell you up to Baathists in Fallujah, who will in turn sell you to al-Qaeda. In turn, cash and weapons flow the other way from al-Qaeda to the Baathists to the criminals. My friend Georges, the French journalist snatched on the road to Najaf, has been missing for a month with no word on release or whether he is still alive."

And what of America's "hope for a quick exit"? Fassihi noted that "cops are being murdered by the dozens every day, over 700 to date, and the insurgents are infiltrating their ranks. The problem is so serious that the U.S.

military has allocated $6 million to buy out 30,000 cops they just trained to get rid of them quietly. . . . Who did this war exactly benefit? Was it worth it? Are we safer because Saddam is holed up and al-Qaeda is running around in Iraq? I heard an educated Iraqi say today that if Saddam Hussein were allowed to run for elections he would get the majority of the vote. This is truly sad. . . ."

Making clear what can only, at best, appear between lines in her published dispatches, Fassihi concluded, "One could argue that Iraq is already lost beyond salvation. For those of us on the ground it's hard to imagine what if anything could salvage it from its violent downward spiral. The genie of terrorism, chaos, and mayhem has been unleashed onto this country as a result of American mistakes and it can't be put back into a bottle."

NOVEMBER

It was unclear, when Americans went to the polls in November, whether they felt they were given any kind of clear choice on Iraq. Sen. John Kerry had pretty much fumbled the issue, but the president had bungled the occupation so thoroughly—and his WMD excuse for the war had turned out to be bogus—that a repudiation seemed in order. A new survey, however, revealed that a vast majority of Bush's backers continued to believe, contrary to evidence, that Saddam had strong links to al-Qaeda—and possessed WMD or a major program for making them. Equally interesting, the new survey found that if the Bush supporters knew (and chose to accept) the truth, some of them might feel quite differently about the war. Asked whether we should have gone to war if Iraq was not making WMD or providing strong support to al-Qaeda, 58 percent of Bush supporters said no. Bush narrowly won re-election on Nov. 2. Almost immediately he ordered a new U.S. assault on Fallujah—partly to promote stability for the scheduled January elections in Iraq.

From Fallujah to Landstuhl: What About the Wounded?

NOVEMBER 11, 2004

Dozens of embedded reporters re-enlisted this week, and hundreds of newspapers recounted the U.S. invasion of the insurgent stronghold of Fallujah (which turned out to be not quite as strong as expected) as if it might prove to be yet another turning point in the war. The embeds, however, might have considered covering another death zone: the American tragedy unfolding at the military's Landstuhl Regional Medical Center in Germany, where most of the seriously wounded U.S. troops in Iraq are taken.

As of Saturday, according to hospital officials, at least 413 U.S. military personnel had been airlifted to the facility from Iraq since the start of the offensive, forcing them to add beds and expand their operations. And the pace has only slacked off slightly since the U.S. commanders announced on Saturday that they had seized the entire city. An additional 46 troops from Iraq were en route to the hospital Monday, Landstuhl spokeswoman Marie Shaw said.

To be fair to the brave men and women serving in Iraq, shouldn't the press place a few embeds at Landstuhl? While American fatalities receive major play in press accounts, you have to look deeply to find the numbers on the wounded and maimed. You don't get airlifted to Landstuhl for a nick or scratch. A hospital spokeswoman told *Stars and Stripes* today that at least half the damage came from burns, blasts, and gunshots, with spinal and brain injuries and "traumatic amputations" among them.

As bad as it is in Fallujah, imagine if most of the rebels had actually stood and fought? Having been warned for weeks of the coming attack, and knowing it would be tied to the results of the U.S. election, many melted away, perhaps to Mosul. Of course, if the assault had not been postponed until after the White House was re-secured, perhaps that mass flight could have been prevented (not that any newspapers I've seen are pressing this point).

Even so, the American toll is bad enough. As for the Iraqis in Fallujah: Air Force Gen. Richard Myers, chairman of the Joint Chiefs, said Thursday there have been "hardly any, if any, civilian casualties so far." This has already been disproven, but the scope remains unclear, partly because medical relief teams are still not being allowed into the city.

One thing we do know: For the Iraqi civilians still in the city and in the refugee camps, a humanitarian crisis is unfolding, according to local officials. There's no water, little food, and too much disease. And when the smoke clears, it will be interesting to discover whether battered Fallujah will become known as the Hue of Iraq.

Jackie Spinner, *The Washington Post* embed with the Marines in Fallujah, said in an online chat from the battleground (the mind boggles how they managed that): "No one I've talked to believes that solving the Fallujah problem will end the violence in Iraq. But, as one Marine officer told me, not solving the Fallujah problem will not end it either."

Well, that just about covers it.

Spinner also relayed without comment the official military explanation for why it seized a Fallujah hospital, and tied up all its doctors, on the first day of the invasion: They had to make sure the docs were not "insurgents" and also, "One of the persistent problems for the military . . . was the misreporting of civilian dead and wounded by the propaganda machines at the hospitals." This comes just weeks after the Allawi government itself released figures showing thousands of civilian casualties in the country, with estimates from others reaching into the tens of thousands.

Given Gen. Myers's claims today of no civilian casualties in this week's assault, it is odd that the Marines told Spinner that they had secured the "propaganda" hospital first "to make sure that civilians had access to medical care during the offensive."

What's to be done if the chaos continues in Iraq? Thursday, *New York Times* columnist Thomas Friedman joined his paper's editorial board in calling for more combat boots on the ground, two divisions worth. Now, where are those boots going to come from? An editorial in the *Times* earlier this week suggested that all the military had to do was raise "recruitment quotas" and, presto, enlistees would appear. Why? With the promise of 40,000 more troops in Iraq, the editorial declared, these young men wouldn't worry so much about their safety if they got sent there. Strength in numbers.

Just don't show them any footage from Landstuhl.

FIVE DAYS LATER, A FOLLOW-UP:

How the press portrays the aftermath of the Battle of Fallujah may determine what happens next in Iraq. In the days ahead, therefore, the media must look carefully at both the strategic benefits and the human toll of the offensive. While the issues are endlessly complex, they boil down to the simple, age-old question: Does the end justify the means?

A glorious victory to some may look like Bush's Guernica to others. In a report from the city for *The New York Times*, Robert F. Worth on Wednesday described Fallujah as "this post-apocalyptic wasteland" and "like a film that is set sometime on the other side of Armageddon."

With the fight easing—though by no means finished—embedded reporters can see more of (what's left of) the city and independent journalists are now braving the scattered gunfire. What they learn, the pictures they take, and the lessons they draw, will help shape public opinion as the administration ponders "Fallujah-type solutions" for routing insurgents from Ramadi, Samarra, Mosul, and other inflamed cities.

Jackie Spinner, *The Washington Post* embed, wrote on Tuesday: "Even the dogs have started to die." But she also quoted Marine Brig. Gen. Dennis J. Hejlik: "This is what we do. This is what we do well. . . . What I saw out here is a bunch of professional Marines and soldiers who were protecting the property of the Iraqi people."

This stood in contrast to another Tuesday report, by Dexter Filkins, of *The New York Times*. It described horrific conditions in the battered city: "obliterated mosques, cratered houses and ground-up streets." Filkins observed that "the American military faces the urgent but almost paradoxical imperative of rebuilding the city it just destroyed. . . . The devastation that the battle has wrought will not be easy to repair. The human and political effects of that devastation could rapidly spread far beyond Fallujah."

Filkins also showed what Col. Tucker's "combat firepower" actually looked like on the street: a tank firing a round at a single sniper, turning him "into rubble" as well as punching a hole in a minaret of a mosque. One insurgent remained alive in the mosque, so the military called for a pair of 500-pound bombs to be dropped from the sky, "and the mosque was no more."

Of course, an enemy shooting from a mosque may be fair game. But leveling a mosque is not likely to win the hearts and minds of the Fallujahans who will soon see it. Or, as Col. Michael Olivier told Robert Worth of the *Times*: "First we blow up your house, then we pay you to rebuild it." Equally disturbing: While we are starting to get a sense of the human effects of the "means," we still have no idea of how, when, or whether this will ever "end."

November would be the deadliest month for U.S. troops yet, with 137 falling dead. In a sign of the times, E&P reported that The Washington Post *was contemplating dropping its use of the word "postwar" to describe the current period in Iraq—and no wonder.*

Shoot the Messenger (Literally)

NOVEMBER 22, 2004

"The hardest thing," Darrin Mortenson told me over the phone from California, "was, after everything I've done, to be called a traitor." Among the things he's done: serve his country as an infantry sergeant and take two tours of duty in Iraq as an embedded reporter for the *North County Times* of suburban San Diego. But this week, in defending embattled NBC television reporter Kevin Sites—the man behind the now-famous video from Fallujah showing a U.S. Marine executing a badly injured insurgent—abuse is coming Mortenson's way in waves.

"Yeah," he told me, "I'm getting my butt kicked around here a bit. I try not to take it personally." Sites, still in Iraq with the Marines, is getting it even worse, from conservative commentators here at home and the troops (his former buddies) over there. "Sites wrote me first thing this morning," Mortenson informed me. "He seemed pretty down."

Mortenson, 36, had met Sites this past spring, during the first, aborted assault on Fallujah, and found him to be a fair and diligent journalist, and one who had previously covered wars in Afghanistan and Kosovo. He shared with me some of the e-mail he has received since writing a lengthy defense of his friend on Sunday:

• "That you would consider the death of a terrorist as something bad tells me all I need to know about you."

• "Sorry, I may be old-fashioned, but I prefer Ernie Pyle. At least it seemed as though he wanted Americans to win."

• "Go back to Iraq, with a target on your back."

• "If you go back over I hope they take your head."

• "Now each and every embed is in enemy territory. What I mean is, a reporter in the combat zones of Iraq now has no friends. . . . There is probably not a marine or soldier who will even attempt to save you if they don't accidentally shoot you first."

All this abuse came to Mortenson for daring to point out that the blame-the-messenger mentality, "which is always a sign of weakness in a democracy, is contagious and miserable. . . . When the news is good, everyone hails those hardworking reporters who live in the dirt and danger to accompany the troops, as long as their reports make us feel good. But when the images make us uncomfortable or force us to ask questions, we blame the media. . . . War brings out the very best and the worst in men, especially when both sides claim they have God on their side."

According to reports he'd heard from the field, Sites's relationship with the troops there is "doomed" and he "was last seen at the base camp near Fallujah eating alone in the chow hall, shunned." Mortenson told me he could relate to Sites's plight, because he'd been punished by the Marines during his embed tours for including certain unpleasant truths in a handful of stories. His phone messages and e-mails since Sunday have been running 70/30 negative, but "journalists have written from Iraq and Europe to thank me for backing up Sites," he said.

The soft-spoken Mortenson, a former military man himself, can't help but feel deeply conflicted. "Part of me wants to call for all of my fellow embedded reporters to come home, pack up, and forget about those hellish places where American troops serve and fight," he wrote near the end of his Sunday article. "The American people don't want to hear about it. Come home. It's not worth the risk. It's not worth a single hair on your noble and hardworking heads. Let them fend for themselves with government propaganda on one side and Al Jazeera on the other.

"Then, when the troops' sacrifices go untold, and we have no idea what's going on in the world and the military falls out of our gaze and to the bottom of the congressional budget, sit back in safety and listen to the armchair critics holler: 'Where were the media?'"

But his friend Kevin Sites was even more eloquent in an entry on his blog Sunday, which he addressed directly to the "Devil Dog" Marines he still travels with: "So here, ultimately, is how it all plays out: when the Iraqi man in the mosque posed a threat, he was your enemy; when he was subdued, he was your responsibility; when he was killed in front of my eyes and my camera, the story of his death became my responsibility.

"The burdens of war, as you so well know, are unforgiving for all of us."

DECEMBER

Despite the grim outlook, most reporters still failed to directly challenge the architects of the war when given the chance. When they did attempt to pin them down, the questions were often sidestepped or mocked. No one got away with this more regularly than Donald Rumsfeld. His artful evasions were even put in verse form and reprinted in a book of "poetry." But one enterprising reporter figured out one way to get to the bottom of one issue, at least. It led to one of the most famous quotes of the entire war: Rumsfeld declared that "you have to go to war with the army you have, not the army you might want."

Rumsfeld Caught with "Armor" Down

December 9, 2004

The day after U.S. soldiers directly questioning Secretary of Defense Rumsfeld about the lack of armored vehicles in Iraq made national news, an e-mail from a *Chattanooga* (Tenn.) *Times Free Press* embedded reporter ignited even more interest. In the e-mail, sent to another staffer at the paper (and obtained by *E&P*), Lee Pitts describes how he helped make the tough questioning in Kuwait happen: "I was told yesterday that only soldiers could ask questions, so I brought two of them along with me as my escorts."

The story was headlined this way at the Drudge Report: "Rumsfeld Set Up; Reporter Planted Questions with Soldier." But Tom Griscom, the Chattanooga newspaper's publisher and executive editor, commended the reporter's work today, telling The Associated Press that the question was one that members of the unit and their families wanted answered. Specialist Thomas Wilson, a scout with the Tennessee National Guard, asked the key question at the gathering. His picture appears on the front page of today's *New York Times*.

In the e-mail, Pitts notes that he had previously written two stories on the lack of armored vehicles in Iraq and "it felt good to hand it off to the national press." (One of his stories, exposing the fact that soldiers were scrounging for junk metal to bolt to vehicles, was published earlier Wednesday.) He added: "The soldier who asked the question said he felt good b/c he took his complaints to the top."

Excerpts from the text of the e-mail:

"I just had one of my best days as a journalist today. As luck would have it, our journey north was delayed just long enough so I could attend a visit today here by Defense Secretary Rumsfeld. Beforehand we worked on questions to ask Rumsfeld about the appalling lack of armor their vehicles going into combat have. While waiting for the VIP, I went and found the Sgt. in charge of the microphone for the question and answer session and made sure he knew to get my guys out of the crowd.

"So during the Q&A session, one of my guys was the second person called on. When he asked Rumsfeld why after two years here soldiers are still having to dig through trash bins to find rusted scrap metal and cracked ballistic windows for their Humvees, the place erupted in cheers so loud that Rumsfeld had to ask the guy to repeat his question. Then Rumsfeld answered something about it being 'not a lack of desire or money but a logistics/physics problem.' . . .

"Then he asked a three star general standing behind him, the commander of all ground forces here, to also answer the question. The general said it was a problem he is working on.

"The great part was that after the event was over, the throng of national media following Rumsfeld (*The New York Times*, AP, all the major networks) swarmed to the two soldiers I brought from the unit I am embedded with. . . . The national media asked if they were the guys with the armor problem and then stuck cameras in their faces.

"The *New York Times* reporter asked me to e-mail him the stories I had already done on it, but I said he could search for them himself on the Internet and he better not steal any of my lines. I have been trying to get this story out for weeks, as soon as I found out I would be on an unarmored truck, and my paper published two stories on it. But it felt good to hand it off to the national press. I believe lives are at stake with so many soldiers going across the border riding with scrap metal as protection. It may be too late for the unit I am with, but hopefully not for those who come after.

"The press officer in charge of my regiment, the 278th, came up to me afterward and asked if my story would be positive. I replied that I would write the truth."

2005

JANUARY

Hopes for the January 30 elections faded after the leading Sunni groups announced a pullout and boycott. Five embedded reporters had been expelled by the military recently, apparently for breaking rules. Still, I worried that fears about embeds shading their coverage in favor of the soldiers they bunked with had been realized. An article written by an embed in early January quoted an unnamed Marine lieutenant in Ramadi: "If anyone gets too close to us we fucking waste them. It's kind of a shame, because it means we've killed a lot of innocent people." But this came from a British reporter, traveling with American forces, writing for The Economist. *Few American embeds had passed along a quote like that, and I wondered why. According to that same Marine lieutenant: "It gets to the point where you can't wait to see guys with guns, so you start shooting everybody. It gets to the point where you don't mind the bad stuff you do." The question was: Do American soldiers only talk and act like this around foreign journalists, or were our embeds only telling half the story?*

Meanwhile, another official report declared that there were no WMD in Iraq, and a new Gallup poll showed that exactly 50 percent of Americans now called the invasion a "mistake." Yet officials who pro-moted a suspect war still seemed to get less flak than did a famous news anchor for promoting a suspect TV news story.

Rathergate vs. Weaponsgate

JANUARY 13, 2005

It's already clear that yesterday's official announcement that really, for sure—no kidding—there are no weapons of mass destruction in Iraq will get much less play in the media than the report on the *60 Minutes* fiasco released on Monday. That's odd, since the news stories share one important element: Neither was exactly a whopping surprise. Actually, there's something else: Neither scandal would have ever happened if journalists had done a better job at the outset.

So how did the press react this morning to closing the book on WMD? Most major papers I've seen, with several exceptions, did not play it on the front page. *The New York Times* ran a microscopic item on A16. It did devote an editorial to the subject, and, after mocking the White House and TV commentators, the *Times* acknowledged "our own failures to deconstruct all the spin and faulty intelligence." Then it went back to bashing the "fantasies of feckless intelligence analysts" and holding President Bush strictly accountable for the fact that 40 percent of Americans still think WMD are there.

But everyone was having a tough time explaining their original embrace of the WMD scenario. On the *NewsHour with Jim Lehrer* on Thursday night, Secretary of State Colin Powell admitted that the evidence on WMD in Iraq that he presented to the U.N. was "not correct," but later in the interview called the same evidence "solid, and it was something that we could rely on." No wonder Stephen Colbert, on *The Daily Show* a few hours later, said it was Saddam Hussein's fault for not *having* the weapons.

While awaiting the fallout from the WMD non-finding finding, the blogosphere, as usual, rushed forward with some instant commentary. The blog known as The Poor Man quickly posted a revealing "quantitative" analysis yesterday, comparing Rathergate with the claims of Saddam's WMD. Here are some highlights, which I've slightly revised, with "R" standing for Rathergate and "WMD" for Weaponsgate. This is not to minimize the egregious *60 Minutes* failings, but to highlight the lack of accountability for the egregious WMD claims:

Investigation recently concluded
R: Yes
WMD: Yes
Number of firings resulting
R: 4
WMD: 0
Use of highly questionable documents
R: Yes
WMD: Yes

Media spread questionable information
R: Yes
WMD: Yes
Central claim completely disproven
R: No
WMD: Yes
Number of wars started partly because of flawed journalism
R: 0
WMD: 1
Cost to American taxpayer
R: $0
WMD: $150 billion, so far
Number of American soldiers killed as a result
R: 0
WMD: 1,357, as of now
Number of Iraqi civilians killed as a result
R: 0
WMD: 10,000 to 100,000
Number of al-Qaeda training camps destroyed as a result
R: 0
WMD: 0
U.S. reputation abroad severely damaged as a result
R: No
WMD: Yes
CIA agents outed in effort to prevent or punish disclosure
R: 0
WMD: 1
Resulting government contracts for Halliburton
R: $0
WMD: $10 billion
Apologies issued by CBS: 2+
Apologies issued by the White House: 0
Medals of Freedom Awarded to those who played key role
R: 0
WMD: 3

Key producer unwilling to admit wrongdoing
R: Mary Mapes
WMD: Judith Miller

As the Iraqi elections approached, Knight Ridder's Tom Lasseter and Jonathan Landay offered an overall assessment of the situation and concluded that the U.S. "won't win the war." Their colleague, famed military reporter Joe Galloway, suggested in his column that the U.S. should simply come home, making him one of the first well-known pundits to go that far.

Declare Victory—and Pull Out

JANUARY 25, 2005

No one can accuse Joe Galloway of being anti-military, "French," or unpatriotic (although some may try). Few reporters speak more convincingly of loving the men and women in uniform. Now a columnist for Knight Ridder, he served four journalistic tours in Vietnam and was the only civilian awarded the Bronze Star during that war, for rescuing wounded American soldiers. He's covered numerous conflicts since, including the Gulf War and the 2003 invasion of Iraq, and co-authored the acclaimed book *We Were Soldiers Once . . . and Young*.

So when he says the United States should declare victory in Iraq and start to withdraw, it has a certain credibility.

When I talked to Galloway by telephone recently, he was in Colorado, about to head home to Virginia after several days of maneuvers with the 3rd Armored Calvary Regiment from Fort Carson, which is shipping out to Iraq in a few weeks. It was shortly after his column advocating a pullout moved on the KR wire. "When I go to Walter Reed Hospital," he tells me, "where some of the 10,000 wounded from Iraq end up, I go ward to ward and bed to bed, and reach out to shake a hand, and someone puts a stump in it. These are the best kids we've ever had in the military and this is the best Army and Marine Corps I've seen in my 40 years of marching with them. And I tell you, this war is not worth one of their lives, let alone 1,400 of them."

A Gallup poll in mid-January showed that 46 percent of all Americans now want to start removing some or all troops from Iraq. More than 50 percent now consider the decision to invade Iraq a mistake. Yet publicly calling for a pull-out, even at a slow pace, remains so controversial that very few of Galloway's fellow columnists or editorial writers have dared embrace the idea.

You can't even write about it without having your patriotism or your manhood threatened. Just before Christmas, when I penned a short piece for *E&P Online* on Al Neuharth's call for a pullout "sooner rather than later" in *USA Today*, I received hundreds of angry letters, many of them calling him (and sometimes me) a traitor. Some expressed the wish that Neuharth would be tried and executed. The fact that he was a decorated soldier in World War II didn't do him much good.

Galloway tells me he's gotten mostly positive feedback to his column, from soldiers, retired generals, and mothers of 18-year-olds from Texas informing him, "I'm not going to see my son killed in that war." But John Walcott, Knight Ridder's Washington bureau chief, says, "We have gotten some angry e-mails, some of them arguing that any criticism of administration policy undermines the morale and mission of U.S. troops in Iraq."

That Jan. 5 column had opened this way: "There may be 50 ways to leave your lover, but there may be only one good way out of the deepening disaster that is Iraq: Hold the elections on Jan. 30, declare victory, and begin leaving." His reasoning: There's no way to truly win and no way Americans will be willing to pay the price of a stalemate, particularly since the war was based on "false premises and bogus assumptions."

A stern critic of how the war was fought from the beginning, Galloway last year called for the dismissal of Donald Rumsfeld and Paul Wolfowitz. Those who reject withdrawal, he warns, continue to embrace the Vietnam syndrome; maybe the war was a mistake, but now we're there and we have to make the best of it.

"I say, bullshit, we can start to leave now," Galloway declares. "We can argue we overthrew Saddam and freed Iraq. This would give us a fig leaf to cover our nakedness as we get out." He points out that Robert McNamara recognized our cause in Vietnam was futile in 1965 but told President Johnson we could not cut and run. "We only had 1,100 dead in Vietnam then, less than we have now in Iraq," Galloway says, bitterly. "That's just one panel on the wall of the

Vietnam Memorial. Instead, we 'stayed the course' and now there are 58,000 names on that wall."

Yet he doesn't expect the press or the public, still reflecting a "9/11 mentality," to suddenly rise up against the war. The United States finally had to change course on Vietnam because of the draft and the high casualty rate. Soldiers in Iraq have not yet rebelled, partly because they are not draftees, and partly because, Galloway explains, "the ordinary soldier sees his friends die and he has to believe it is for something. Even if no one can explain what cause he is fighting for, he will fight and die for the other guy."

———————————————————

MARCH

After the polls closed in Iraq on January 30, the press, by and large, followed the White House line in declaring another "turning point," focusing on the strong turnout but not the Sunni boycott or the actual results, which promised a growing sectarian struggle. The death toll for Americans reached 1,500 in early March.

Reporters Air Grievances

MARCH 20, 2005

It's hard to know quite what to make of a survey of 210 journalists involved in coverage of Iraq released on Friday by American University's School of Communications. Drilling deeply into it over the weekend, I found some very revealing, if buried, comments by respondents. Here's one: "Our one raging controversy was over an interview with members of a departing National Guard unit. Our reporter, a Navy veteran of the Gulf War, quoted some of the troops as expressing fear. That provoked enormous outrage from higher-ups—to the point where we were barred from even setting foot on armory grounds in our own town."

Then there were the sweeping condemnations: "Mass media coverage in the U.S.—particularly cable—is horrible." Asked why material was revised, harming the truth, one said the editors "felt it was too negative toward the U.S. effort." Another said it was "toned down because our sources in the military wouldn't be pleased with overly critical articles."

While those responding to the survey remain anonymous, the researchers revealed that they came from both print and broadcast, that 35 percent said they had been in Iraq during the war or the aftermath and, of that group, about half had been embedded with U.S. troops. The report summarized the numerical findings this way: "Many media outlets have self-censored their reporting on the conflict in Iraq because of concern about public reaction to graphic images and details about the war." Many respondents reported no problems, but most troubling was a finding that nearly one in six of those who covered the war "said on one or more occasions their organizations edited material for publication and they did not believe the final version accurately represented the story."

To get to the heart of the matter, I clicked down deep into the often pithy individual statements by respondents, who presumably felt they could speak frankly on the rare occasions in the survey where the researcher asked them if they wanted to "add additional comments." Here are some excerpts:

Asked about specific incidents that had set off a spirited newsroom debate:
• "We had a photo of a child who was horribly mangled by a land mine. The photographer argued that it was part of war and everyone should see what war looks like."
• "The bombing of civilian areas around Iraq."
• "There was a lot of debate about how to write about the case for war made by the Bush administration and how credible it was."
• "Publish pictures of dead GIs on war anniversary."

Asking how certain disputes were resolved elicited these responses:
• "In general, coverage downplayed civilian casualties and promoted a pro-U.S. viewpoint. No U.S. media showed abuses by U.S. military carried out on regular basis."
• "Friendly fire incidents were to show only injured Americans, and no reference made to possible mistakes involving civilians."
• "On some occasions, the reports were subtly edited to make them less negative and more in line with official views."
• "The real damage of the war on the civilian population was uniformly omitted."
• "There was excessive pressure to show the 'good news' in Iraq."

Regarding the use of photos:
One said, "I think we sanitized the images too much so that people do not see the reality of war." Another referred to "plenty of Uday and Qusay [Saddam's sons] after death—not American coffins." A third complained about

failure to publish images that "indicate that Americans are in fact getting killed and maimed over there." A fourth noted that his or her news outlet "followed Pentagon wishes in not showing pictures of U.S. casualties."

But the most brutally honest opinions were expressed at the very end of the survey, when respondents were asked, "Are there any other comments you would like to make?" Among the replies:

- "The human cost of the war has been routinely omitted from most U.S. broadcasts. The American people has definitely not gotten the entire picture of the war's devastation and the infernal conditions in Iraq today as a result of our invasion."
- "We have heard, second-hand, that our corporate president has told producers to keep Iraq war coverage 'positive.'"
- "I was fortunate to not be embedded during the war when I think of the most blatant cases of self-censorship. I have heard many stories, from colleagues who were embedded, of execution of prisoners (including the wounded), of abuse of civilians, or cruelty and brutality by U.S. forces that were never reported."
- "As long as you are not at the front, you can not trust anyone. Unless you cross-search foreign papers."
- "My main reason for filling out this survey is that I have been distressed at the way the 'big boys' have covered the war, the prelude to war and its aftermath. I think too many bought into the administration line. U.K. press has been considerably better in covering the humanitarian outcome and the mistakes and errors in judgment by U.S. forces. . . . But the lack of coverage of Iraqi war dead, etc., and the only recent questioning of the administration line is very disturbing."
- "It seems to me that the American TV network coverage of the war and its aftermath was pretty disgraceful. There was virtually no skepticism about official claims. Americans who relied on TV for their news would have been utterly surprised by the current turmoil. I don't think that's true of British viewers."
- "Our news organization failed to subject the administration's various allegations to sufficient scrutiny and continues to do so. I believe this is primarily because it reflects—and does not challenge—the positions of

those in power. . . . [O]ur organization, like many others, completely failed in its responsibility to challenge the assertions of the White House. In short, it was not an independent voice intelligently assessing charges that would lead to war but instead a megaphone for a misguided policy. This was done presumably because our editors saw the story this way themselves and also I believe because they edit stories for 'Middle America' and they assumed that this is what Middle America thought as well—a great failure of the U.S. media that will no doubt be repeated."

I would add: Only if we allow it.

———————————————

MAY

On March 21, the libertarian-leaning Orange County (Calif.) Register *became the largest U.S. paper to call for the beginning of withdrawal from Iraq. Ten days later, the Silberman-Robb Commission declared that the intelligence community "was dead wrong in almost all of its pre-war judgments." Around May 1, the so-called "Downing Street Memo" emerged in the British press and, after an appalling delay, several days later in the U.S. media. It suggested that the "fix" was in. This private report on a July 23, 2002, U.S.-British planning session before the war revealed that Bush desperately wanted to remove Saddam but evidence for WMD and Iraqi links to terrorism was "thin," so intelligence and facts had to be "fixed around the policy" of "inevitable" invasion. A Gallup poll in late April showed that exactly half of all Americans now felt that Bush had deliberately misled them on WMD in Iraq, and 57 percent said they felt the decision to invade was a "mistake"—even though they were still being denied a true picture of the carnage in this war.*

The Great Photo "Cover-up"

MAY 21, 2005

A remarkable survey by the *Los Angeles Times* of six leading newspapers and two newsmagazines during a recent six-month period found almost no pictures from Iraq of Americans killed in action. The publications ran only 44 photos of the wounded. "Many photographers and editors believe they are delivering Americans an incomplete portrait of the violence that has killed 1,797 U.S. service members and their West allies and wounded 12,516 Americans," James Rainey of the *Times* concluded.

Pim Van Hemmen, assistant managing editor for photography at *The Star-Ledger* in Newark, N.J., told Rainey, "We in the news business are not doing a very good job of showing our readers what has really happened over there."

The survey covered the period from Sept. 1, 2004, until Feb. 28, 2005. During that time, 559 Americans and Western allies died, but readers of the *Los Angeles Times, The New York Times, St. Louis Post-Dispatch, The Washington Post,* and *The Atlanta Journal-Constitution* did not see a single photo of a dead U.S. serviceman. Nor did readers of *Time* and *Newsweek*. *The Seattle Times* carried a photo three days before Christmas of a dead U.S. soldier, killed in the mess hall bombing, but his body was covered.

The *L.A. Times* and *The New York Times* each carried 10 photos of the wounded; the other six publications combined had a total of only 24. That means that for six months, in eight top publications, only 44 such pictures appeared—when thousands of soldiers were injured. "I feel we still aren't seeing the kind of pictures we need to see to tell the American people about this war and the costs of the war," Steve Stroud, deputy director of photography at the *Los Angeles Times*, told Rainey.

A notable exception: Last year, AP photographer John B. Moore—one of a team of AP photographers in Iraq who won a Pulitzer in the breaking news category this year—got exclusive access to a U.S. military hospital in Baghdad and was able to photograph the dead and wounded. One striking image that he captured showed medics attempting to resuscitate a dying soldier.

"We made an effort not to show the faces," the AP's photo chief, Santiago Lyon, tells *E&P*, "but when we sent them out, in the U.S. a lot of major papers chose not to run them. Those papers and other media subscribe to our feed. They're paying a flat rate, and can run as many or as few as they choose. In this case, they chose not to."

Lyon feels the reluctance of U.S. newspapers to publish those images is not an issue on which AP should comment, even though gritty war images are shown much more widely in Europe. "We're providing photos and text to our subscribers, and it's up to them to use pictures as they see fit," he observes. "We've covered our mission. Of course, as a journalist, I think the truth needs to be told."

The publications have run many photos of Iraqi victims, with 55 pictures of the dead and wounded appearing in *The New York Times* in that same period, for example. But the *L.A. Times* survey also found that publications are much more likely to publish photos of "grieving"—scenes captured at funerals, memorials, and hospitals. *The Washington Post*, for example, published no photos of dead Americans, only six of the wounded, but 25 of "grieving."

"There can be horrible images, but war is horrible and we need to understand that," Chris Hondros, a veteran war photog, told Rainey. "I think if we are going to start a war, we ought to be willing to show the consequences of that war."

E&P had followed the controversy over Pat Tillman's death in Afghanistan for many months, focusing on how the press was misled by the military but also was all too willing to go along with the story, as it had much earlier in the case of Jessica Lynch. A new report on the "cover-up" came as TV bloviators were still blathering about the Gitmo Koran-flushing incident misreported by Newsweek.

No Pat Answers in the Tillman Case

MAY 25, 2005

Where, in the week after the Great *Newsweek* Error, is the comparable outrage in the press, in the rightwing blogosphere, and at the White House over the military's outright lying in the cover-up of the death of former NFL star Pat Tillman? Where are the calls for apologies to the public and the firing of those responsible? Who is demanding that the media never trust the Pentagon's word unless backed up by numerous named and credible sources?

Where is a Scott McClellan lecture on ethics and credibility?

The Tillman scandal is back in the news, thanks not to the military coming clean but because of a newspaper account. Ironically, the newspaper in question, *The Washington Post*—which has taken the lead on this story since last December—is corporate big brother to *Newsweek*.

The *Post*'s Josh White reported this week that Tillman's parents are now ripping the Army, saying that the military's investigation into their son's 2004 "friendly fire" death in Afghanistan was a sham based on "lies" and that the Army cover-up made it harder for them to deal with their loss. They are speaking out now because they have finally had a chance to look at the full records of the military probe. "Tillman's mother and father said in interviews that they believe the military and the government created a heroic tale about how their son died to foster a patriotic response across the country," White reported.

While military officials lying to the parents have gained wide publicity in the past two days, hardly anyone has mentioned that they also lied to the public and to the press, which dutifully carried one report after another based on the Pentagon's spin. It had happened many times before, as in the *faux* Jessica Lynch incident in Iraq.

Tillman was killed in a barrage of gunfire from his own men, mistaken for the enemy on a hillside near the Pakistan border. "Immediately," the *Post* reported, "the Army kept the soldiers on the ground quiet and told Tillman's family and the public that he was killed by enemy fire while storming a hill, barking orders to his fellow Rangers." Tillman posthumously received the Silver Star for his "actions."

The latest military investigation, exposed by the *Post* earlier this month, "showed that soldiers in Afghanistan knew almost immediately that they had killed Tillman by mistake in what they believed was a firefight with enemies on a tight canyon road. The investigation also revealed that soldiers later burned Tillman's uniform and body armor."

Patrick Tillman, Sr., the father—a lawyer, as it happens—said he blames high-ranking Army officers for presenting "outright lies" to the family and to the public. "After it happened, all the people in positions of authority went out of their way to script this," he told the *Post*. "They purposely interfered with the investigation, they covered it up. I think they thought they could control it, and they realized that their recruiting efforts were going to go to hell in a hand-basket if the truth about his death got out.

"They blew up their poster boy." He added: "Maybe lying's not a big deal any more. Pat's dead, and this isn't going to bring him back. But these guys should have been held up to scrutiny, right up the chain of command, and no one has."

Mary Tillman, the mother, complained to the *Post* that the government used her son for weeks after his death. She said she was particularly offended when President Bush offered a taped memorial message to Tillman at a Cardinals football game shortly before the presidential election last fall.

Newsweek made a bad mistake in its recent report on Koran abuse at Guantanamo. But it was a mistake, not outright lying. Yet the same critics who blasted the magazine—and the media in general—are not demanding that same contrition or penalties for anyone in the military. One *Newsweek* critic after another has asked in the past week that the media come up with just one case where they erred on the side of making the military look good, not bad. One hopes the Tillman example takes care of that request, though there are, of course, many others.

It is worth looking back at how Steve Coll of *The Washington Post* last December described the early weeks of the Pentagon spin on Tillman. "Just days after Pat Tillman died from friendly fire on a desolate ridge in southeastern Afghanistan," Coll wrote then, "the U.S. Army Special Operations Command released a brief account of his last moments. The April 30, 2004, statement awarded Tillman a posthumous Silver Star for combat valor and described how a section of his Ranger platoon came under attack.

"'He ordered his team to dismount and then maneuvered the Rangers up a hill near the enemy's location,' the release said. 'As they crested the hill, Tillman directed his team into firing positions and personally provided suppressive fire. . . . Tillman's voice was heard issuing commands to take the fight to the enemy forces.'

"It was a stirring tale and fitting eulogy for the Army's most famous volunteer in the war on terrorism, a charismatic former pro football star whose reticence, courage, and handsome beret-draped face captured for many Americans the best aspects of the country's post–Sept. 11 character.

"It was also a distorted and incomplete narrative, according to dozens of internal Army documents obtained by *The Washington Post* that describe Tillman's death by fratricide after a chain of botched communications, a misguided order to divide his platoon over the objection of its leader, and undisciplined firing by fellow Rangers.

"The Army's public release made no mention of friendly fire, even though at the time it was issued, investigators in Afghanistan had already taken at least 14 sworn statements from Tillman's platoon members that made clear the true causes of his death.

"But the Army's published account not only withheld all evidence of fratricide, but also exaggerated Tillman's role and stripped his actions of their context. . . . The Army's April 30 news release was just one episode in a broader Army effort to manage the uncomfortable facts of Pat Tillman's death, according to internal records and interviews."

JULY

Battles continued at a bloody level, with reports of more foreign fighters—absent from Iraq until the U.S. invasion—arriving every week. Yet many in the media and in public office remained in a state of denial. On May 30, Vice President Cheney told Larry King, "I think they're in the last throes, if you will, of the insurgency." President Bush called the Iraq adventure America's "golden moment." John Tierney requested in his New York Times column that the media give us a "respite from gore" from Iraq. On June 5, Tim Russert on Meet the Press referred to the "now-famous Downing Street memo," but in reality the mainstream media in the U.S. had barely mentioned it. Byron Calame, public editor at The New York Times, wrote that coverage of the memo at the paper had "languished" and readers were left "pretty much in the dark."

On another track, the investigation of the Plame/CIA leak case was continuing, with journalists still in the crosshairs. Time magazine's Matt Cooper finally gave up his source, Karl Rove (after Time, Inc., gave up his notes). In early July, prosecutor Patrick Fitzgerald rejected Judith Miller's plea to serve at home any sentence she might get for contempt by noting that anyone "who can handle the desert in wartime" ought to be able to survive a few weeks in the pokey. She was sentenced to jail for contempt on July 6, exactly two years after Joe Wilson's op-ed that started it all.

Plame Gets the "-Gate"

JULY 15, 2005

Today, July 15, 2005, may go down in history as the day when what has previously been known as the "Plame Affair" or the "CIA leak scandal" finally gets that most coveted of all scandal suffixes: the "-gate." So now we have: Plamegate. And with the eye-raising reports today detailing Karl Rove's conversation with Robert Novak, six days before he wrote his fateful Plame column, we are suddenly into "what-did-the-president-know-and-when-did-he-know-it" territory.

Plamegate. It's about time. Think about it: We had a Liddy then and a Libby now. It can't be just coincidence.

At *The New York Times*, the new duo on this case—David Johnston and Richard Stevenson—raised the specter of Watergate in one paragraph today when they noted that the latest news puts front and center the issue the White House "has never addressed": The president's knowledge of any of this. If the *Times* pair stay on the case, will they be the new Woodward & Bernstein? Somehow Johnston & Stevenson doesn't have quite the same ring to it, though it is early, and other candidates may apply.

And as in 1972 and 1973, a story that seemed fairly well contained, and threatening to become old hat, suddenly may spread, like an octopus, as testimony gets leaked, the press wakes from its torpor, and allegations appear that the White House may have been engaged in some kind of "cover-up" as bad as the possible crime at the center of the story. It's far from proven so far, but: Is there a cancer on the presidency?

These Watergate links may seem like stretching the point, but you will have to forgive me: In a column about Rove today, John Dean, Mr. Cancer on the President himself, cites a recent *E&P* column on the case.

In the middle of this decade, everything old is new again, or is it vice versa? Two years ago, when I was one of the first journalists to predict that the conflict in Iraq could become another Vietnam, many (okay, most) laughed. The analogy was never precise, and still isn't, and yet: Who is laughing now? Certainly not Bush, Rumsfeld, or Cheney, or the tens of thousands of U.S. troops still languishing over there, not to mention their dead comrades, and the deceased Iraqis.

In any event, the next few weeks should be riveting. Now that we know that Rove was one of Novak's sources, and that Novak had two of them, surely speculation will center on the office of Vice President Cheney and his aide "Scooter" Libby. What kind of name is "Scooter" anyway?

But more than anything, the question that will be asked today and this weekend is: What did the president know, etc.? Or is it possible the entire smear-Wilson campaign originated in the Oval Office, or the veep's chambers? Is former spokesman/chief spinner Ari Fleischer endangered? Will Rove keep his job?

Who is the source for all the press revelations today? Likely not a new "Deep Throat." *The New York Times* opened by calling him someone who had been briefed on all of this, the AP raised that to someone in the "legal profession," while *The Washington Post* went all the way and called him a "lawyer." Speculation focuses on Rove's attorney, who, if this is true, probably thinks most of this helps his client's cause.

And as a sidelight: If Rove is telling the truth, and he heard about Plame first from another journalist before talking to Novak, who was that reporter? Rove apparently claimed amnesia on that matter before the grand jury. Then there's this amusing (if plausible) comment by *Congressional Quarterly's* Craig Crawford: "So, now we have leakers leaking the leak investigation. Fitzgerald might have to put the whole press corps in jail before it's over with. . . ."

With few graphic images of the bloody violence in Iraq showing up on TV and on front pages—at least in America—some photographers voiced concern. Moises Saman of Newsday *told E&P that he believed that so few pictures are appearing in American papers because of a double standard that he says reflects the nature of our society. "Americans understand we are at war—but not many people want to see the real consequences, especially when they involve one of your own," he said. "I think some publications cater to this sentiment by trying not to anger subscribers and advertisers with harsh 'in-your-face' coverage of the true nature of war." Of course, many shocking photos from Abu Ghraib had been aired—but the worst had not yet seen the light of day.*

Why the Pentagon Is Blocking Abu Ghraib Images
JULY 23, 2005

So, what is shown on the 87 photographs and four videos from Abu Ghraib prison that the Pentagon, in an eleventh-hour move, blocked from release this weekend? One clue: Defense Secretary Donald Rumsfeld told Congress last year, after viewing a large cache of unreleased images: "I mean, I looked at them last night, and they're hard to believe." They show acts "that can only be described as blatantly sadistic, cruel, and inhumane," he added.

A Republican senator suggested the same day they contained scenes of "rape and murder." No wonder Rumsfeld commented then, "If these are released to the public, obviously it's going to make matters worse."

Yesterday, news emerged that lawyers for the Pentagon had refused to cooperate with a federal judge's order to release dozens of unseen photographs and videos from Abu Ghraib prison in Iraq by Saturday. The photos were among thousands turned over by the key "whistleblower" in the scandal, Spc. Joseph M. Darby. Just a few that were released to the press sparked the Abu Ghraib abuse scandal last year, and the video images are said to be even more shocking.

The Pentagon lawyers said in a letter sent to the federal court in Manhattan that they would file a sealed brief explaining their reasons for not turning over the material. They had been ordered to do so by a federal judge in response to a FOIA lawsuit filed by the American Civil Liberties Union. The ACLU accused the government Friday of putting another legal roadblock in the way of its bid to allow the public to see the images of the prisoner abuse scandal. One Pentagon lawyer has argued that they should not be released because they would only add to the humiliation of the prisoners. But the ACLU has said the faces of the victims can easily be "redacted."

To get a sense of what may be shown in these images, I went back to press reports from when the Abu Ghraib abuse scandal was still front page news. This is how CNN reported it on May 8, 2004, in a typical account that day: "U.S. Defense Secretary Donald Rumsfeld revealed Friday that videos and 'a lot more pictures' exist of the abuse of Iraqis held at Abu Ghraib prison. 'If these are released to the public, obviously it's going to make matters worse,' Rumsfeld told the Senate Armed Services Committee. 'I mean, I looked at them last night, and they're hard to believe.'

"The embattled defense secretary fielded sharp and skeptical questions from lawmakers as he testified about the growing prisoner abuse scandal. A military report about that abuse describes detainees being threatened, sodomized with a chemical light and forced into sexually humiliating poses. . . .

"A report by Maj. Gen. Antonio Taguba on the abuse at the prison outside Baghdad says videotapes and photographs show naked detainees, and that groups of men were forced to masturbate while being photographed and videotaped. Taguba also found evidence of a 'male MP guard having sex with a female detainee.' Rumsfeld told Congress the unrevealed photos and videos contain acts 'that can only be described as blatantly sadistic, cruel and inhuman.'"

The military later screened some of the images for lawmakers, who said they showed, among other things, attack dogs snarling at cowed prisoners, Iraqi women forced to expose their breasts, and naked prisoners forced to have sex with each other.

In the same period, reporter Seymour Hersh, who helped uncover the scandal, said in a speech before an ACLU convention: "Some of the worst that happened that you don't know about, okay? Videos, there are women there. Some of you may have read they were passing letters, communications out to their men. . . . The women were passing messages saying, 'Please come and kill me, because of what's happened.'

"They are in total terror it's going to come out."

AUGUST

On July 27, the top U.S. military leader in Iraq said there could be "fairly substantial" withdrawals of some of the 135,000 U.S. troops in the country as early as the following spring. By now, Cindy Sheehan had become a household name, having set up an encampment near the Bush ranch in Crawford, Texas. It had taken two years, but finally the media were focusing on a parent of a soldier slain in Iraq who did not continue to back the mission there. She clearly did not buy the notion that we had to win in Iraq or her son's life would be a waste. I was amazed to discover that in my April 2004 column, when I listed the names of the dead that appeared in that day's New York Times, *the toll that day included not only Bill Mitchell's son Mike but Cindy Sheehan's son Casey.*

Reporters covering Bush at his ranch wrote amusingly of tagging along on one of his bike rides there, as he continued to refuse to meet with Sheehan. One revealed that USA Today *writer Sal Ruibal stopped by a tree to take a leak. Maybe that's why they call them the "dog days" of August.*

Cindy Sheehan and the Lost Boys

AUGUST 12, 2005

With the U.S. death toll in Iraq approaching 2,000, producing a like number of grieving families, what were the odds that the one father I know personally in that mournful position would end up at Cindy Sheehan's side in Crawford, Texas, this week? Since he's been protesting the war before it began—and before he lost his son—I probably shouldn't have been so surprised.

Yesterday, visiting the Web site of *The Lone Star Iconoclast* (better known as "George Bush's hometown paper") in Crawford, I came across a firsthand account of a visit by the publisher and editor of that paper, W. Leon Smith, to the Sheehan encampment. She is the woman now famous for demanding to meet with the president to find out from him why her son had to die in Iraq last year, and for what.

Smith, on his suddenly popular Web site, recounted in Q&A form his interview that day with a man who had also lost a son in Iraq and had flown in from California to stand with Sheehan. Lo and behold, the interview subject was none other than Bill Mitchell (no relation), who I interviewed on several occasions last year. There was even a picture of the two men chatting, so I finally got to see what Bill looks like: thin, fair, with a moustache.

I'd read a fair amount about Sheehan, and knew Bill's story very well, but still I was shocked when I read in the interview that Mitchell's son Mike had died on the same day, April 4, 2004, as Sheehan's son Casey, and in the same Sadr City incident. Then Bill said something about the two boys probably not ever meeting—until their coffins likely left Iraq on the same plane. Elsewhere in the interview, Mitchell, who lives in Atascadero, Calif., explained that his life was still in turmoil because of his son's death. But he felt he should continue to speak out because the parents of the dead "have a certain credibility. We're not someone up there that's just espousing some belief. We're victims of the war like many other people are."

I caught up with Bill via cell phone this afternoon, as he completed a drive back to the central coast of California. Bill tells me he was "running only on adrenaline" after a week of getting only two to four hours of sleep a night, if that. And no wonder, with Bush neighbors shooting off guns across the road or mowing down hundreds of crosses erected in honor of dead soldiers in the middle of the night.

"I did about 20 interviews a day," he reveals. "So did the other Gold Star parents. It was a real media frenzy, and a far cry from months ago when only the 'alternative'-type papers were interested. There was even a live thing going with a Waco TV station when that guy ran over the crosses. We've got a well-equipped media center. It was the most incredible week of my life, I'll tell you."

Photos of Bill, often next to or holding one of those crosses, appeared in *The New York Times* and many other papers. He told me he'll be heading back to Texas after a few days at home, and organizing (he hopes) many others to accompany him in buses or vans. Then he plans to travel to Washington, D.C., when, as expected, "Camp Casey"—from the name of Sheehan's deceased son—relocates to Lafayette Park after Labor Day. "We've got momentum, dude," he exclaims (remember, he is from California). A few days ago, he explained, there were 10 families at the Sheehan site who had lost relatives in Iraq, and another 15 with loved ones there now. The media have it partly wrong, he asserts. "It's not about Cindy," he says. "It's so much more."

Just last week, I learned, in a letter from his daughter Christine, that over a year ago she had taken my list of names in that first April 2004 column and tried to contact the families of all the others who died. Some, according to Bill, did not respond at all, or voiced unwavering support for the war, which helped give their son's death greater meaning, they thought. Only Cindy Sheehan, a fellow Californian over in Vacaville, responded with an open mind.

Referring to Sheehan, Christine wrote me last week: "We have been in constant contact with her from almost the beginning. . . . She is like a second mom to me, and since she has yet to have grandbabies of her own, she wants to know if she can claim my two boys as her grandchildren. . . . I always say that she and the other Gold Star Families for Peace members are the greatest people I wish I never knew."

Mitchell, 53, an Army vet who had opposed the war from the beginning, spoke at peace rallies after his son's death, and traveled with Sheehan, even to Washington a couple months ago. "We paid our own way, using what we call our 'blood money' from our sons' deaths," he says. Much of the rest of the blood money is going toward paying for his son's fiancée Bianca, who lives in Germany, to get her master's degree in sociology. Or, as Bill puts it, "Mike is going to make sure she gets her degree."

One day recently, Bill says he got a call from a woman in the U.S. Army in Germany, who said she and many others in the military were with him. "When my son was killed, I said he had died in vain," Bill explains. "Now I feel the tide is turning, the mood changing. Now I feel that with incredible people, and incredible numbers of people, pulling together, the story of my son's life and death will actually save many other lives."

OCTOBER

In late August, still on vacation, Bush claimed that those who protest the Iraq conflict don't want the U.S. to win the war on terror. Perhaps this applied to those pesky reporters who kept revealing grim news from Iraq? In any case, the death toll for journalists had reached 66—topping the Vietnam numbers. In the wake of the administration's hapless—some would say criminally negligent—response to the post-Katrina flooding of New Orleans, new questions were raised about the president's pattern of dithering in times of war or crisis. I wrote a column calling his hurricane response "My Pet Goat—The Sequel." On Sept. 7, Colin Powell came as close to an apology as he might ever get, telling ABC News that his WMD presentation to the U.N. in 2003 "is a blot. . . . It was painful. It's painful now." Judith Miller had her own problems, apparently losing spirit and weight in jail, despite visits from the likes of John Bolton.

The Scooter and Judy Soap Opera: "As the Aspens Turn"
OCTOBER 6, 2005

After its starring role Wednesday night on *The Daily Show*, the Sept. 15 "aspens are already turning" letter from Lewis "Scooter" Libby to Judy Miller (in jail) has now reached a new level of infamy. Next stop: *SNL,* a book of Libby poems, then maybe the movie, starring Harrison Ford and Annette Bening?

On his Oct. 5 show, Jon Stewart graded Libby's prose a "D" on merit, and suggested that he might flunk Miller on general principles. David Ignatius of *The Washington Post* probed the letter's journalistic meaning, a *New York Observer* headline referred to it as a "love letter," while others suggested Libby could be indicted for coaching the witness, even if he didn't out Valerie Plame.

I'm proud to say that I was the first to print the full text of the letter, at E&P Online, early last Saturday. It had appeared until then only in PDF form on *The New York Times* site. Within hours, the blogs were linking, and posters were finding codes and conspiracies in Scooter's suggestion that the aspens that Judy supposedly knows and loves out West would be "turning" together this fall because they are, after all, connected at the roots.

Some bloggers recalled a significant meeting of neo-cons and/or Iraqi exiles in Aspen, Colo., that Miller might have attended. And so on. I scoffed at first, but today I read a confidential letter from a top Washington editor who seemed to think there was something to this code business. So, silly me, for thinking otherwise about Libby's closing passage: "Your reporting, and you, are missed. Out West, where you vacation, the aspens will already be turning. They turn in clusters, because their roots connect them. Come back to work—and life."

One blogger declared that Libby and Miller had obviously conspired to nail Karl Rove: "Since all neo-cons are connected by their roots and grow in clusters, why pull the roots out of two neo-cons, when you can pull the roots out of only one (Karl Rove) and overall still have a healthier forest of (neo-cons) aspens."

Above ground, columnist Gene Lyons pondered "that metaphor for a moment" and then decided: "Here's all I know: If Hillary Clinton had written Susan McDougal a letter like that, the Washington press would have exploded with indignation. Or would the TV talking heads be predicting indictments?"

Ignatius, on the other hand, treated the note like no big deal, writing in the *Post*: "The warm tone of the letter from White House insider Lewis 'Scooter' Libby to Judith Miller of *The New York Times* conveyed an essential reality of reporter-source relationships, which we in the media sometimes tend to play down: These are often relationships between like-minded people who care about the same issues and who become—dare I say it?—friendly. . . .

"It's obvious that Libby cares about Miller and wants her to return to reporting on issues they both see as important. That sort of personal connection between reporter and source may strike some people as sinister, but it's the mother's milk of journalism. That's why people tell us things: Because we listen, and often sound sympathetic."

Well, I'll give him that: Miller was certainly sympathetic to Libby, his delusions of weapons of mass destruction in Iraq, and his drive for an invasion that may be this country's greatest blunder in decades and already caused the deaths of tens of thousands. In fact, she helped him sell it. No code needed to figure that out.

Last night, Jon Stewart, perhaps forgetting Pol Pot, gave Scooter an award for "Man with Silliest Name Who Generated Mass Killing," or something like that. Funny. Not so much.

Just hours after that column appeared, Miller emerged—she had finally asked Scooter Libby for permission to testify, and his OK served as her get-out-of-jail card. Many of her colleagues at the Times *criticized her, anonymously, but four* Times *columnists explained to E&P that they had not written about her role because they didn't really know enough about it. They denied they had been pressured into silence. In a memo to staff, Bill Keller, apparently feeling that Judy had handled herself well, hit "armchair critics" who continued to criticize her and the paper's unbending support for her. Still, he promised a major* Times *report on her involvement in the leak case. When it appeared, I was first to review it fully online.*

Times Drops Bombshell—on Judy Miller

OCTOBER 15, 2005

Shortly after 3:30 p.m. today, *The New York Times* delivered its promised article probing Judith Miller's involvement in the Plame case. It reveals many devastating new details about her experience—and dissent within the newspaper about her role and the way the *Times* handled her case. The article details how the paper's defense of Miller, coming from the top, crippled its coverage of the Plame case and humiliated the paper's reporters on numerous occasions.

Among other things, the 5,800-word article discloses that in the same notebook that Miller belatedly turned over to the federal prosecutor last month, chronicling her July 8, 2003, interview with I. Lewis Libby, she wrote the name "Valerie Flame." She surely meant Valerie Plame, but when she testified for a second time in the case this week, she could not recall who mentioned that name to her, the *Times* said. She said she "didn't think" she heard it from Libby, a longtime friend and source.

The *Times* article is accompanied by Miller's own first-person account of her grand jury testimony. In it, she admits that the federal prosecutor "asked if I could recall discussing the Wilson-Plame connection with other sources. I said I had, though I could not recall any by name or when those conversations occurred."

In this memoir, Miller also claims that she simply "could not recall" where the "Valerie Flame" notation came from, "when I wrote it or why the name was misspelled." But her notes from her earlier talk with Libby, on June 23, 2003— belatedly turned over to the prosecutor last week after she found them under a desk—also "leave open the possibility" that Libby told her that former Ambassador Joseph Wilson's wife worked at the CIA, though perhaps not using the name "Plame."

The article concludes with this frank and brutal assessment: "The *Times* incurred millions of dollars in legal fees in Ms. Miller's case. It limited its own ability to cover aspects of one of the biggest scandals of the day. Even as the paper asked for the public's support, it was unable to answer its questions."

Yet it follows that paragraph with Executive Editor Bill Keller's view: "It's too early to judge."

Perhaps that's because, the article notes, "In two interviews, Ms. Miller generally would not discuss her interactions with editors, elaborate on the written accounts of her grand jury testimony or allow reporters to review her notes." Thus, the probe appears to be less than the "full accounting"—with full Miller cooperation—that the editors promised.

Just as surprising, the article reveals that Keller and the publisher of the *Times*, Arthur Sulzberger, did not even review her notes. Keller said he learned about the "Valerie Flame" notation only this month. Sulzberger knew nothing about it until told by his reporters on Thursday.

The article (written by Don Van Natta, Jr., Adam Liptak, and Clifford J. Levy) says that Miller is taking some time off but "hopes to return to the newsroom," and will write a book about the case. Meanwhile, newsroom leaders expressed frustration about the coverage at the *Times* (or lack of) during the entire ordeal. Asked what she regretted about the paper's coverage, Jill Abramson, a managing editor, said: "The entire thing."

Saturday's story says that Miller was a "divisive figure" in the newsroom and a "few colleagues refused to work with her." Doug Frantz, former chief investigations editor at the paper, said that Miller called herself "Miss Run Amok," meaning, she said, "I can do whatever I want." The story also paints a less-than-flattering picture of Keller. At one point it dryly observes:

"Throughout this year, reporters at the paper spent weeks trying to determine the identity of Ms. Miller's source. All the while, Mr. Keller knew it, but declined to tell his own reporters."

During the crucial July 8, 2003, talk with Libby, the Veep's man told her that Plame worked on weapons intelligence and arms control, and Miller allegedly took this to mean that she was not covert, but she didn't really know one way or the other.

Revealing her working methods, perhaps too clearly, she writes today that at this meeting, Libby wanted to modify their prior understanding that she would attribute information from him to an unnamed "senior administration official." Now, in talking about Wilson, he requested that he be identified only as a "former Hill staffer." This was obviously to deflect attention from the Cheney office's effort to hurt Wilson. But Miller admits, "I agreed to the new ground rules because I knew that Mr. Libby had once worked on Capitol Hill."

Two days after her third chat with Libby, Robert Novak exposed Plame. In her first-person account, Miller writes that when asked by the prosecutor what she thought about the Novak column that outed Plame as a CIA agent, "I told the grand jury I was annoyed at having been beaten on a story."

For the first time this clearly, Miller, in Saturday's article, admits, "WMD—I got it totally wrong," but then goes on to say that "all" of the other journalists, and experts and analysts, also were wrong. "I did the best job I could," she said. Of course, not "all" did get it wrong.

The article reveals, also for the first time, that Keller took her off Iraq and weapons issues after he became editor in July 2003. Nevertheless, he admits, "she kept drifting on her own back into the national security realm," making one wonder who was in charge of her.

In a somewhat amusing sidelight, Miller at the end of her piece addresses the much-discussed "aspens are already turning" letter from Libby last month that some thought was written in code or somehow had something to do with Aspen, Colo. Well, the Aspen part is right, Miller confirms, recalling a conference in that city in 2003 and an unexpected encounter with Libby—in cowboy hat and sunglasses—shortly afterward.

At last report, Miller was still scheduled to receive a First Amendment Award given by the Society of Professional Journalists at their convention on Tuesday.

Beyond my review, most commentary on the Times *probe was muted or generally positive in the first day or so. Bill Keller, who was abroad and had not seen fit to come home to deal with this crisis, said that everyone should close the book on this episode. But as my critical assessment gained attention, others joined in. By October 18, we were reporting that "the Gray Lady's newsroom is buzzing over what the paper did not report, the future of its publisher and editor, and who might ultimately take the fall for 'letting Judy run amok.'" Three days after that, Keller, backtracking, admitted in a memo that the paper had erred in not owning up to the errors by Miller and others in their WMD reporting for so long, raising suspicions (a point made by E&P about a dozen times) that the paper was "putting the defense of a reporter above the duty to its readers." He also suggested that Miller had misled her editors on certain points about the CIA leak case.*

Time to End Miller's High Life

OCTOBER 23, 2005

In case you wondered: The Judy Miller Saga is front-page news in Italy, too. On my second day there last week, I managed to spot coverage not only in the *International Herald Tribune* but also in the Italian papers. Maybe, like many in the American press, the Italians resent Miller for helping to push their country into a war. But now, the scandal has gotten even more interesting—and disturbing—with Miller's angry response late Sunday to the critique by the newspaper's public editor.

In that fresh e-mail, among other things, she calls Executive Editor Bill Keller's memo to *New York Times* staff last Friday "ugly," bluntly attacks the veracity of Jill Abramson (the key managing editor in this mess), and lamely defends her various ethical lapses. What does someone at the *Times* have to do to get fired? After Judy's latest e-mail, it appears that either Miller goes, or Keller and Abramson need to walk away themselves.

When I left the U.S. on Monday, I felt a bit lonely out on the limb. Just hours after the *Times* had published its account of the official leak that led Miller to jail, I called on Keller to fire her. (He'd tried reassigning her once before, but Ms. Run Amok somehow wandered into the national security field again, behind his back.) Few joined me in this. Returning from abroad, I found that viewing Miller's dismissal as warranted, or at least inevitable, was now approaching conventional wisdom—but not yet within key offices at the *Times*.

Keller's initial response to his paper's 6,000-word Miller probe was let's-turn-the-page. After several staffers explained to him what the piece really meant, he finally came out with his much-needed and long-delayed mea culpa on Friday. But he made no mention of getting rid of his pet albatross—though this was before she talked back to him, and his public editor, in the just-published e-mails.

Maureen Dowd, at last, got around to criticizing Miller on Saturday, calling her everything from journalism's Becky Sharp to a "Woman of Mass Destruction," but hinted that she deserved to keep drawing a check from the *Times* so long as she didn't get to write about national security. Then Public Editor Barney Calame offered his critique on Sunday, again suggesting that something be done about the lady, maybe make her an editor, but they didn't necessarily have to get rid of her. He also quoted Arthur Sulzberger, Jr.'s revelation that he had already talked to Judy about "new limits" on her employment, but not dismissal.

Why not? She's brought dishonor to the paper for so long and in so many ways, you have to wonder: How and why does she get to keep her job? Apparently many *Times* staffers are asking the same question. Some even wonder why Keller still has a job there.

David Halberstam, the ex–*Times* reporter, had it right when he told my colleague Joe Strupp today, "I think it is shocking that this young woman who has been a known identified landmine for a long time seems to have guaranteed loyalty to the office of the Vice President of the United States more than to *The New York Times*."

How can Keller keep Miller on at the *Times*, after complaining that she hadn't played honest with him—especially in light of an Associated Press scoop this weekend that got less attention than it deserved due to all the other Miller dramatics? "The Case of the Missing Notebook," as I called it two weeks ago, has now been solved.

The AP's John Solomon reported that Miller belatedly gave prosecutors her notes of the key June 23 meeting in the CIA leak probe only after being shown White House records of it, according to two lawyers familiar with the investigation. In her first grand jury appearance Sept. 30, Miller did not mention the meeting and retrieved her notes about it only when prosecutors presented her visitor logs showing she had met with Libby in the Old Executive Office Building adjacent to the White House.

I don't know why it took Maureen Dowd so long to criticize Miller. Her column, when it did appear on Saturday, was suitably savage, with its conclusion that returning Miller to the national security beat would put the newspaper itself in imminent danger. But surely Dowd, and Keller, know that the newspaper grows more imperiled every day it fails to order Miller to run amok someplace else, and on someone else's dime.

NOVEMBER

On October 28, Scooter Libby was indicted on five felony charges. About the same time, U.S. Army Lt. Col. Steve Boylan, a military spokesman in Iraq, wrote in a statement, "The 2,000 service members killed in Iraq supporting Operation Iraqi Freedom is not a milestone. It is an artificial mark on the wall set by individuals or groups with specific agendas and ulterior motives." Going against those wishes, several top TV news outlets and newspapers covered fatality number 2,000 prominently, with The New York Times *cheekily using "milestone" right in its headline. In perhaps the most widely reprinted editorial cartoon of the war, Mike Luckovich handwrote the names of each of the 2,000, spelling out the word WHY? Joe Galloway, whose work we had featured since before the war, took a different approach.*

Lunching with Rumsfeld

NOVEMBER 3, 2005

It started Tuesday with ordering a tuna fish sandwich and ended more than an hour later with the guest/reporter telling the Secretary of Defense, "I'm going to keep kicking your butt." And in between? Let Joe Galloway tell you, including this exclusive: What's so funny about Rummy's bathroom?

For at least two years, Knight Ridder military editor and columnist Joe Galloway has been one of the most persistent and harshest critics of Pentagon chief Donald Rumsfeld's handling of the Iraq war, and other military issues, from an informed position. Galloway is one of the celebrated war correspondents of our time, winner of a Bronze Star for valor during the Vietnam conflict, and co-author of the book *We Were Soldiers Once . . . and Young.*

About six weeks ago, perhaps recognizing Galloway's credibility and the growing chorus of criticism from others, Rumsfeld's office invited the correspondent to what it called "a private lunch" at the Pentagon. No one told

Galloway why, but he didn't have to guess. "I knew they weren't planning to give me some kind of ribbon," Galloway told me today.

Asked if he spiffed up for the meeting, Galloway acknowledged that he did "put on a tie," then took the metro to the Pentagon from his apartment on the Potomac in nearby Arlington, Va. Well, as it turned out, the lunch wasn't quite private, as the two men were joined by the chairman of the Joint Chiefs of Staff, two other brass, and a Pentagon spokesman. "Five to one, they had me surrounded," Galloway said. "I've been doing this for 47 years and it was the first time I had a command performance with an audience like that."

How did it go? "I had a fun time," Galloway revealed. "I don't know about the rest of them."

They met in Rumsfeld's "huge" office around a conference table. Galloway had ordered a tuna sandwich on the way in and found that Rummy was also eating tuna, but salad style. When Rumsfeld noticed that Joe had eaten the tuna but left the bread he ribbed him about that—imagine, waste at the Pentagon!

Rumsfeld, Galloway related, was cordial and smiling throughout, but quickly demanded to know why he himself wasn't hearing all the negative stuff about the lack of progress in Iraq and the military grumblings that the writer was picking up on. Galloway reminded him that someone in Rumsfeld's position was not likely to get much bad news passed up the chain of command. Then Rummy questioned his sources, suggesting they were perhaps all retired generals far from the scene. Galloway replied that about half were active duty and many of them "not only active duty, but also work in the Pentagon." Some might even be on Rumsfeld's staff.

As the discussion went on, Galloway continued to raise issues about the state of our military, as the generals argued that "the Army was not broken and things were not going so badly in Iraq." Rumsfeld occasionally took notes on a yellow pad. He "seemed to be enjoying it when I got into it with one of the other guys," Galloway told me. "He would lean back in his chair with a grin and watch us go at it. I had the impression he was listening very carefully to everything and here and there he heard something that might need follow-up. I suspect he will shower a few snowflakes [memos] down on them, maybe starting today."

The Knight Ridder columnist asked whether the U.S. could figure out a better way of fighting the war than sending our troops down the same road only to be blown up by IEDs. Rumsfeld claimed he agreed and had ordered that our emphasis shift even more to training Iraqis. Galloway also pressed him on one of his pet issues—military "bill collectors" going after ex-soldiers who maybe had lost a limb or two in Iraq. Rumsfeld blamed it on the Pentagon computer system but said steps were being taken to address that.

When Rumsfeld took issue with Joe's most recent column, in which he charged that the Pentagon, à la Vietnam, was pushing "body counts," Galloway stood his ground, saying, "If you don't want to do body counts then stop doing them."

After more than an hour, the Pentagon spokesman told his boss, "Sir, we are way out of time," but Galloway thought the meeting could have gone on for another hour or more. As he headed for the door, Rumsfeld guided him to an anteroom to show him a framed letter he found in his late father's belongings. It was written by Defense Secretary James Forrestal to the elder Rumsfeld, thanking him for his service in the Navy during the Pacific War. Rumsfeld has never served in combat himself.

On the way out, the defense secretary said, in parting: "I want you to know that I love soldiers and I care about soldiers. All of us here do." Well, one would hope so.

In parting, Galloway told me, he informed Rumsfeld, "I want you to know that I'm going to keep kicking your butt, to keep you focused." Rumsfeld replied, "That's okay, I can take it."

Two days later now, I asked Joe about Rumsfeld's central belief—that he was getting the true story on Iraq and the state of the military and Galloway was not. "Besides talking to people, I get a tremendous amount of e-mail from people in the military and in the Pentagon who read my column and react to it," he replied. "They are concerned. What I'm hearing is that 99 percent of these readers are 100 percent in favor of what I am writing, and ask me to keep at it. Unfortunately, if I am right, the military is in a lot of trouble."

Anything else you left out of today's column, I wondered? "I got a peek at the bathroom in his office," Galloway said, deadpan, "and he has a bank of cartoons posted there."

As autumn rolled on, little changed, as the administration worked on what it called a "Victory in Iraq" plan that it would roll out at the end of the month (it promised). Judy Miller quit The New York Times *on November 9; in return, the paper ran her farewell letter. Then she went on* Larry King *and claimed she'd never used Ahmad Chalabi as an unnamed source. Two hours later, Arthur Sulzberger turned up on Charlie Rose's PBS show, defending the paper's handling of her reporting and her jailing. By mid-November, a surprising new name had been linked to the CIA leak case—Bob Woodward, who admitted Plame's name had been leaked to him a month before it appeared in print.*

At this point, I wrote another one of my periodic columns wondering when a few major editorial pages would finally turn against the war. Polls showed that 60 percent of the public favored the beginning of a pullout, and Bush's approval rating was stuck around 37 percent. Nicholas Kristof of The New York Times *became one of the few pundits to back withdrawal, sketching a two-year timetable. The administration was more concerned about threatening to legally go after Dana Priest of* The Washington Post *for disclosing that the CIA ran "black sites" abroad for secret interrogation of terror suspects. Then a real earthquake struck, or so it (briefly) seemed.*

Murtha Speaks Out—a "Cronkite Moment"?

NOVEMBER 17, 2005

For months, media watchers have wondered if we would any time soon witness another "Cronkite moment"—some sort of dramatic statement by a mainstream media figure that would turn hearts and minds against an ill-advised war, for good. It hasn't happened. But perhaps a not-very-famous, 73-year-old gentleman named Murtha will be the new Cronkite, who belatedly spoke out against the Vietnam war on national TV in 1968.

A few days ago, newspaper editorial pages were merely trailing their readers in calling for change in direction in Iraq. Now they are even behind a certain conservative congressman from Pennsylvania.

Earlier this week, even pro-war Democrats in Congress, such as Senators Biden and Clinton, asked Bush if he could, please, at least come up with some kind of long-term timetable. It wasn't much and it didn't pass, but that's still more than we have seen from all but a few editorial pages. *The New York Times*, for example, once again Thursday morning came out against any withdrawal or a timetable for exiting.

Now, how will newspapers respond to the angry, moving statement by Rep. John Murtha (D-Pa.) today? The crusty, hawkish former Marine called for an Iraq pullout, starting not in, say, 2007, but ASAP, and introduced a bill to this effect. "Our military has done everything that has been asked of them, the U.S. can not accomplish anything further in Iraq militarily," Murtha said. "It is time to bring them home."

Wisely, he called it a "redeployment," not a pullout, and he said it was not exactly "immediate," but could be largely accomplished by the middle of next year. Asked at a press conference if this did not amount to "cutting and running," Murtha replied that the war had been handled haplessly from the start, and new polls show that even most of the Iraqis want us out.

In response, White House Press Secretary Scott McClellan said, "It is baffling that he is endorsing the policy positions of Michael Moore."

But Rod Dreher, the conservative columnist, quickly posted this at NRO Online, the *National Review* site: "If tough, non-effete guys like Murtha are willing to go this far, and can make the case in ways that Red America can relate to—and listening to him talk was like listening to my dad, who's about the same age, and his hunting buddies—then the president is in big trouble. I'm sure there's going to be an anti-Murtha pile-on in the conservative blogosphere, but from where I sit, conservatives would be fools not to take this man seriously."

This man: After serving in the Marines in the early 1950s, he re-enlisted in 1966 and served in Vietnam, earning a Bronze Star. Today, in a not-so-veiled response to Vice President Cheney's recent attacks on the patriotism of anti-war critics, Murtha said: "I like guys who got five deferments and (have) never been there and send people to war, and then don't like to hear suggestions about what needs to be done."

And on President Bush: "You know, the president said it's tough to win a war. You know, it's tough to WAGE a war. That's where the fallacy's been. To WAGE this war is where the problem's been."

Murtha's statement puts the issue squarely and fairly to editorial and opinion writers. Rise to the challenge. Don't just sit on the fence. Consider his concluding passage: "This war needs to be personalized. As I said before, I have visited with the severely wounded of this war. They are suffering. Because we in Congress are charged with sending our sons and daughters into battle, it is our responsibility, our obligation, to speak out for them. That's why I am speaking out.

"Our military has done everything that has been asked of them, the U.S. can not accomplish anything further in Iraq militarily. It is time to bring them home."

2006

JANUARY

Michael Kinsley of The Washington Post *wrote: "Now, thanks to Rep. John Murtha, it is permissible to say, or at least to ask, 'Why not just get out now? Or at least soon, on a fixed schedule?'" Needless to say, the editorial pages and TV pundits did not rise to the occasion. Many said they backed the general frustration and sentiment behind the Murtha call—but almost none backed his proposal. So you had* USA Today *calling Murtha's plea "understandable" but "misguided," even while re-affirming that the entire war was "a mistake." The* Austin American-Statesman *in Texas said most Americans had "lost confidence" in the president's war leadership, but withdrawal would likely "not be in this nation's best interests at this point." The (New York)* Daily News *declared: "Murtha is right, of course, that the American public is sick of the slog, is 'thirsting for a new direction' and 'wants and deserves real answers.'" But it added that he "is still wrong" about withdrawal. The* Milwaukee Journal-Sentinel *said Murtha is "surely on the right track," but "leaving Iraq now would be a mistake."*

In late November, we learned that the U.S. military was secretly paying Iraqi newspapers to publish stories written by Americans to improve the image of the U.S. occupation. President Bush called progress in Iraq "amazing." On December 17, Sen. Joe Lieberman declared a "turning point" with the U.S. now on the road to success. Exactly three weeks later, 140 Iraqis were killed in one day, one of the bloodiest 24-hour periods since the war began. Then I found myself bumbling into a potential controversy.

What I Did During the Jill Carroll Abduction
JANUARY 12, 2006

Nearly two days have passed since *E&P* reported that an extraordinary "blackout" on reporting a murder and kidnapping in Baghdad had existed in this country for about 40 hours starting Saturday night. Only one publication broke that blackout, unwittingly: *E&P*. The incident, as everyone now knows, involved the abduction of *Christian Science Monitor* stringer Jill Carroll and the brutal killing of one of her translators.

For some reason—perhaps because Carroll is still being held—this revelation has not produced wide commentary in media critic and blog circles, or from within the media industry. Possibly there is some confusion, with many believing that only Carroll's name and affiliation were withheld, when actually it was any mention of the incident. In other words: a total blackout. *USA Today*, for example, posted a brief Associated Press item about the abduction on its Web site Saturday—and then killed the link. And AP stopped moving that item before it appeared just about anywhere.

Or maybe it's just no big deal and it raises no major press issues involving voluntarily holding back information from the public when lives are at stake. A couple of top editors told *E&P*'s Joe Strupp that something like this has happened before, but it's unclear what they are referring to, or how often it has occurred. *Time* magazine said it was merely aimed at giving negotiators and rescuers time to win Carroll's release. We all remember Danny Pearl, of course.

It didn't seem to work. And late Saturday, during the blackout, the U.S. military and Iraqis raided an important mosque searching for clues or perpetrators, and apparently left it in something of a mess afterward.

I'm not sure how I feel about all this myself, but I am amazed there has been so little serious discussion of it, although *E&P* has received many letters from readers posing questions such as: Is it right to organize any press blackout, even for a good cause? Or: Who are they kidding—there can be no such thing as a blackout in the era of the globe-spanning Web?

Rather than say more at this point, I will just recount my very odd personal interaction with this story.

It all began innocently on Sunday. Often I try to do a little work at home every weekend, putting up a few stray or important items that I come across, usually without breaking much of a sweat or raising any ethical dilemmas. This past Sunday morning, in trolling Google News, I came across an AP item, I think from a small TV station's site, about a female American reporter getting abducted in Iraq, while her translator was killed. Her name and affiliation were missing.

I didn't find any other AP pickup, which seemed odd, since the incident supposedly happened on Saturday, but I found a UPI item saying much the same thing, with a couple of added details. This was a pretty hot story for a Sunday morning, and I immediately wrote up and posted a short account, based on the two wire service reports, but labeling the report "unconfirmed" in both the headline and the first graf.

Anxious to learn about any updates, and the name of the reporter, I checked back online every couple hours, and was surprised, and then amazed, to find that the wire service dispatches were not getting picked up anywhere in the U.S. But I did find an Agence France-Presse report from Europe, with a little more detail and a confirmation from a U.S. embassy official.

I hunted some more on the Web and found a mention at one Arab news site that the seized reporter worked for *The Christian Science Monitor*. This was hardly an unimpeachable source, but I went to the *Monitor's* site and quickly discovered that a reporter named Jill Carroll had written stories for the paper from Baghdad just this past week. Then, searching a little more, I found Arab sites or Arab news services identifying the reporter as "Jill Kelly" or phonetically "Jil Carowel" or something like that.

So it seemed clear that someone, somewhere, was putting out the name of Jill Carroll as the victim. But I didn't even ponder printing the name—the sources were just so unknown and untrustworthy, it never entered my mind.

By this time, I was finding extensive coverage of the kidnapping and killing in the British press online, though still without the I.D. of the abductee. But at the end of the night, I still couldn't find any U.S. reporting on this. With a Black Hawk helicopter down, and 12 dead, and other pressing issues, I thought maybe the kidnapping wasn't as big a deal as I might have thought. I assumed officials were asking the media not to print Carroll's name, but it never occurred to me that an organized blackout on the entire incident might be in place—especially on a weekend. If this had been a weekday, of course, we would have made a few phone calls checking this out hours earlier.

Monday morning it really seemed suspicious when *The New York Times* and *The Washington Post* did not mention the abduction at all. Arriving at the office, I asked Joe Strupp to check it out. He reported back, after talking to a *Monitor* spokesman: The paper had asked for, and achieved, a blackout at all major news outlets, and nearly all smaller ones. This I could surely attest to.

But now the *Monitor* was getting a lot of calls about the matter (how long could it last?) and in response was about to send out a release and post a story on its Web site. There seemed no point in even thinking about taking down the *E&P* story, which still did not name the reporter or her paper. The spokesman said we could run with their announcement about 3 P.M. on Monday.

Strupp, meanwhile, was talking to editors at some of the major papers, confirming the blackout. Some of them complained about *E&P* having posted a story on the abduction on our Web site. Strupp truthfully answered: We didn't know anything about a blackout. About this time, we learned from our editor in Chicago, Mark Fitzgerald, that he had received a message on his office answering machine late Saturday from a *Monitor* editor, asking us to avoid the story. But Fitzgerald didn't check his phone messages until Monday.

At 3 P.M. we put up our full story with the first news of the blackout. Meanwhile, we express a fervent wish for the safe, speedy release of Jill Carroll.

FEBRUARY

The embedding of journalists around the U.S. invasion of Iraq was deemed an almost unqualified success by both military officials and journalists who participated in a Pentagon-sponsored study of the program. On January 29, ABC newsman Bob Woodruff and cameraman Doug Vogt were seriously wounded in Iraq. A new poll by a University of Maryland research institute found that most Iraqis supported violent attacks on Americans and more than 70 percent backed some sort of timetable for U.S. withdrawal. Naturally, the subject of how we had gotten into this cauldron returned to the fore.

Oprah "Freys" George W. Bush

FEBRUARY 1, 2006

In the days since Oprah Winfrey sliced and diced writer James Frey on her TV show for misleading the public with lies in his bestselling memoir, many liberal commentators have expressed a single wish: to watch Oprah have the opportunity to do the same with President George W. Bush concerning the alleged lies that got the U.S. into Iraq (2,200 lost American lives ago). Eugene Robinson, *The Washington Post* columnist, observed on Tuesday, "If there were justice in the world, George W. Bush would have to give his State of the Union address from Oprah's couch. . . . Bush should have to face the wrathful, Old Testament Oprah who subjected author James Frey to that awful public smiting the other day."

Syndicated columnist Norman Solomon cited the Winfrey/Frey tussle, then charged, "Yet the journalists who interview Bush aren't willing to question him in similar terms." On *The Daily Show* Monday, Jon Stewart contrasted Oprah's tough questioning of Frey with obsequious TV news treatment of President Bush, Secretary of Defense Donald Rumsfeld, and others. Maureen Dowd compared "disgraced author" Frey with "a commander in chief who keeps writing chapter after chapter of fictionalized propaganda."

So I have taken the liberty of pushing all this dreaming one step beyond, imagining an Oprah sitdown with the president—based almost word for word on the transcript of her session with Frey, with just a few phrases obviously changed here and there. Here it is, without commercial interruption, or claps and boos from the audience. It even has a happy ending.

OPRAH: President Bush is here, and I have to say it is difficult for me to talk to you because I feel really duped. But more importantly, I feel that you betrayed millions of citizens in your statements about WMD in Iraq and Saddam's connection to al-Qaeda. I think it's such a gift to have millions of people to believe in you and your office, and that bothers me greatly. So now, as I sit here today I don't know what is true and I don't know what isn't. Was your description of how Saddam Hussein was about to get nuclear weapons true?

BUSH: He was about to get nuclear weapons, yes.

O: About to?

B: I mean, that was one of the details I altered about him.

O: Okay. And why?

B: Because all the way through the run-up to the war, I altered details about every single one of the WMD possibilities to render them unidentifiable.

O: But why did you lie? Why did you do that?

B: I think one of the coping mechanisms I developed was sort of this image of myself that was greater, probably, than—not probably—that was greater than what I actually was. In order to get through the experience, I thought of myself as being tougher than I was and badder than I was—and it helped me cope. When I was selling the war, instead of being as introspective as I should have been, I clung to that image.

o: And did you cling to that image because that's how you wanted to see yourself? Or did you cling to that image because that would make a better sell job?

b: Probably both.

o: How much of your statements on WMD and Saddam's connections to al-Qaeda were fabricated?

b: Not very much. I mean, all the people are real.

o: But I acted in defense of you and as I said, my judgment was clouded because so many people seemed to have gotten so much out of it. But now I feel that you conned us all. Do you?

b: I don't feel like I conned everyone.

o: You don't.

b: No.

o: Why?

b: Because I still think the war is about WMD and al-Qaeda, and nobody's disputing that I was addicted . . . to fighting Saddam. And it's a battle to overcome that.

o: Your charges about WMD, you said that that was true then. Would you say that today?

b: I had documents that supported it. About nine months after the war, I was speaking to somebody from State. They said that they doubted it happened that way, but that there was a chance that it did—that cases like that are reviewed on an individual basis.

o: This is what I don't get. Because when you were here before, you said that there were about 400 pages of documents. That there were documents and reports. Because I said, "How can you remember such detail?" And that's how you explained it to me.

b: Absolutely.

o: Do you wish you had added a disclaimer?

b: I don't know if I wish I had offered a disclaimer or if I had just talked about certain events in a different way. I think that would have been the more appropriate thing to do than putting in a disclaimer.

o: I appreciate you being here because I believe the truth can set you free. I realize this has been a difficult time for you, and maybe this is the beginning of another kind of truth for you.

b: I think you're absolutely right. I mean, I think this is obvious—this hasn't been a great day for me. It certainly hasn't been a great couple weeks for me. But I think I come out of it better. I feel like I came here and I have been honest with you. I have, you know, essentially admitted to . . . [sigh] . . . lying.

o: Which is not an easy thing to do.

b: No, it's not an easy thing to do in front of an audience full of people and a lot of others watching on TV. I mean, if I come out of this experience with anything, it's being a better person and learning from my mistakes and making sure that I don't repeat them.

o: Good.

MARCH

Everyone had some fun in February after Vice President Cheney on a hunting trip "shot his friend in the face," as the incident came to be known, thanks to The Daily Show. *But in Iraq, they were not using bird-shot. My favorite editorial cartoon of the month came from my local paper in the Hudson Valley,* The Journal News, *which employs a recent Pulitzer winner, Matt Davies. He pictured a barren landscape, looking much like Iraq, with buckshot-riddled bodies strewn across the field, Cheney with his shotgun still smoking, and flying harmlessly overhead a duck labeled "WMD." Cheney looks up at the duck and says, "Damn. Missed."*

Well, that pretty much said it all. Yet one of the top American correspondents in Iraq, Tom Lasseter of Knight Ridder, still managed to say quite a bit more, in a gripping, and depressing, article distributed on February 16. E&P had profiled Lasseter and his work numerous times in the past two years, and last we heard he was supposed to be back home in the USA, but there he was, still risking life, limb, and, no doubt, sanity during embeds in Iraq—unlike many American reporters who mainly stayed in Baghdad due to the very real dangers in the field. (The Boston Globe was the latest major news outlet to close its bureau entirely.) Lasseter often got ordinary grunts to speak honest truths. His most recent piece focused strictly on Samarra, a city that had lost half of its population since the U.S. supposedly pacified the area more than a year ago. Then real hell broke out there, and beyond, with effects felt for more than a year.

Appointment in Samarra
MARCH 1, 2006

Two weeks ago, I wrote a column alerting readers to a report by Knight Ridder's longtime Baghdad correspondent Tom Lasseter. He had returned from an embed mission to little-visited Samarra and, in his usual way, offered a remarkably frank look at a city that was taken by the U.S. last year but never really pacified. Well, timing is everything. A few days later, on February 22, insurgents blew the Golden Dome off the main mosque there and a near–civil war has raged since, with hundreds killed—many executed—nearly every day in sectarian violence.

Lasseter's mid-February dispatch proved prescient, but what surprised me most of all was that he was still out there risking his life. When we heard from him last autumn, he was planning to wind up his long, award-winning stint in Iraq in January 2006 and move to Washington, D.C., to work for the KR bureau there. So what was he doing in mid-February, still in Iraq, filing another wrenching dispatch, embedded with U.S. troops in Samarra? What's with this guy? And how does he manage to get all of these stories, and revealing quotes, from military personnel when few others can? His assignment in Samarra caused me to ask him how it came about.

From Baghdad, he replied that he had been curious about Samarra for quite some time. Was it indeed pacified last year, as claimed by the U.S., or more like still-boiling Ramadi? After expressing his interest to the public affairs chief for the 101st Airborne, he got the OK to hitch a ride in a helicopter to the city in January.

Lasseter wrote in this e-mail that he was "pretty surprised by the level of destruction in the town." Its population of over 200,000 had been cut in half. Despite being surrounded by a seven-mile-long security wall, it was beset by an increasing number of explosions set off by insurgents. An officer mentioned to him that a platoon of soldiers was living in an abandoned schoolhouse in the middle of the city. Lasseter told him that's where he wanted to go. "I always try to get as close to the ground as possible; it gives me a feel for the place that is hard to get while staying at larger, more comfortable bases," he told me.

After hitching a ride to the schoolhouse, or Patrol Base Uvanni, Lasseter spent about a week and a half living with the guys "and going out with them in Samarra on foot or in a Humvee. I find it really helpful, especially at the beginning of an embed, to accompany troops on every patrol mission possible. I want to see what they're seeing as they see it and hear what they have to say. It also shows them, in a quiet way, that I'm willing to go wherever they go and not ask for any special accommodations.

"I eat what they eat," Lasseter continued, "sleep when they sleep and when they wake up in the middle of the night, grab their flak vests and rush out the door, I do the same. Sometimes that means sitting in a Humvee and doing absolutely nothing and returning to pass out without getting much in the way of notes. And sometimes that means a big gunfight or a soldier saying something profound about his experience in Iraq.

"It's hard to tell the way things will work; big raids can produce very little, and a walk down the street can lead you into something big. My approach is to almost always just go out the door with the soldiers and find out." He calls this "getting down in the dirt with them."

So what did he find out in his Samarra stay? "Bloodshed is destroying the city and driving a wedge between the Iraqis who live there and the U.S. troops who are trying to keep order," he reported. In one of those brutally honest quotes Lasseter inevitably seems to gather, Maj. Curtis Strange said, "It's apocalyptic out there. Life has definitely gotten worse. You see Samarra and you almost want to build a new city and move all these people there."

After much more in this vein, Lasseter described in vivid detail how a .50-caliber machine gun, manned by a 21-year-old Texan named Michael Pena on the roof of the schoolhouse, blasted an unarmed civilian on the street into oblivion. Horrified soldiers rushed to the Iraqi, or what was left of him—his organs were now slithering out—and watched him die, as he praised God and muttered, "Why? Why?"

"Haji, I don't know," an American soldier replied, with Lasseter right there.

A few days later, Lasseter found the gunner, Pena, still manning the machine gun on the same roof. "No one told me why I'm putting my life on the line in Samarra, and you know why they didn't?" Pena asked. "Because there is no f—— reason."

So we now know how Lasseter got that story. But how much longer will he continue in the war zone? "I'm not sure," he wrote to me. "I was supposed to leave late last year, but in looking at the year ahead I realized that I am not done reporting here. I would like to devote some time to embedding with U.S. units as the debate continues about troop drawdown in Iraq. This has been true the whole time I've been here, but it really does feel like a critical moment in the American experience in Iraq."

He added, "I think that you have to be there to know it."

Gen. Peter Pace told Tim Russert on Meet the Press *that, contrary to much evidence, things were actually "going well" in Iraq, adding, inanely, "though I wouldn't put a smiley face on it." This is the man who chaired the Joint Chiefs of Staff. On March 11, as sectarian slayings continued unchecked,* The Washington Post *reported that the president, once again, was going on the "offensive" to explain his war strategy.*

David Brooks Plays Rummy

MARCH 16, 2006

Given the recent events in Iraq—hell, given the past two years—you would think pundits who agitated for an attack on Iraq, largely on false pretenses, would by now be on their knees begging the American public for forgiveness. With nearly 60 percent of their fellow Americans now calling the war a "mistake" and agitating for troop withdrawals—and the president's approval rating still heading south, thanks to their war—it would seem to be the right thing to do. We won't even mention the death or maiming of more than 10,000 young Americans.

In fact, several prominent pro-warriors (from Francis Fukuyama to William F. Buckley) have gone halfway there in recent weeks, but a column by David Brooks in *The New York Times* today reveals the fallback position for the unapologetic: blame Rumsfeld. The war was a swell idea that the Pentagon chief somehow screwed up.

Of course, he did screw it up, and if a Secretary of Defense could be impeached, he'd probably be in the dock by now. But from the pro-war pundits, blaming Rummy is mainly a way to avoid taking responsibility for their own tragic and profound misjudgments.

Brooks opens his column today with: "Some weeks nothing happens; some weeks change history. The week of March 24, 2003, was one of those pivotal weeks." There you have it right at the start. The week that changed history was not the week Bush took us into war, but the following week when Rumsfeld started to mess it up, by not listening to generals who said they would need more troops to handle a surprising, and surprisingly strong, insurgency.

This presumes, of course, that even if Rumsfeld had sent more troops, the country would have been pacified, sectarianism stilled, and the country blossoming secular democracy today, with Americans troops long gone.

About 2,000 of those now buried in the ground would be enjoying life with their friends and families instead. Still, it's a neat way of saying: War good, Rummy bad.

It also ignores that there were voices predicting a strong insurgency before the invasion that Brooks and his brethren ignored at the time.

Brooks emphasizes that many of his fellow pundits had it right at the time in urging more boots on the ground. They were "prescient," he relates. But Rumsfeld and his crowd "got things wrong, and the pundits often got things right." He doesn't cite any of his own views at the time, obviously hoping that readers will place him among those pundits who "got things right." And also: forget that he was a strong supporter of the invasion. In fact, he bears special blame, not only for his writing, but for serving as senior editor of the most influential pro-war publication, *The Weekly Standard*.

He may want you to forget what he wrote three years ago, but here's a trip down memory lane with Our Mr. Brooks.

From his column in *The Weekly Standard*, March 10, 2003:

"The American commentariat is gravely concerned. Over the past week, George W. Bush has shown a disturbing tendency not to waffle when it comes to Iraq. There has been an appalling clarity and coherence to his position. There has been a reckless tendency not to be murky, hesitant, or evasive. Naturally, questions are being raised about President Bush's leadership skills.

"Meanwhile, among the smart set, Hamlet-like indecision has become the intellectual fashion. The liberal columnist E. J. Dionne wrote in *The Washington Post* that he is uncomfortable with the pro- and anti-war camps. He praised the doubters and raised his colors on behalf of 'heroic ambivalence.' *The New York Times*, venturing deep into the territory of self-parody, ran a full-page editorial calling for 'still more discussion' on whether or not to go to war.

"In certain circles, it is not only important what opinion you hold, but how you hold it. It is important to be seen dancing with complexity, sliding among shades of gray. Any poor rube can come to a simple conclusion—that President Saddam Hussein is a menace who must be disarmed—but the refined ratiocinators want to be seen luxuriating amid the difficulties, donning the jewels of nuance, even to the point of self-paralysis.

"But those who actually have to lead and protect, and actually have to build one step on another, have to bring some questions to a close. Bush gave Saddam time to disarm. Saddam did not. Hence, the issue of whether to disarm him forcibly is settled. The French and the Germans and the domestic critics may keep debating, which is their luxury, but the people who actually make the decisions have moved on to more practical concerns. . . ."

FROM HIS *WEEKLY STANDARD* COLUMN TWO WEEKS LATER:

"The president has remained resolute. Momentum to liberate Iraq continues to build. The situation has clarified, and history will allow clear judgments about which leaders and which institutions were up to the challenge posed by Saddam and which were not.

"Over the past 12 years the United States has sought to disarm or depose Saddam—more forcefully since September 11 than before. Throughout that time, France and Russia have sought to undermine sanctions and fend off the ousting of Saddam. They opposed Clinton's efforts to bomb Saddam, just as they oppose Bush's push for regime change. Through the fog and verbiage, that is the essential confrontation. Events will show who was right, George W. Bush or Jacques Chirac.

"What matters, and what ultimately sprang the U.N. trap, is American resolve. The administration simply wouldn't let up. It didn't matter how Hans Blix muddied the waters with his reports on this or that weapons system. Under the U.N. resolutions, it was up to Saddam to disarm, administration officials repeated ad nauseam, and he wasn't doing it. It was and is sheer relentlessness that has driven us to where we are today.

"Which is ironic. We are in this situation because the first Bush administration was not relentless in its pursuit of Saddam Hussein. That is a mistake this Bush administration will not repeat."

Update: Three days after the above was written, on the third anniversary of the invasion, Brooks's own paper, in an editorial, gave him a little slap: "Many who supported the invasion have taken this anniversary to argue that it all would have been worthwhile if things had been run better. . . . We doubt it. The last three years have shown how little our national leaders understood Iraq, and have reminded us how badly attempts at liberation from the outside have gone in the past. Given where we are now, the question of whether a botched invasion created a lost opportunity might be moot, except for one thing. The man who did the botching, Donald Rumsfeld, is still the secretary of defense."

---

*A new Gallup poll showed that nearly 6 in 10 Americans still believed Iraq had WMD when the war started and 39 percent believed that Saddam was personally involved with the 9/11 attacks. On March 19—ironically, the third anniversary of the U.S. invasion—*Time *magazine revealed that U.S. Marines had killed at least 15 unarmed Iraqi civilians in a village called Haditha (the number later climbed to 24). Marking the anniversary, Bush promised to "finish the mission" with "complete victory," and urged the public to remain steadfast. That had never been much of a problem for newspaper editorial pages.*

On Third Anniversary: Editorials Dither While Iraq Dies

MARCH 19, 2006

Anyone who hoped that the third anniversary of the U.S. invasion of Iraq would inspire leading newspapers to finally editorialize for a radical change in the White House's war policy has to be disappointed, again. From this evidence, the editorial boards appear to be as clueless about what to do as are Mr. Bush and Mr. Rumsfeld.

Reading the editorials, which mainly call for more of the same, puts you in a time warp: They could have been, perhaps were, written one year ago, maybe two. There's always a "turning point" to count on, from the transfer of power to this-time-we-mean-it-we-are-really-forming-a-unity-government. Reviving a Vietnam-era phrase, it is the nation's editorial voice that is the "pitiful, helpless giant," even as the American and Iraqi publics, alike, call for the start of a withdrawal. Even conservative godfather William F. Buckley recently threw in the towel on the war.

On the other hand, the same newspapers—and many others—produced for the third anniversary on Sunday tough-minded and vital war coverage likely to make any thinking reader cry out, in the direction of Washington, "Enough!" But that's nothing new. Reporters for most papers long ago revealed that the

U.S. presence is Iraq is doing some good, but more harm. Then the editorial page proclaims: Let's stick around for more.

As with their news coverage, the editorials are often harshly critical of the war and the administration. They inevitably say the right things. Yet, after all that, they claim, despite no real evidence, that things will only get worse if we start even a very slow pullout or, gosh—after three years with no end in sight—set some kind of timetable for same.

The New York Times, for example, cogently lays out everything that has gone criminally wrong, with little hope for improvement, but concludes with this ringing call for . . . what? "The Iraq debacle ought to serve as a humbling lesson for future generations of American leaders—although, if our leaders were capable of being humbled, they could have simply looked back to Vietnam," the *Times* declares. "For the present, our goal must be to minimize the damage, through the urgent diplomacy of the current ambassador and forceful reminders that American forces are not prepared to remain for one day in a country whose leaders prefer civil war to peaceful compromise."

"Urgent diplomacy" and "forceful reminders": In other words, leave it to the incompetent gangs in Washington and Baghdad that the editorial has just eviscerated.

Here is what the *Times* wrote on the first anniversary of the war in 2004: "Right now, our highest priority is making the best of a very disturbing situation." The "possibility" of "an Iraq flung into chaos and civil war, open to manipulation by every unscrupulous political figure and terrorist group in the Middle East, is too awful to contemplate."

Two years later, we've got it.

The hawkish *Washington Post*, for its part, did not run an editorial on the war on Sunday. It did offer the next worst thing: an op-ed by Donald Rumsfeld. "Turning our backs on postwar Iraq today would be the modern equivalent of handing postwar Germany back to the Nazis," he wrote.

What about the *Los Angeles Times*? No help there. It boasted that it "will resist the temptation to be fashionable and will take this opportunity to at least concede that the Bush administration's actions were rooted in a strain of American idealism most often identified with Woodrow Wilson." And: "Much of the mocking by Bush critics about the supposed absurdity of the administration's claims about weapons of mass destruction is revisionist nonsense."

Think about all that for a minute. Then ponder that while the *L.A. Times* calls Iraq a "quagmire" and says U.S. leaders are completely out of ideas, it concludes with this unconscionable call to inaction: "As it enters its fourth year, the war in Iraq defies simplistic characterizations from both ends of the political spectrum. The heroism of U.S. forces and of ordinary Iraqis going about their daily lives is inspiring. But the future of Iraq remains shrouded in gray uncertainty." And that's it.

Sen. Chuck Hagel (R-Neb.) said today on ABC: "And this mindless kind of banter about, well, if we leave, the whole place falls apart; we can't leave; we can't even think about leaving. Wait a minute: You just showed on your screen the cost to the American people of the last three years. It's helping bankrupt this country, by the way. We didn't think about any of that—and not just the high cost of lives and the continuation of that, but our standing in the world."

Chuck Hagel said that, and *The New York Times* and *L.A. Times* can't?

Even the folks at Knight Ridder, the chain that produced some of the toughest pre-war and war coverage, prove toothless in an editorial published in many of its papers today. And what of Knight Ridder's likely new owner, McClatchy? That chain's California papers offered their own pointless assessment: "Bush has painted himself and this country into a dangerous corner from which no exit is in sight, save more years of bloodshed and misery in Iraq on the one hand or, on the other, a hasty U.S. departure that would dishonor America and leave Iraqis to cope with the tragedy visited upon them. It's been a long three years. How many more await?"

Plenty more, if newspaper editorial pages (with a few brave exceptions) have anything to say about it.

APRIL

Perhaps bolstered by the absence of editorial calls for withdrawal, Bush at a press conference said troops would remain in Iraq until at least 2009, when he leaves office. On March 30, Jill Carroll, The Christian Science Monitor reporter, was finally freed, unharmed, by her captors. Appearing on CBS News, a former top CIA official, Tyler Drumheller, said that Bush was told before the war by a high-level Iraqi informant that Saddam did not possess WMD. Meanwhile, Seymour Hersh raised new fears by reporting in the The New Yorker that the U.S. had plans in place for the possible bombing of Iran.

Since the start of the war, some of the most caustic and, in the end, accurate commentary had appeared on Comedy Central's The Daily Show and spinoff The Colbert Report. The skepticism expressed there about the war seemed more in sync with public opinion than much in the mainstream media. Still, it seemed risky—if inspired—for the White House Correspondents Association to invite the nervy Stephen Colbert to be the comic "entertainment" at this year's celebrity-stuffed dinner, especially with President Bush in the house. These fun-and-games events, where newsmen mingle with those they cover regularly, always seemed a bit improper, and who could forget the hee-hawing over Bush's video search for those dang missing WMD at a similar dinner two years earlier. But Colbert, appearing in his on-screen Bill O'Reilly–like persona, really shook things up by not just lampooning but actually mocking the president—and the assembled press. Working off the C-SPAN feed, I provided the first online report, and it proved to be our most popular single article of the year.

Even Stephen: Colbert Roasts President—and the Press
APRIL 29, 2006
A blistering comedy "tribute" to President Bush by Comedy Central's faux talk-show host Stephen Colbert at the White House Correspondent Dinner tonight

left George and Laura Bush unsmiling at its close. Earlier, the president had delivered his talk to the 2,700 attendees, including many celebrities and top officials, with the help of a Bush impersonator.

Colbert, who spoke in the guise of his talk-show character, who ostensibly supports the president strongly, urged Bush to ignore his low approval ratings, saying they were based on reality, "and reality has a well-known liberal bias." He attacked those in the press who claim that the shake-up at the White House was merely rearranging the deck chairs on the *Titanic*. "This administration is soaring, not sinking," he said. "If anything, they are rearranging the deck chairs on the *Hindenburg*."

Colbert told Bush he could end the problem of protests by retired generals by refusing to let them retire. He compared Bush to Rocky Balboa in the "Rocky" movies, always getting punched in the face—"and Apollo Creed is everything else in the world." Turning to the war, he declared, "I believe that the government that governs best is a government that governs least, and by these standards we have set up a fabulous government in Iraq."

He noted former Ambassador Joseph Wilson in the crowd, just three tables away from Karl Rove, and that he had brought Valerie Plame. Then, worried that he had named her, he corrected himself, as Bush aides might do, "Uh, I mean . . . he brought Joseph Wilson's wife."

Colbert also made biting cracks about missing WMD, "photo ops" on aircraft carriers and at hurricane disasters, melting glaciers, and Vice President Cheney shooting people in the face. He advised the crowd, "If anybody needs anything at their tables, speak slowly and clearly into your table numbers and somebody from the N.S.A. will be right over with a cocktail."

Observing that Bush sticks to his principles, he said, "When the president decides something on Monday, he still believes it on Wednesday—no matter what happened Tuesday."

Also lampooning the press, Colbert complained that he was "surrounded by the liberal media who are destroying this country, except for Fox News. Fox believes in presenting both sides of the story—the president's side and the vice president's side." In another slap at the news channel, he said: "I give people the truth, unfiltered by rational argument. I call it the No Fact Zone." Then he warned: "Fox News, I own the copyright on that term."

He also reflected on the alleged good old days for the president, when the media was still swallowing the WMD story. Addressing the reporters, he said, "Let's review the rules. Here's how it works. The president makes decisions, he's the decider. The press secretary announces those decisions, and you people of the press type those decisions down. Make, announce, type. Put them through a spell-check and go home. Get to know your family again. Make love to your wife.

"Write that novel you got kicking around in your head. You know, the one about the intrepid Washington reporter with the courage to stand up to the administration. You know—fiction."

He claimed that the Secret Service name for Bush's new press secretary is "Snow Job."

Colbert closed his routine with a video fantasy where he gets to be White House press secretary, complete with a special "Gannon" button on his podium. By the end, he had to run from Helen Thomas and her questions about why the U.S. really invaded Iraq and killed all those people.

As Colbert walked from the podium, when it was over, the president and First Lady gave him quick nods, unsmiling. The president shook his hand and tapped his elbow, and left immediately. Those seated near Bush told *E&P*'s Joe Strupp, who was in the room, that Bush had quickly turned from an amused guest to an obviously offended target as Colbert's comments brought up his low approval ratings and problems in Iraq.

Several veterans of past dinners, who requested anonymity, said the presentation was more directed at attacking the president than in the past. One noted that Bush quickly turned unhappy: "You could see he stopped smiling about halfway through Colbert."

Strupp had observed that quite a few sitting near him looked a little uncomfortable at times, perhaps feeling the material was a little too biting—or too much speaking "truthiness" (a word Colbert popularized) to power.

Asked by *E&P* after it was over if he thought he'd been too harsh, Colbert said, "Not at all." Was he trying to make a point politically, or just get laughs? "Just for laughs," he said. Helen Thomas told Strupp her segment with Colbert was "just for fun."

After the gathering, Snow, while nursing a Heineken outside the *Chicago Tribune* reception, declined to comment on Colbert. "I'm not doing entertainment reviews," he said. "I thought the president was great, though."

Earlier, the president had addressed the crowd with a Bush impersonator alongside, with the near-Bush speaking precisely and the real Bush deliberately mispronouncing words, such as the inevitable "nuclear." At the close, Bush called the imposter "a fine talent. In fact, he did all my debates with Senator Kerry." The low-brow routine went over well with the crowd.

Among attendees at the black tie event: Morgan Fairchild, quarterback Ben Roethlisberger, Justice Antonin Scalia, George Clooney, and Jeff "Skunk" Baxter of the Doobie Brothers—in a kilt.

MAY

As we expected, the Beltway pundits did not take kindly to Colbert's brand of humor. Richard Cohen, the Washington Post *columnist (usually described as liberal) who had been so wrong on the war, called Colbert's routine "not funny." In fact, he was "lame and insulting." Colbert was "rude," Cohen complained. "He took advantage of President Bush's 'sense of decorum' and 'civility' that kept the president from 'rising in a huff and leaving.'" Colbert was "more than rude. He was a bully." And to those who called Colbert brave: Actually, he showed no courage because in this country when you openly criticize the president you don't get tossed "into a dungeon" or lose your job.*

A cultural icon from a different era had also roused himself politically. Neil Young had recorded a powerful anti-war album, Living with War, *featuring a little ditty called "Let's Impeach the President." In a column, I noted that his father once was a prominent newspaper reporter in Canada, so maybe Neil had learned some journalistic skills at home. As days passed, it seemed like the rocker was outperforming our pundits.*

Neil Young and the Restless
MAY 9, 2006

For centuries, The Press acted as surrogate for The People. Now, at least in regard to the Iraq war, the reverse often seems to be true. While reporters and TV commentators continue to tiptoe around the question of whether Bush administration officials, right up to the president, deliberately misled the nation into the war, average and not-so-average citizens—such as rocker Neil Young—have raised the charge of "lies" and caused a stir usually reserved for reporters. Is America, or just my own head, about to explode over Iraq?

The latest example of citizen journalism occurred Thursday, with former CIA analyst Ray McGovern's persistent questioning of Pentagon chief Donald

Rumsfeld at a forum in Atlanta. CNN's Anderson Cooper, interviewing McGovern later, told him he had gone where most reporters had failed to tread. Whether Anderson meant this as self-criticism was impossible to tell.

This comes on the heels of satirist Stephen Colbert's caustic routine at the White House Correspondents Association dinner on Saturday—publicized primarily by Web sites and blogs—and this week's streaming-on-line debut of Neil Young's *Living with War* album, which proposes impeaching the president "for lying" (and "for spying"). It has already earned more than a million Internet listeners, and on Saturday reached Number Three in sales at Amazon. "Don't need no more lies," Young sings repeatedly in one song.

McGovern, Colbert, and Young are hardly grassroots Americans, but we also have the recent example of Harry Taylor, who on April 6 rose at a town meeting in Charlotte, N.C., and asked the president about his domestic spying program, among other things, saying he was "ashamed" of the nation's leader. But this "people pressure" has been the story of the war at home all along, at least in personal probing of the engineers of the disaster. It was a U.S. soldier, after all, whose questioning of Rumsfeld in 2004 about the lack of adequate armor for personnel and vehicles in Iraq brought that issue to national attention.

Even on the editorial pages, it has required at virtually every newspaper an outside contributor to propose a radical change in direction on Iraq. Witness the op-ed on Thursday in the *Los Angeles Times* by retired Gen. William E. Odom, calling for the start of an American withdrawal. For more than a day it was the most e-mailed story at the paper's Web site—just as the belated story on Colbert in *The New York Times* was Number One at that site for 24 hours or more.

While reporters have produced acres of tough journalism on issues related to the war, they have generally failed to ask Bush and Rumsfeld truly pointed questions (saving that experience for punching bag Scott McClellan), and refuse to use the word "lie" in news stories and editorials. At the same time, the public now has many more opportunities to act as press hounds, at public forums that either did not exist or at least were not televised years ago.

Still, it would be nice to see reporters following ex–CIA analyst McGovern's example on Thursday, directing chapter-and-verse examples of misleading statements, or downright lies, at Bush, Rumsfeld, Cheney, and others whenever they get a chance. Certainly, every poll shows that the American public is behind them on this—or, should I say, ahead of them?

Now it will be fun to watch the media reaction to the CD release of the Neil Young anti-Bush broadside next week. (It's the first major album to "go there" since Steve Earle's *The Revolution Starts Now*.) A *Washington Post* music critic has already weighed in with a pan, declaring, bizarrely, "The urgency is somewhat strange, given that the album doesn't appear to be inspired by any recent events." Huh?

If you are a Neil Young fan—politics aside—you will no doubt appreciate his return to slashing guitar work and full-throated singing. The lyrics are consistently biting, always topical, and occasionally humorous, with war the focus but with side trips to American consumerism and environmentalism. He even refers to the prohibition against the media showing pictures of coffins returning from Iraq: "Thousands of bodies in the ground/Brought home in boxes to a trumpet's sound/No one sees them coming home that way/Thousands buried in the ground." And in another song: "More boxes covered in flags/But I can't see them on TV."

Neil closes with "America the Beautful" sung by a 100-voice choir. It's true, Young is a Canadian, but he has now lived in this country (and paid zillions in taxes) for four decades, which should count for something.

The best song is not "Impeach the President," which includes audio clips of embarrassing Bush statements ("We'll smoke them out," etc.), but rather the blistering "Shock and Awe," which includes not only specific anti-war lyrics but the more philosophical "history is a cruel judge of overconfidence." It mocks Bush right where it hurts: "Back in the days of Mission Accomplished/Our chief was landing on the deck."

The press response will be fascinating, but, no matter what, it is not likely to top John Gibson's gaffe on Fox News this week. On April 28, Gibson blasted Young, charging that he must be suffering from "amnesia" about the terrorist attacks of 9/11. He suggested that Young go see the new movie, *United 93*, about the hijacked flight that went down in Pennsylvania that day. Gibson even offered to buy Young a ticket.

Whoops. It was Neil Young who wrote one of the highest-profile songs about 9/11, right after the tragedy—"Let's Roll," which paid tribute to the passengers on United 93.

It turned out that Young's album was largely inspired by a photograph that he spotted in USA Today *showing a flying hospital for wounded soldiers. The photographer, who worked for the* Detroit Free Press, *told us he was honored, but said Pearl Jam, not Neil, was his musical fave. Judy Miller, meanwhile, had returned to the WMD beat, with a long piece in* The Wall Street Journal—*this time focusing on Libya. Howell Raines's new memoir appeared, but the former* New York Times *editor accepted little blame for how he had handled "Miss Run Amok" during the pre-war period—in fact, he did not mention her once. The most prominent "liberal hawk" on the war at Raines's old paper, or anywhere, was also refusing to face the facts.*

A History of the "Friedman Unit"

MAY 18, 2006

For weeks now, liberal bloggers have proposed a new measurement to mark the mildly optimistic, if farfetched, pronouncements on Iraq coming from many pundits, Republicans, and White House spokesmen: the "Friedman Unit" or "F.U." It equals six months, and is named after famed *New York Times* columnist Thomas Friedman, a longtime supporter of the war who, for nearly three years, has repeatedly declared that things would likely turn around there if we just give it another six months.

Friedman Unit has even gained a lengthy entry at Wikipedia. It calls it a "tongue-in-cheek neologism. . . . The term has been used in general to describe any pronouncement of a critical period for the U.S. occupation of Iraq."

Now the press watchdog group Fairness and Accuracy in Reporting (FAIR) has assembled a full review of Friedman's pronouncements in this vein. "A review of Friedman's punditry reveals a long series of similar do-or-die dates that never seem to get any closer," said FAIR, which compiled excerpts from Friedman's columns and broadcast remarks. It tracks the birth of the Friedman Unit to his *Times* column on November 30, 2003, which held this quote: "The next six months in Iraq—which will determine the prospects for democracy-building there—are the most important six months in U.S. foreign policy in a long, long time."

Then, on CBS's *Face the Nation*, on Oct. 3, 2004, he declared: "What we're gonna find out, Bob, in the next six to nine months is whether we have liberated a country or uncorked a civil war."

Six weeks after that, in the *Times*, he declared: "Improv time is over. This is crunch time. Iraq will be won or lost in the next few months. But it won't be won with high rhetoric. It will be won on the ground in a war over the last mile."

And away we go:

• "I think we're in the end game now. . . . I think we're in a six-month window here where it's going to become very clear and this is all going to pre-empt I think the next congressional election—that's my own feeling— let alone the presidential one." (NBC's *Meet the Press*, Sept. 25, 2005)

• "We've teed up this situation for Iraqis, and I think the next six months really are going to determine whether this country is going to collapse into three parts or more or whether it's going to come together." (*Face the Nation*, Dec. 18, 2005)

• "The only thing I am certain of is that in the wake of this election, Iraq will be what Iraqis make of it—and the next six months will tell us a lot. I remain guardedly hopeful." (*The New York Times*, Dec. 21, 2005)

• "I think that we're going to know after six to nine months whether this project has any chance of succeeding. In which case, I think the American people as a whole will want to play it out or whether it really is a fool's errand." (*Oprah Winfrey Show*, Jan. 23, 2006)

• "I think we are in the end game. The next six to nine months are going to tell whether we can produce a decent outcome in Iraq." (NBC's *Today*, March 2, 2006)

• "Can Iraqis get this government together? If they do, I think the American public will continue to want to support the effort there to try to produce a decent, stable Iraq. But if they don't, then I think the bottom is going to fall out of public support here for the whole Iraq endeavor. So one way or another, I think we're in the end game in the sense it's going to be decided in the next weeks or months whether there's an Iraq there worth investing in. And that is something only Iraqis can tell us." (CNN, April 23, 2006)

• "Well, I think that we're going to find out, Chris, in the next year to six months—probably sooner—whether a decent outcome is possible there, and I think we're going to have to just let this play out." (MSNBC's *Hardball*, May 11, 2006)

JUNE

On May 25, Iraqi Prime Minister al-Maliki vowed that Iraqi troops would be ready to handle security for the entire country by the end of 2007, but war leaders Bush and Blair announced that no coalition withdrawals were expected any time soon. The number of journalists killed in Iraq reached 71, topping the total for all of World War II. Another poignant Memorial Day arrived, this time with the American death toll in Iraq well past 2,400 lives, with over 18,000 injured. Just over six months had passed since Rep. Murtha called for the beginning of a U.S. pullout in Iraq. No major papers backed that position in their Memorial Day editorials. The New York Times, for example, after ripping Bush's handling of the war, concluded weakly: "It's time for Mr. Bush either to chart a course that can actually be followed, or admit that there is none." The Washington Post said that Iraq's "new government and its army . . . should be given a chance to tackle the insurgency and stabilize the country with U.S. support." It observed that there "is also a new plan to pacify Baghdad."

Media Slow to Probe Haditha

June 4, 2006

By now, it's clear that the U.S. military engaged in some kind of cover-up of an alleged massacre in Haditha. Following the November killings, it took months for an official investigation to begin. But even as reporters explore the story now, with impressive and detailed probes that often end up on the front page, the question must be asked: Did the press also drop the ball in probing the killings? Or was the usual roadblock—the danger of spending a lot of time in hellish Anbar province—just too difficult to overcome?

In any case, have editors and reporters back home, for three years now, shown too little interest in possible—some would say likely—American atrocities in the heat of horrible pressures in Iraq?

An Associated Press story from Baghdad on Sunday quoted Hassan Bazaz, a Baghdad University political scientist, complaining that strong interest now being shown by Western news media in the alleged U.S. misconduct is only now catching up with common views in Iraq. "There is nothing new or surprising for Iraqis," said Bazaz. "The problem is that the outside world has been isolated from what happens on the ground in Iraq. What the media say now is only a fraction of what happens every day." This is pretty much what Iraqi Prime Minister al-Maliki said on Friday.

Of course, dangerous conditions for reporters in Iraq have been well chronicled—especially in this space. It's hard to criticize anyone for not being eager to trek out to Haditha and get shot at (or worse), and it's not known if villagers would have spoken frankly to any reporter months ago. But what about those covering war-related issues back in the safety of the USA?

Clues about the general lack of interest in American misconduct in Iraq—here at home—appear in Thomas Ricks's *Washington Post* story on Haditha on Sunday. Near the end, he traces the now-familiar timeline: Haditha killings in November, *Time* magazine story in March, very quiet again until Rep. John Murtha (D-Pa.) told reporters on May 17 the shocking news (after he was briefed on the incident) that what happened in Haditha was "much worse than reported in *Time* magazine." Murtha stated that the investigations would reveal that our troops overreacted and they killed innocent civilians in cold blood.

But here's what happened next, according to Ricks: "The reporters present barely focused on what Murtha had said. When the congressman finished his statement, the first reporter asked about Iraqi security forces. The second asked about U.S. troop withdrawals. The third asked about congressional support for Murtha's resolution calling for a U.S. pullout from Iraq.

"Finally, the fourth asked about Haditha. Murtha responded with a bit more detail: 'They actually went into the houses and killed women and children. And there was about twice as many as originally reported by *Time*.' Even then, his comments captured little attention and were not front-page news. It took a few days for the horror of what Murtha was talking about to sink in."

This is shocking, on one level, but, on another, not surprising, because the media had pretty much ignored the Haditha story after noting *Time*'s scoop back in March.

The New York Times, for example, covered the *Time* revelations on March 17. On April 6, Haditha briefly appeared in a story, without any reference to the *Time* probe, and a week later another story mentioned the possible massacre in one sentence. Nothing else appeared in the paper until May 19—after Murtha's talk. Nothing appeared in any opinion columns there either.

The Washington Post carried two stories just after the *Time* scoop—then nothing else until Murtha's remarks. The *Los Angeles Times*, after covering the *Time* revelations, returned for an April 8 story on three commanders at Haditha being relieved of duty, and that's it. A search of AP archives mirrors the record of the *L.A. Times* in that period.

Throughout the war there have been scattered reports of U.S. wrongdoing in the field, ranging from hair-trigger shootings of civilians to running Iraqi vehicles off the road when they did not get out of the way of a convoy fast enough. The Knight Ridder Baghdad bureau has been relatively aggressive on this front, and others have covered dozens of tragic episodes—but, by and large, the media's reports have been downplayed and rarely followed up.

On Sunday, John Burns of *The New York Times* described what he called "harsh Marine battle tactics" in Iraq. "Reporters' experiences with the Marines," he related, "even more than with the Army, show they resort quickly to using heavy artillery or laser-guided bombs when rooting out insurgents who have taken refuge among civilians, with inevitable results." Yet many of these same embeds do not report—or at least rarely emphasize—these "inevitable results."

One problem: News organizations are cutting back on sending reporters to Iraq, a true scandal. Another: Some outlets that are not scaling back are having trouble getting volunteers to go.

The media, like political figures of all persuasions, have tried to separate the war from the warriors. This is a very good thing, except when it is carried too far—into blanket and largely unquestioning support for the conduct of our boys. Surely, the vast majority behave nobly, but is that number really 99.9 percent as both Donald Rumsfeld and Wesley Clark asserted last week? Given the incredible conditions of facing a faceless enemy? Impossible.

In any case, after Haditha, finally—after three years—we see a torrent of stories, on the home front, focusing on possible abuses, past and present.

Just one example was Mark Mazzetti's Sunday story in *The New York Times*. "Military experts," he revealed, "say that the first principle of counterinsurgency warfare, and its greatest difficulty, is to separate enemy fighters from the local population from which they draw strength. But as details emerge about the killings of Iraqi civilians in Haditha and Hamandiyah, it seems increasingly clear that some American troops have come to see the population itself as the enemy." But this is nothing like Vietnam, right?

Mazzetti closes his story by noting that Charles Moskos, a sociologist at Northwestern University and a frequent Pentagon consultant, had said "temporary insanity" sometimes set in for soldiers and marines who daily watched their close friends die in battle. The frustration and sense of powerlessness, according to Moskos, often leads combat troops to direct their venom at innocent civilians they assume are aiding the insurgents—and sometimes even at young children. "If they feel that a local town is covertly involved in the killing of G.I.'s," he said, "that's when people lose their sense of right and wrong."

Of course, this has likely been true since 2003.

On June 8, Abu Musab al-Zarqawi, leader of al-Qaeda in Iraq, was killed during a U.S. air raid and his bloody corpse displayed for photographers. TV newcasts and newspapers—suddenly not squeamish—aired the close-up images, as some pundits and administration officials again proclaimed a possible "turning point" had arrived.

Dead and Loving It: Media Air Graphic Images of Zarqawi

JUNE 9, 2006

As shown on TV screens, Web sites, and front pages, few editors are reticent to display graphic close-up images of the dead head of slain terrorist Abu Musab al-Zarqawi. The vast majority of papers, as they had done on the Web the day before, carried at the top of their front pages a large image of the bloodied face of Zarqawi. Leading the pack, not surprisingly, was the *New York Post*, which devoted its full front page to the dead head, with the headline "Gotcha!" and a quote bubble leading from Zarqawi's mouth with him saying, "Warm up the virgins."

As noted by some commentators, this was in stark contrast to newspapers' general ban on showing pictures of dead U.S. soldiers or Iraqi civilians.

But several papers, with the same opportunity to display the deceased terrorist, chose for whatever reason to avoid that on their front pages. Among others that did not use a death photo on their front pages (again, very much in the minority), were the *San Francisco Chronicle*, *Des Moines Register*, and *The Christian Science Monitor*. Perhaps we will learn eventually if any of these papers felt showing the close-up of a dead man—even if he was one of the world's most notorious killers—violated their standards of decency, or if they broke from the pack for other reasons.

But in considering the wide showcasing of the death photo, *Washington Post* staff writer Philip Kennicott on Friday wondered if, "as with so many images in this war, it is loaded with the potential to backfire." It might add to his martyr status—"and it reminds others how much this war has been about cycles of killing, retribution, tribal and sectarian violence, and the most primitive destructive urges. . . .

"And now we gaze on Zarqawi's face one last time, as he reminds us that the new product wasn't so new; the war turned out to have all too much of what wars have always had in them, death, destruction, and chaos. Zarqawi's head forces us to confront once again the most primitive dynamic of war: It's an eye for an eye, or a head for a head. . . .

"What began as a war of necessity, premised on the slam-dunk certainty that Saddam Hussein was staring us down with weapons of mass destruction, eventually became a war of ideas. If there were no weapons, then at least it was a war of liberation, bringing freedom and democracy to a land in desperate need of both. And when that war devolved into clouds of dust and pools of blood as the country broke into religious and ethnic factions, and the rule of law was extinguished by terrorists and militias, the war of ideas began to seem more like another thing—a war of trophies.

"We may not have victory. Iraq may be a living hell both for those who are fighting to make it better and for those who live there. But we bring home the occasional politically expedient marker of 'progress.' Major combat operations are over. We got Saddam's sons. We got Saddam. Now we have Zarqawi. The trophy case fills: elections, a constitution, a new government—everything but peace and stability for an exhausted nation of Iraqis who have died by the tens of thousands during the evolution of this war.

"Zarqawi is gone, and good riddance. But there's nothing in the image of his face that deserves a frame. It's a small thing, to be sure. But it suggests a cynicism about this war that is profoundly distressing. Our political and military leaders simply can't resist packaging the war and wrapping it up in a bow."

The Sun in Baltimore interviewed Philip Seib, author of *Beyond the Front Lines: How the News Media Cover a World Shaped by War*. He said, "I think it's important for the American media not to turn this into a *Star Search* kind of a thing where you have one super-celebrity in al-Zarqawi and you make a huge deal out of it, when the fact is that the insurgency is so much more complicated. . . .

"I'm not saying al-Zarqawi's death is trivial—it's an important development—but parts of the media just get caught up in it and are falling all over themselves to show the dead body and the bombs and make it into much more than it is in terms of its importance to the overall insurgency and military effort."

In the aftermath of the Haditha revelations, almost every day brought some kind of report on an alleged atrocity in Iraq, large or small, founded or unfounded. One had to wonder if there just happened to be an uptick in such incidents or there had been many all along and they were just getting military, and media, attention after Haditha. Also surfacing: something with the mysterious name "solatia."

The Cost of Killing Civilians

JUNE 10, 2006

Long before revelations about Haditha, I was always amazed, if not surprised, when newspapers routinely took at face value reports from the military on the results of a raid, air strike, or firefight in Iraq: you know, "15 insurgents were killed," and so forth. After more than three years of fighting a shadowy enemy in Iraq—not to mention the Vietnam experience—you would think the strong chance that a few civilians were among the dead would inspire more skepticism.

It is extremely risky for individual reporters to travel to insurgent hotbeds to secure the true facts—but at least their papers, and the wire services, could use the word "claimed" or "asserted" when referring to the military's report, or add, "could not be independently confirmed." This, of course, is only the truth.

I've long felt this way, but perhaps this approach now has gained some traction following the Haditha revelations—remember, the initial accounts carried in all papers was that only "insurgents" were killed there. Then, this past week, came shocking reports in *The Boston Globe* and, yesterday, in *The New York Times*, about U.S. payoffs to thousands of families of civilians we have killed or maimed. The *Times* even provided a city-by-city chart today tracing the recent payments—more than $6 million just in Baghdad last year—and observes that the Marines have made the bulk of the payments.

The custom, not unique to Iraq, is known as "solatia"—it means families receive financial compensation for physical damage or a loss of life. The practice has earned more attention in recent weeks, with news that the U.S. military paid about $2,500 per victim to families in Haditha following the alleged massacre there last November. But how common is the practice? And how many deaths do the numbers seem to suggest?

A chilling report from *The Boston Globe* on Thursday revealed that the amount of cash the U.S. military has paid to families of Iraqi civilians killed or badly injured in operations involving American troops "skyrocketed from just under $5 million in 2004 to almost $20 million last year, according to Pentagon financial data." The payments can range from several hundred dollars for a severed limb to a standard of $2,500 for loss of life. This, of course, is a little less than the price of a good used car. There is no explanation on how that top figure was arrived at.

Globe reporter Bryan Bender observed: "If each of the payments made in 2005 was the maximum $2,500 for an Iraqi death, it would amount to 8,000 fatalities. But it's unknown exactly how many payments were made or for what amount."

Defense Department officials stressed to Bender that the payments shouldn't be seen as an admission of guilt or responsibility. But Bender observed that "the fourfold increase in condolence payments raises new questions about the extent to which Iraqi civilians have been the victims of U.S. firepower."

A report earlier this week by Tom Lasseter for Knight Ridder described the accidental death of three civilians, a woman and two men, in a U.S. raid of an insurgent hotspot south of Baghdad one week ago. That story closed with the military indicating it would probably be making compensation payments to families—and an Army captain saying he wasn't looking forward to making that visit to hand out the money.

Senator Edward M. Kennedy (D-Mass.), a member of the Senate Armed

Services Committee, is pushing for a broader investigation into condolence payments. "The dramatic rise in condolence payments raises many questions of accountability and process—and serve as a warning sign for incidents like Haditha," Kennedy told the *Globe*.

Compensation payments come from the Commanders Emergency Response Program, which allows commanders to make payments to help win the hearts and minds of Iraqis affected by the war. But is it possible that the ability to make the payoffs encourages the military to feel that this closes the book on a civilian killing or true atrocity? Bender notes that "some experts have said that the commanding officers who approved the Haditha condolence payments should have asked more questions about what happened that day—and whether the Marines were responsible."

The charts in today's *Times* seem to show that the payoffs, already high, soared in January, with more than $4 million shelled out in that month alone. And the carnage has only increased since.

A top Iraqi official said U.S. troop strength should be under 100,000 by the end of the year and most of the remaining troops should go home by the end of 2007. Timothy McNulty, ombudsman for the Chicago Tribune, *revealed that a survey found that in the past three years, the war has steadily been moving off the front pages of major newspapers. Even celebrities, such as Bruce Springsteen, couldn't do much to counter that trend. I went way back with The Boss—having co-authored the first magazine article about him anywhere, for the legendary* Crawdaddy *magazine, in early 1973—and always kept an eye on his political activities. Breaking tradition, he'd endorsed John Kerry in 2004 and even went out on one of the fund-raising tours for him. Now he spoke out again.*

Bruce Springsteen vs. Ann Coulter

JUNE 23, 2006

Ann Coulter has used her latest column to repeat some of the controversial language she has used in her new book, on TV appearances, and elsewhere. "I

dedicate this column to John Murtha, the reason soldiers invented fragging,"
Coulter began. A spokeswoman for her syndicate, Universal, told *E&P* that it
does not censor columnists and, in any case, the "fragging" comment had not
appeared in one of her columns—until now.

"In response to the arguments of my opponents, I say: Waaaaaaaah! Boo
hoo hoo!" Coulter continued. "If you're upset about what I said about the
Witches of East Brunswick [the activist 9/11 widows], try turning the page.
Surely, I must have offended more than those four harpies. . . .”

Murtha is the hawkish Congressman—and former Marine officer—who
now opposes the Iraq war, while "fragging" is the term for soldiers killing their
own officers. Appearing on the *Hannity & Colmes* show on Fox News this week,
she declared that if Murtha "did get fragged, he'd finally deserve one of those
Purple Hearts."

Coulter also discussed abortion in her latest column. She wrote: "Liberals
don't care about women. They care about destroying human life. To them, 2,200
military deaths in the entire course of a war in Iraq is unconscionable, but 1.3
million aborted babies in America every year is something to celebrate." Actually,
more than 2,500 American soldiers have died in the war, and many more Iraqis.

After mentioning *New York Times* columnist Maureen Dowd, Coulter called
the paper's Op-Ed section "the cartoon pages." (She didn't mention if that
description applied to the days when columnists David Brooks and John
Tierney appeared.) Coulter's conclusion: "Finally, a word to those of you out
there who have yet to be offended by something I have written or said: Please
be patient. I am working as fast as I can."

Apparently my old friend Bruce Springsteen doesn't have to wait for that.
Appearing on CNN today to promote his current tour and album of Pete Seeger
songs, Springsteen—who was about as apolitical as they come when I knew him
well back in the 1970s—took note of the new Coulter controversy in responding to a question about whether musicians should speak out on politics.

Springsteen was asked by Soledad O'Brien if getting flak about his political
views, such as backing John Kerry in 2004, made him wonder if musicians
should try so hard to be taken seriously on topical issues.

"They should let Ann Coulter do it instead?" he mused, with a chuckle.
Then he said, "You can turn on the idiots rambling on, on cable television,
every night of the week—and they say musicians shouldn't speak up? It's insane,

it's funny," he said, with that inimitable booming laugh. He called politics "an organic part of what I'm doing. . . . It's called common sense. I don't even see it as politics at this point."

As for the Iraq war, he commented, "You don't take your country into a major war on circumstantial evidence—you lose your job for that. That's my opinion, and I don't have a problem voicing that. Some people have a problem with that, others don't."

He revealed that some former fans have even mailed records back to him. Records? What are they?

SEPTEMBER

At the end of June, one of the most sickening American atrocities yet came to light: the murder of an Iraqi family, apparently by American soldiers, who raped a teenage girl and then set her on fire back in March. Five G.I.'s were charged in the case. The Los Angeles Times *set the Iraqi death toll since the U.S. invasion at over 50,000, mainly civilians, based on morgue reports; other estimates went much higher. Gallup found two out of three Americans backing the start of a withdrawal, but as Leonard Cohen once observed: "Come on back to the war—it's just beginning." Sectarian slaughter continued—a record 3,500 civilians died in July. Meanwhile, Frank Rich in* The New York Times *noted, "On the Big Three networks' evening newscasts, the time devoted to Iraq has fallen 60 percent between 2003 and this spring, as clocked by the television monitor, the Tyndall Report. On Thursday, Brian Williams of NBC read aloud a 'shame on you' e-mail complaint from the parents of two military sons anguished that his broadcast had so little news about the war."*

On August 19, it had been 1,249 days since the war began—surpassing the length of the U.S. involvement in World War II. Nevertheless, on August 21, Bush said, "We're not leaving so long as I am president." A new National Intelligence Estimate found that the Iraq war had actually increased the terror threat and "helped spawn a new generation of Islamic radicalism."

A Comma or a Coma?

SEPTEMBER 24, 2006

In a CNN interview just aired, Wolf Blitzer asked the president about the latest setbacks in Iraq and indications that civil war may be at hand. Bush, with a slight smile, replied, "Yes, you see—you see it on TV, and that's the power of an enemy that is willing to kill innocent people. But there's also an unbelievable will and resiliency by the Iraqi people. . . . I like to tell people when the final history is written on Iraq, it will look like just a comma because there is— my point is, there's a strong will for democracy."

Even for Bushisms, this is an odd one. Maybe he meant "coma." No, that would be too negative.

A comma as a metaphor perhaps? If so, for what? All that bloodshed as merely a comma—a pause in a long sentence—leading to a hopeful phrase or conclusion? Comma, "and they all lived happily ever after"? Or maybe, comma, "and then we bombed Iran"?

Of course, one can think of other punctuation that might be apt, including "?" for the 140,000 Americans still deployed there, "!" for the cries of the gravely injured, and "$" for Halliburton and other contractors. Or perhaps, as in the comics pages, when an angry character really wants to curse: "!@#%^&*()#*"

Like many others, I was initially confused—though appalled—when President Bush stated that the Iraq war will be viewed as "just a comma." Perhaps he meant to say "asterisk" but did not know how to pronounce it. Or maybe he meant "blip" or "footnote"—though that wouldn't make the sentiment any less revolting, especially for the thousands of dead. In any case, if you watch the CNN video, you will see the president stumbling a bit after making that statement, as if he hadn't quite finished the thought or phrase, or was afraid to.

That sent me googling in search of an answer, which I believe I have found. This is it: He likely meant to finish it off by suggesting that, looking back, the Iraq war will be viewed as "just a comma, not a period." Not surprisingly, this is rooted in current Christian teaching, often in reference to Jesus' death, or more generally as "Don't put a period where God puts a comma."

Where does this come from? Not directly from the scripture, apparently. A quote by comedienne Gracie Allen is cited on many religious Web sites: "Never place a period where God has placed a comma." United Church of Christ parishes in Massachusetts were recently urged to put that quote on banners during Lent and color in the words as the weeks went by.

Of course, many of us of a certain age remember Gracie Allen, the actual and TV wife of the legendary George Burns. Memo to the president: She was the batty one who often talked nonsense. Or as a minister at a United Church of Christ in Los Angeles recently put it, admiringly: "She would have said whatever came to her mind in a full voice, and lived out its conviction." Sound familiar?

Rev. Philip Blackwell of the First United Methodist Church in Chicago opened a sermon last year with this: "I am wearing a comma lapel pin that was given to me by my good friend and United Church of Christ minister, Chuck Wildman. The comma is part of the most recent advertising campaign of the UCC. The punch line is, 'Don't put a period where God has put a comma.' That's a good line. I asked Chuck who said that, which famous theologian. And he replied, 'Gracie Allen.' Some of us remember Burns and Allen. Gracie Allen at her theological best."

An article in the *St. Petersburg Times* in November 2005 described a new TV commercial by the UCC—not a conservative, but a progressive church—which featured a large comma. "Weighing in on the commercial," the article concluded, "evangelist Pat Robertson is said to have remarked, 'Never place a comma where God has placed a period. God has spoken!'"

And so has the president. Did he fail to finish his thought—linking the comma to the period—for fear of invoking his Christianity in discussing a murderous war? Or did he want to avoid being linked to Gracie Allen?

OCTOBER

A poll had found that Americans aren't the only ones who want a U.S. pullout to begin: 71 percent of Iraqis also back this idea. Another poll revealed that 58 percent of Americans felt the Bush administration deliberately misled the public about the war, but pundits still refused to use the word "lie." U.S. casualties were spiking as sectarian violence continued to grow. Bob Woodward's third book on the war, State of Denial, *emerged with a much more critical version of the events leading up to the war and the administration's handling of the conflict since. Some critics suggested that Woodward had been in a state of denial about the war himself for many years, but he explained that he had just learned more as time passed. He also defended holding back some of the scoops from his own newspaper until they appeared in the book.*

Will the Media Finally Count the Dead?

OCTOBER 11, 2006

From the beginning, the U.S. military refused to count—and the American media rarely probed—civilian casualties as the result of our invasion of Iraq in 2003. For the longest time, these deaths were rarely mentioned at all. In recent months, they do gain notice nearly every day or two, usually in relation to several dozen bodies discovered around Baghdad with holes drilled in their skulls or showing other forms of torture. We also now learn about U.S. soldiers arrested for killing innocent civilians. Even so, the press almost never attempts to quantify the Iraqi death toll.

Now today comes a shocking study from the Johns Hopkins Bloomberg School of Public Health—to be published Thursday by *The Lancet*, a leading medical journal—based on very detailed (and no doubt dangerous) fieldwork. It suggests that upwards of 600,000 Iraqis may have met a violent or otherwise war-related end since the U.S. arrived in March 2003. Even now, however,

The Associated Press casts a very skeptical eye on the study, emphasizing the views of one expert who charges that it is nothing but "politics," with the November election approaching.

The expert is Anthony Cordesman, who actually is a respected voice on military matters (he recently said flatly that a civil war is indeed raging in Iraq). But *The Washington Post*, fortunately, quickly found others with far more experience in studying civilian casualties who basically endorsed the validity, if not necessarily the findings, of the Johns Hopkins study.

The AP report by Malcolm Ritter called the study "controversial" right in its first sentence, then went on to cite Cordesman as the only critic—presto, instant controversy. Ritter also noted that the invaluable Web site Iraq Body Count, which has tried to keep a running tally, places the number of dead at 50,000, but this is based strictly on confirmed media reports. The Johns Hopkins count, based on extrapolations from door-to-door surveys in 18 provinces, finds a minimum figure of 426,000.

The last guess coming from President Bush was 30,000. Today, asked about this at a press conference, Bush declined to amend his figure, called the new survey not "credible," and added inanely: "I am, you know, amazed that this is a society which so wants to be free that they're willing to—you know, that there's a level of violence that they tolerate." He meant Iraq, but he could just as easily have been talking about America.

The Washington Post, meanwhile, interviewed Ronald Waldman, an epidemiologist at Columbia University who worked at the Centers for Disease Control and Prevention for many years. He called the Johns Hopkins survey method "tried and true," and added that "this is the best estimate of mortality we have." Sarah Leah Whitson, an official of Human Rights Watch in New York, told the *Post*, "We have no reason to question the findings or the accuracy" of the survey.

When I was doing my own field research a few decades ago in another place devastated by violent death—Hiroshima—I found that the most valuable and chilling moment of all came on virtually the first day, when I climbed a hill overlooking the rebuilt city. It resides in a natural bowl formed by the hills, and I found it all too easy to imagine nearly everything spread out below me, including all the people, dead and gone. So here is a list of 11 American cities with a population of just under or just over 600,000. It may be that the Johns Hopkins numbers are on the high side. But think of these cities disappearing: Austin, Baltimore, Denver, Boston, Seattle, Milwaukee, Memphis, Washington, D.C., Fort Worth, Portland, Las Vegas.

Relating to all this, NBC correspondent Jane Arraf posted the following last night at the network's Blogging Baghdad site:

"Some readers and viewers think we journalists are exaggerating about the situation in Iraq. I can almost understand that, because who would want to believe that things are this bad? Particularly when so many people here started out with such good intentions.

"I'm more puzzled by comments that the violence isn't any worse than any American city. Really? In which American city do 60 bullet-riddled bodies turn up on a given day? In which city do the headless bodies of ordinary citizens turn up every single day? In which city would it not be news if neighborhood school children were blown up? In which neighborhood would you look the other way if gunmen came into restaurants and shot dead the customers?

"Day-to-day life here for Iraqis is so far removed from the comfortable existence we live in the United States that it is almost literally unimaginable. . . . I don't know a single family here that hasn't had a relative, neighbor, or friend die violently. In places where there's been all-out fighting going on, I've interviewed parents who buried their dead child in the yard because it was too dangerous to go to the morgue.

"Imagine the worst day you've ever had in your life, add a regular dose of terror, and you'll begin to get an idea of what it's like every day for a lot of people here."

The number of embedded journalists in Iraq had fallen to only a handful. Some blamed restrictions on reporting and pressure by some commanders to avoid negative coverage. Electricity levels in Baghdad were now at the lowest level since the invasion. After more than 30 months of defending the war, conservative pundit Jonah Goldberg admitted that the decision to invade was a "mistake." Bush, meeting with a group of other conservative columnists at the White House, told them, "This war is on the TV screen every night. And I'm wise enough not to blame the media for anything, but I also understand it's created quite a headwind—the TV screens do."

Bush Among Friends

OCTOBER 26, 2006

If you've ever fantasized about what it would be like to eavesdrop on our president chatting with some of his strongest fans in the media, then your decidedly odd dream has come true. President Bush met with eight leading conservative TV and print pundits on Wednesday afternoon, and a transcript has just been released.

It's a fascinating fly-on-the-wall replay, nearly all on the record—as the president explains, "I'm a skeptical off-the-record" guy. Surprisingly, there's less joking around than at most press conferences, although he does call Larry Kudlow of CNBC "Kuds" and claims he is a "blood and guts" guy. Clearly among friends (Krauthammer, Henninger, Blankley, and the rest), Bush states, "al-Qaeda is lethal as hell," and then instructs, "scratch the 'hell'—it's lethal." Later he urges, "Don't be writing—don't write me down as hopelessly naive and trying to always put lipstick on the pig."

And there were, for me at least, some surprising revelations. Bush says, for example, that Gen. John Abizaid ("one of the really great thinkers") was the one who "came up with" the recent construct about the enemy in Iraq, "If we leave, they will follow us here." Bush then explains that this is what makes the Iraq struggle "really different from other wars we've been in." This completely over-looks the official U.S. line in trying to halt communism in Vietnam and Korea, not to mention the Nazis and the Japanese in World War II.

"I'm not a good faker," Bush declares elsewhere.

Another revealing moment comes when Bush flatly declares that only "25 percent or so" of Americans want the U.S. out of Iraq. In fact, a Gallup poll released this week shows that the number is actually 54 percent who want us out quickly—within a year at most. Bush also mischaracterizes the war opponents, saying they "just don't believe in war," as if they are all pacifists. Then he goes on: "I believe when you get attacked and somebody declares war on you, you fight back. And that's what we're doing." Of course, this ignores the fact that Iraq did not declare war on us—but it's been so long now, maybe he's just forgotten.

A critical moment arrives when Bush announces, "And I'm trying to figure out a matrix that says things are getting better. I think that one way to measure is less violence than before, I guess. We'll have to see what happens here after Ramadan. I believe these people—oh, I was going to tell you Abizaid believes Ramadan, no question, caused them to be more violent because he says there's some kind of reward during Ramadan for violence."

Memo to the president: Ramadan ended three days ago and the number of Americans killed continues to surge, with at least five killed in the past day alone.

But Bush calls the war "a struggle of good versus evil," adding, "Maybe it's not nuanced enough for some of the thinkers and all that stuff—that's fine. But that's exactly what a lot of people like me think."

Sometimes the columnists, just trying to be helpful, offered Bush suggestions on how to sell the war on terror. This happened after the president described the enemy, bizarrely, in the broadest terms: "We will press and press and press to protect ourselves. And this stuff about how Iraq is causing the enemy—whatever excuse they need, they have made up their mind to attack, and they grab on to things to kind of justify. But if it's not Iraq, it's Israel. If it's not Israel, it's the Crusades. If it's not the Crusades, it is the cartoon. I'm not kidding you. I'm not kidding you."

This provokes "laughter," according to the transcript. But Bush presses on. "They are cold-blooded killers."

"If it's not the Crusades, it's the cartoon—that's a good slogan," one of his guests suggests.

Another suggestion comes from "Kuds" Kudlow, who opens his questioning by practically begging the president to let him come away with at least one tiny bit of positive spin about Iraq.

KUDS: I want to go on the air tonight, I want some good news. I need some good news, sir.

BUSH: Yes, I do, too.

KUDS: I really do.

BUSH: You're talking to Noah about the flood. I do, too. . . .

KUDS: You said if we leave Iraq they'll come after us—

BUSH: Yes.

KUDS: We've heard you say that quite specifically. So maybe that's a sign of victory, is that they haven't come here.

With such high-quality advice, it's no wonder Bush closed the meeting, after 63 minutes, by saying, "Okay, guys, I hope you enjoyed it. I enjoyed it. We ought to do this more often."

NOVEMBER

A classified military briefing reported that Iraq was "edging toward chaos." No wonder that fewer than one in five Americans in a poll said that they felt the U.S. was winning in Iraq. Prospects for Republican candidates in the upcoming midterm elections now appeared bleak, as anti-war candidates seemed to be surging nearly everywhere. More than 100 American service members were killed in October. Since the beginning of the war, I had charted not just the official American death toll but the number of accidental deaths, the wounded, the soaring number suffering from post-traumatic shock—and the dozens of suicides. The suicide rate in Iraq remained above the military average, but one case struck me as especially tragic, and revealing.

She Killed Herself—After Objecting to Torture Techniques
NOVEMBER 1, 2006

The media, in reporting on U.S. casualties in Iraq or Afghanistan, too often accept the official version. The Pat Tillman friendly-fire incident has now drawn wide attention, but dozens of other cases undoubtedly remain hidden. With a little more digging, I have discovered that one of the first female soldiers killed in Iraq died by her own hand after objecting to interrogation methods used on prisoners.

She was Army specialist Alyssa Peterson, 27, a Flagstaff, Ariz., native serving with C Company, 311th Military Intelligence BN, 101st Airborne. Peterson was an Arabic-speaking interrogator assigned to the prison at our air base in troubled Tal Afar in northwestern Iraq. According to official records, she died on Sept. 15, 2003, from a "non-hostile weapons discharge."

She was only the third American woman killed in Iraq, so her death drew wide press attention. A "non-hostile weapons discharge" leading to death is not unusual in Iraq, often quite accidental, so this one apparently raised few eyebrows. *The Arizona Republic*, three days after her death, reported that Army officials "said that a number of possible scenarios are being considered, including Peterson's own weapon discharging, the weapon of another soldier discharging, or the accidental shooting of Peterson by an Iraqi civilian."

But in this case, a longtime radio and newspaper reporter named Kevin Elston, not satisfied with the public story, decided to probe deeper in 2005, "just on a hunch," he told *E&P* today. He made "hundreds of phone calls" to the military and couldn't get anywhere, so he filed a Freedom of Information Act [FOIA] request. When the documents of the official investigation of her death arrived, they contained bombshell revelations. Here's what the Flagstaff public radio station, KNAU, where Elston now works, reported (it has not yet drawn any national attention) yesterday:

"Peterson objected to the interrogation techniques used on prisoners. She refused to participate after only two nights working in the unit known as the cage. Army spokespersons for her unit have refused to describe the interrogation techniques Alyssa objected to. They say all records of those techniques have now been destroyed." She was then assigned to the base gate, where she monitored Iraqi guards, and sent to suicide prevention training. "But on the night of September 15th, 2003, Army investigators concluded she shot and killed herself with her service rifle," the documents disclose.

The Army talked to some of Peterson's colleagues. Asked to summarize their comments, Elston told *E&P*: "The reactions to the suicide were that she was having a difficult time separating her personal feelings from her professional duties. That was the consistent point in the testimonies, that she objected to the interrogation techniques, without describing what those techniques were."

Elston said that the documents also refer to a suicide note found on her body, which suggested that she found it ironic that suicide prevention training had taught her how to commit suicide. He has now filed another FOIA request for a copy of the actual note.

Peterson, a devout Mormon, had graduated from Flagstaff High School and earned a psychology degree from Northern Arizona University on a military scholarship. She was trained in interrogation techniques at Fort Huachuca in Arizona, and was sent to the Middle East in 2003.

In the past, I've found that a search of "fallen heroes" message boards often turns up revealing, or chilling, details about deceased soldiers. At one tribute site on the Web, Mary W. Black of Flagstaff wrote, "The very day Alyssa died, her Father was talking to me at the Post Office where we both work, in Flagstaff, Ariz., telling me he had a premonition and was very worried about his daughter who was in the military on the other side of the world. The next day he was notified while on the job by two Army officers. Never has a daughter been so missed or so loved than she was and has been by her father since that fateful September day in 2003. He has been the most broken man I have ever seen."

An A.W. from Los Angeles wrote: "I met Alyssa only once during a weekend surfing trip while she was at DLI. Although our encounter was brief, she made a lasting impression. We did not know each other well, but I was blown away by her genuine, sincere, sweet nature. . . . I was devastated to hear of her death. I couldn't understand why it had to happen to such a wonderful person."

Finally, Daryl K. Tabor of Ashland City, Tenn., who had met her as a journalist in Iraq for the *Kentucky New Era* paper: "Since learning of her death, I cannot get the image of the last time I saw her out of my mind. We were walking out of the tent in Kuwait to be briefed on our flights into Iraq as I stepped aside to let her out first. Her smile was brighter than the hot desert sun. Peterson was the only soldier I interacted with that I know died in Iraq. I am truly sorry I had to know any."

A report today in *The Arizona Daily Sun* of Flagstaff reveals that Spc. Peterson's mother, Bobbi Peterson, reached at her home in northern Arizona, said that neither she nor her husband Richard has received any official documents that contained information outlined in the KNAU report. "Until she and Richard have had an opportunity to read the documents, she said she is unable to comment," the newspaper reported.

In other words: Like the press and the public, even the parents had been kept in the dark.

An Iraqi tribunal sentenced Saddam Hussein to death by hanging for "crimes against humanity." A group of influential publications for the military, including the Army Times, *called for the resignation of a high*

American official—Donald Rumsfeld. Tony Snow called this a "shabby piece of work" and claimed that the president would "shrug it off." After the election debacle, however, Rumsfeld resigned on November 8, as Republicans wondered why Bush couldn't have pushed him out the door sooner, which might have prevented their loss of Congress. My column on Alyssa Peterson had drawn one of the largest batches of e-mail from readers since the start of the war. It occurred to me that another woman, who had gained considerable publicity for her book about Iraq, might have known the deceased soldier.

Kayla and Alyssa: Why One Survived

NOVEMBER 8, 2006

They served in the same battalion in Iraq at the same time. Kayla Williams spoke with Alyssa Peterson about the young woman's troubles a week before she died—and afterward, attended her memorial service. Williams even has her own interrogation horror story to tell. So what, in Williams's view, caused Alyssa Peterson to put a bullet in her head in September 2003 after just a few weeks in Iraq? And why were the press and the public not told about it?

The death of Alyssa Peterson, 27—a former Mormon missionary—is unspeakably sad, and what was fully in her mind will never be known, especially since her parents apparently knew little about her death until four days ago. The press, which has rarely challenged the official version of Iraq fatalities, has not probed the incident, to this day. But this tragedy also begs the question: Which interrogation techniques drew her ire?

And were they of such a nature that this might explain why this young woman of faith and, reportedly, good nature would suddenly turn a gun on herself? The official Army investigation notes that all papers relating to the interrogations have been destroyed. But what do we know about what was going on in Iraq in 2003, beyond credible claims that treatment of prisoners was being "Gitmo-ized"?

Perhaps the most specific testimony that may relate to Alyssa Peterson comes from another Arabic-speaking female U.S. soldier who also served in the 101st Airborne at that time in the same region of Iraq. She even wrote a book partly about it. This is former Army sergeant Kayla Williams, author of the 2005 memoir *Love My Rifle More Than You.* Much of the media publicity about the book focused on her accounts of sexual tension or harassment in Iraq, but it also holds several key passages about interrogations.

In the book, Williams, now 29 and out of the Army, described how she had been recruited to briefly take part in over-the-line interrogations. Like Peterson, she protested torture techniques—such as throwing lit cigarettes at prisoners—and was quickly shifted away. But she told me Friday that she is still haunted by the experience and wonders if she objected strongly enough. She also wonders if she could have done more to help Alyssa Peterson after their brief chat just before she died.

Williams and Peterson were both interpreters—but only the latter was in "human intelligence," that is, trained to take part in interrogations. They met by chance when Williams, who had been on a mission, came back to the base in Tal Afar in September 2003 before heading off again. A civilian interpreter asked her to speak to Peterson, who seemed troubled. Like others, Williams found her to be a "sweet girl." Williams asked if she wanted to go to dinner, but Peterson was not free—maybe next time, but of course time ran out.

Their one conversation, Williams told me, centered on personal, not military, problems, and it's hard to tell where it fit in the suicide timeline. According to records of an Army probe that were obtained by radio reporter Kevin Elston, Peterson had protested, and asked out of, interrogations after just two days in what was known as "the cage"—and killed herself shortly after that. This protest might have all transpired just after her encounter with Williams, or it might have happened before and she did not mention it—they did not really know each other.

Peterson's suicide on Sept. 15—reported to the press and public as death by "non-hostile gunshot," usually meaning an accident—was the only fatality suffered by the battalion during their entire time in Iraq, Williams reports. At the memorial service, everyone knew the cause of her death. They were surprised and "frustrated," she comments, since Peterson had only been in Iraq a few weeks and many of them had been there six months, going back to the U.S. invasion, and had not cracked.

Shortly after that, Williams (a three-year Army vet at the time) was sent to the 2nd Brigade's Support Area in Mosul, and she described what happened next in her book. Brought into "the cage" one day on a special mission, she saw fellow soldiers hitting a naked prisoner in the face. "It's one thing to make fun of someone and attempt to humiliate him. With words. That's one thing. But flicking lit cigarettes at somebody—like burning him—that's illegal," Williams writes. Soldiers later told her that "the old rules no longer applied because this was a different world. This was a new kind of war."

Here's what she told Soledad O'Brien of CNN on Sept. 26 of this year: "I was asked to assist. And what I saw was that individuals who were doing interrogations had slipped over a line and were really doing things that were inappropriate. There were prisoners that were burned with lit cigarettes.

"They stripped prisoners naked and then removed their blindfolds so that I was the first thing they saw. And then we were supposed to mock them and degrade their manhood. And it really didn't seem to make a lot of sense to me. I didn't know if this was standard. But it did not seem to work. And it really made me feel like we were losing that crucial moral higher ground, and we weren't behaving in the way that Americans are supposed to behave." As soon as that day ended, after a couple of these sessions, she told a superior she would never do it again.

In another CNN interview, on Oct. 8, 2005, she explained: "I sat through it at the time. But after it was over I did approach the non-commissioned officer in charge and told him I think you may be violating the Geneva Conventions. . . . He said he knew and I said I wouldn't participate again and he respected that, but I was really, really stunned. . . ."

So, given all this, what does Williams think pushed Alyssa Peterson to shoot herself one week after their only meeting? The great unknown, of course, is what Peterson was asked to witness or do in interrogations. We do know that she refused to have anything more to do with that after two days—or one day longer than it took for Williams to reach her breaking point.

Properly, Williams points out that it's rarely one factor that leads to suicide, and Peterson had some personal problems, to be sure. "It's always a bunch of things coming together to the point you feel so overwhelmed that there's no way out," Williams says. "I witnessed abuse, I felt uncomfortable with it, but I didn't kill myself, because I could see the bigger context.

"I felt a lot of angst about whether I had an obligation to report it, and had any way to report it. Was it classified? Who should I turn to?" Perhaps Alyssa Peterson felt in the same box. "It also made me think," Williams says, "what are we as humans, that we do this to each other? It made me question my humanity and the humanity of all Americans. It was difficult, and to this day I can no longer think

I am a really good person and will do the right thing in the right situation." Such an experience might have been truly shattering to the deeply religious Peterson.

Referring to that day in Mosul, Williams says, "I did protest but only to the person in charge and I did not file a report up the chain of command." Yet, after recounting her experience there, she asks: "Can that lead to suicide? That's such an act of desperation, helplessness, it has to be more than that." She concludes, "In general, interrogation is not fun, even if you follow the rules. And I didn't see any good intelligence being gained. The other problem is that, in situations like that, you have people that are not terrorists being picked up and being questioned. And, if you treat an innocent person like that, they walk out a terrorist."

Or, maybe in this case, if an innocent person witnesses such a thing, some may walk out as a likely suicide.

In the wake of the election results, pundits from left and right predicted that the president would use the upcoming report by his Iraq Study Group as a nonpartisan safety raft to change course and perhaps order the start of a withdrawal. But some insiders suggested that, on the contrary, Bush seemed likely to call for sending more troops to Iraq, no matter what his Iraq Study Group suggested. Thomas Ricks of The Washington Post *reported the options, memorably, as "Go Big, Go Long, or Get Out." His colleague at the* Post, *Richard Cohen, joined the formerly hawkish who now admitted they had been very wrong on the war. He had once declared that the U.S. had "no choice" but to invade Iraq, partly for "therapeutic" reasons—but now declared that soldiers had a right to feel "duped" because of the "exaggerations" that led to war. But these words would no longer offer any solace to Linda Michel and her husband.*

She Outlived Iraq—Then Killed Herself at Home

November 23, 2006

Her name doesn't show up on any official or media list of American military deaths in the Iraq war, by hostile or non-hostile fire, who died in that country or in hospitals in Europe or back home in the USA. But Iraq killed her just as certainly. She is Jeanne "Linda" Michel, a Navy medic. She came home last month to her husband and three kids, delighted to be back in her suburban home of Clifton Park in upstate New York. Michel, 33, would be discharged from the Navy in a few weeks, finishing her five years of duty. Two weeks after she got home, she shot and killed herself.

"She had come through a lot and she had always risen to challenges," her husband, Frantz Michel, who has also served in Iraq, lamented last week. Now he asks why the Navy didn't do more to help her.

All deaths are tragic, especially when young lives are lost in an unnecessary war after all hope for a meaningful victory has passed. Those of us of a certain age—boomers-verging-on-geezers—may recall the early 1970s when stories of suicides and crippling mental trauma associated with Vietnam veterans belatedly emerged in the press. No doubt some of that was triggered by the growing realization that countless soldiers had died, and were still dying, in vain—wasted, in every sense of the word.

We are witnessing the same phenomenon today in regard to Iraq, with newspapers only now, at last, starting to look behind the routine (and seemingly endless) reporting of American fatalities—and finding that many are not what they seem to be.

A fine story about Michel appeared in the Albany, N.Y., *Times Union*, written by Kate Gurnett. It came after the paper had carried her death notice without any mention of the suicide (she simply "died suddenly"), which may be customary, but highly misleading. So how did Gurnett get that follow-up story? She tells me that the paper had received several calls from neighbors who were troubled by what had happened to Michel. Gurnett, as luck would have it, had just returned from a state Mental Health Association meeting where there was much talk of Iraq returnees suffering mental illness, along with reports of three recent vet suicides in an area just north of Albany.

Gurnett talked to friends of the dead medic and visited tribute message boards, where those who served with her had expressed utter surprise. Only then did she sit down with the woman's husband. It turned out that Linda had worked at a strife-torn prison in Iraq where riots had taken place and prisoners had been killed. Suffering from depression, she was given the anti-depressant Paxil—which was cut off when she returned home, a step known to often have disastrous consequences.

Frantz Michel blamed the Navy for not giving his wife the help she needed to cope, and asked the haunting question: Should someone who needed Paxil be anywhere near a combat zone to start with? Of her suicide, he said, "She would never leave her children," revealing her shattered emotional state in deciding to do just that.

"I wanted to tell her story," Gurnett now recalls. "I thought she deserved at least that. I really did not want her to be forgotten, to just go away and quietly die in the corner of her house all alone, no one knowing what happened to her. It was compelling on so many levels." It also made the reporter realize, with regard to the death toll in Iraq, that "there is a lot there that we're not seeing." This is a concern I have been raising for more than three years. For example, Gurnett asks, "how many of those accidental weapons discharges are actually suicide?"

Here at home, and rarely mentioned in the press, tens of thousands of Iraq and Afghanistan vets are being treated for post-traumatic stress disorder. Vets in "overwhelming" numbers "come home and get reams of information" on how to cope with mental distress, but "they can't make sense of this documentation," Gurnett reports. Since her story ran, she has received a lot of mail from readers who had "a really bad time with withdrawal from Paxil." She also heard from Michel's supervisor in Iraq, who said her death "left him feeling so lost—how could this have happened?"

The military, meanwhile, knows it's got a problem, she observes: "They help you navigate around the bureaucrats who want to cover stuff up. Like at a corrupt police force, it's denial, distortion, and disinformation." She also points to the media's reluctance to show images of fallen soldiers in the field. "That says it right there," she says. "It's total denial." Newspapers, she adds, are not doing enough overall to probe the untold number of lives fractured by Iraq: "If we're going to be the fourth estate, we need to investigate and devote staff to this. I think newspapers are making enough money—they should not be cutting staff and instead should be doing more investigating.

"It's why we're here."

DECEMBER

Debate broke out across the media over whether to refer to the conflict in Iraq, with sectarian violence still raging, as a "civil war." NBC News adopted the "civil war" usage, but The Washington Post *and many others, as usual, lagged behind public opinion, as polls showed that two in three Americans did believe it was a civil war. Maureen Dowd in* The New York Times *observed that editors at her paper, along with other news outlets, "have been figuring out if it's time to break with the administration's use of euphemisms like 'sectarian conflict.' How long can you have an ever-descending descent without actually reaching the civil war? Some analysts are calling it genocide or clash of civilizations, arguing that civil war is too genteel a term for the butchery that is destroying a nation before our very eyes."*

Nicholas Kristof, also in a Times *column, hailed reporters on the ground in Baghdad, often criticized for being "negative"—actually, they have been proven right on the war. And Thomas Friedman at last junked postponing a judgment for another Friedman Unit (six months): Now he declared we should immediately set a fixed date for a pullout, even if it's down the road a bit. The Iraq Study Group's "Baker-Hamilton" report then emerged, urging a change in direction in Iraq; but, as many feared, the White House offered only a mild embrace—while emphasizing that the president has ordered his own report, due in a few weeks, before he took the next step, now likely to be some kind of "surge" in troops.*

The Last Soldier to Die for a Mistake
DECEMBER 10, 2006

In the wake of the November elections, the release of the Baker-Hamilton report, and the latest surge in American fatalities in Iraq, a familiar phrase has resurfaced in the press. It's an updating of John Kerry's famous question in 1971, as a Vietnam veterans' leader, "How do you ask someone to be the last

American soldier to die for a mistake?" Indeed, today's *Washington Post* features an article by Christian Davenport and Joshua Partlow about the emerging split among military families over that very question. It's a profound change. Until now, the general sentiment in those quarters has been: Stay in Iraq and accomplish something so my loved one did not die or get badly wounded "in vain."

All of this has caused me to wonder: Well, who *was* the last soldier to die for the Vietnam mistake?

To my surprise, with a little research, I discovered that there is a consensus on who that individual was. We'll get to his name in a moment, but what's most relevant is that he died almost five years after that "mistake" was widely acknowledged. How many will die from now until the last American perishes in Iraq? Gallup and other polls show that a clear majority of Americans have already labeled the Iraq invasion a "mistake."

We are at a haunting juncture in the Iraq war. Forgive me for another "back in the day" reference, but I recall very well that the public only turned strongly against the Vietnam conflict with the mass realization that young American lives were not only being lost but truly wasted. Contrary to myth, this did not happen promptly after Walter Cronkite's war-doubting monologue on CBS in 1968.

Now, a woman named Beverly Fabri says in today's *Washington Post*, almost three years after her 19-year-old son, Army Pvt. Bryan Nicholas Spry, was killed, "I'm beginning to feel like he just died in vain, I really am." That's because she believes, "We are not going to win this war. And we shouldn't have gotten involved with it in the first place."

Another echo of Vietnam: press reports of military officers in Iraq saying, off the record, that they are cutting down, or eliminating, certain patrols because they no longer think the effort is worth the death of any of their men. What's next in this Vietnam flashback? Fragging of officers who do send their men foolishly into harm's way?

Now, who was that last American to die in Vietnam?

According to Arlington National Cemetery, and numerous other sources, he was Army Lt. Col. William B. Nolde, a 43-year-old father of five. He was killed Jan. 27, 1973, near An Loc—just 11 hours before the U.S. signed the Paris Peace Accords—when an artillery shell exploded nearby.

This is how *Time* magazine reported it the following week: "The last hours of the Viet Nam War took a cruel human toll. Communist and South

Vietnamese casualties ran into the thousands. Four U.S. airmen joined the missing-in-action list when their two aircraft were downed on the last day. Another four Americans were known to have been killed—including Lt. Colonel William B. Nolde, 43, of Mt. Pleasant, Mich., who was cut down in an artillery barrage at An Loc only eleven hours before the ceasefire. He was the 45,941st American to have died by enemy action in Viet Nam since 1961."

His Wikipedia entry opens: "Born in Menominee, Michigan, Nolde was a professor of military science at Central Michigan University before joining the army. As an officer, he served in both the Korean War and the Vietnam War, acting as an advisor to the South Vietnamese forces in the latter. . . .

"While other Americans lost their lives after the truce was enacted, these were not recorded as combat casualties. During his time in the armed forces, he had accumulated four medals, including the Bronze Star and Legion of Merit."

His full military funeral was so momentous—it included the same riderless horse that accompanied President Kennedy's coffin—it was covered on the front page of *The New York Times* on Feb. 6, 1973. That story began, "The Army buried one of its own today, Bill Nolde. And with him, it laid to rest—symbolically, at least—its years of torment in Vietnam."

How many more years of torment and wasted lives remain in Iraq?

———

On December 19, The Washington Post *revealed that the White House was, indeed, likely to announce a "surge" of up to 30,000 troops for Iraq, "over the unanimous disagreement of the Joint Chiefs of Staff." The same day, Joe Galloway concluded: "Double down, Mr. President? Or get smart?" Army Gen. John Abizaid, commander of troops in the Middle East, announced his retirement the following day. At least we wouldn't have Saddam Hussein to kick around anymore. But was that a plus, or a minus?*

Media Leave Audience Hanging

DECEMBER 31, 2006

With the videotaped execution of Saddam Hussein last night, newspaper, online, and TV editors in the U.S. debated what, if anything, to show of the act. As promised, video and photos of the event were aired on Iraq TV a few hours after the 10 P.M. ET execution. When the time came, a photo from the video was quickly posted on cable news outlets in the U.S. and at the top of the Web sites of *The New York Times, Los Angeles Times*, and *The Washington Post*, showing Saddam with the noose being fitted around his neck.

They chose not to run another photo that shows Hussein after the execution. *USA Today's* site, however, carried three pictures in a gallery, with a second photo of the noose-fitting scene—and a shot of Saddam on the floor after the act, with blood near his mouth.

The New York Times later put up a 70-second video of Saddam getting the noose fitted around his neck, stopping short of the actual hanging. (The video screen was adjacent to an ad for the current movie about crazed strongman Idi Amin, *The Last King of Scotland*.) *The Washington Post* also put up the same video, somewhat less prominently.

Fox News may have been first to air footage on American TV, also stopping the images just before the hanging. CNN International also apparently aired it at the same time. CNN, among others, put up over a minute of footage on its Web site, leading to the actual hanging, showing an oddly calm and dignified Hussein ready to meet his fate. It was preceded by a warning of "graphic" images to come.

Early this morning, The Associated Press also showed a close-up of Saddam on the floor after the hanging, with a little blood near his mouth, and it was quickly posted at Yahoo News and the Drudge Report. The caption read: "This video image released by the Biladi TV stations, which are affiliated with the Dawa party of Prime Minister Nouri al-Maliki, appears to show the body of former Iraqi leader Saddam Hussein wrapped in a white shroud following his execution."

Bob Murphy, the senior vice president of ABC News, said that ABC News would not allow its Web site to show anything more than what is permitted on television. "The decision will be for all of ABC News," Murphy told the *Times*. "What is excluded for ABC News on television will be excluded for all ABC News outlets." The *Times* report concluded: "And a representative from YouTube did not respond to questions about the policy of that popular video site, which has previously offered videos with graphic battle footage from Iraq." Amazingly, YouTube in short order has become a major player in the news business.

In a statement delivered with no apparent irony, Iraqi Prime Minister Nouri al-Maliki said, "Our respect for human rights requires us to execute him."

Earlier Friday, in an editorial, *The New York Times* observed, "This week began with a story of British and Iraqi soldiers storming a police station that hid a secret dungeon in Basra. More than 100 men, many of them viciously tortured, were rescued from almost certain execution. . . . Toppling Saddam Hussein did not automatically create a new and better Iraq. Executing him won't either."

By chance, today brought another milestone that cannot be disputed: The reported 3,000th American military fatality in Iraq. It comes at the end of the bloodiest month for American forces since the first siege of Fallujah in November 2004.

Update: One day after becoming the only major U.S. paper to carry a graphic photo of Saddam Hussein after his execution on its front page—and above the fold, at that—*The New York Times* took up the question of TV networks debating whether to run a cellphone video of the dictator in his moment of death. Bill Carter wrote on Monday, "No national American television organization has thus far allowed the moment of the drop to be shown. But the same niceties were not observed on numerous Web sites, which have posted the complete video, including the moment that Mr. Hussein, noose around his neck, falls, and a close-up of his face afterward." The article noted that the networks carried the footage—but cutting off before his death was shown, some explaining that they did so because the accompanying audio was newsworthy. Carter did not mention his paper's decision to run the photo above the fold on its front page the previous day.

2007

JANUARY

Since mid-November, I had been warning that Bush was bent on sending more troops to Iraq, but pundits and editorialists didn't seem very alarmed about the prospect, even though it promised to be one of the true (not fake) "turning points" in the war—perhaps Number One at that. In any case, the media largely bought into the proponents' "surge" slogan rather than the more appropriate "escalation," which some Democrats promoted. What is the time limit, I asked in early January, for a "surge" to recede before it seems semi-permanent? A few months, as the White House has suggested? Or a year or more, as some of its outside backers demand, saying that anything less would be futile? How many troops would indicate a mere "surge" versus a "large buildup"? Would 30,000 or less qualify for surge, but 40,000 or more represent a "large buildup"? A new round of polls came out, showing that public support for adding troops was practically nil, but this didn't seem to stiffen the spines of the Democrats—or the pundits. If the war didn't "belong" to the opinion shapers before, it certainly did now.

Surge Protectors

JANUARY 6, 2007

As a critical turning point in the nearly four-year-old Iraq war nears, the editorial pages of the largest U.S. newspapers have been surprisingly—even appallingly—silent on President Bush's likely decision to send thousands of more troops to the country. It follows a long pattern, however, of editorialists and TV talking heads strongly criticizing the conduct of the war—without advocating a major change in direction. Now it comes at what appears to be a crucial point, with Democrats in Congress, overcoming their own timidity on the issue, finally emerging Friday with opposition to the buildup, setting up a possible battle royal in the days ahead.

Newspapers, at least in their editorials, have chosen to retreat to the sidelines. This comes even as hawkish conservatives such as Oliver North and David Brooks, and dozens of other op-ed contributors, have come out against the idea, and polls show that 11 percent or less of the public back the idea. Even General Casey has opposed the escalation. Then there are the new revelations that the troops we already have in Iraq are not properly equipped or protected. That would seem to set the stage for editorials taking a strong stand, for or against.

But very few—hardly any—editorial pages have said much of anything about the well-publicized "surge" idea, pro or con. I mean: Say *something*. Didn't they see this coming? It's like sleepwalking into the abyss. Even if they finally declare themselves in the next day or two, it will come much too late, since the president seems to have made up his mind and just shook up his cast of commanders to assemble a more sympathetic crew.

The editorial page of *The New York Times* has said nothing this week, beyond noting the "bleak realities" in Iraq. Other papers often critical of the war, the *Los Angeles Times*, *The Boston Globe*, and *USA Today*—among others— have also been silent. Oddly, all of them hailed the recent Iraq Study Group report, which opposed an escalation.

The Washington Post, hawkish in the past, has not even roused itself to say anything. Perhaps it is hopelessly torn. Even its conservative columnist, Charles Krauthammer, criticized how the Iraqis executed Saddam on Friday, concluding: "We should not be surging American troops in defense of such a government." But the paper, we've learned, will run a major op-ed on Sunday by Sen. John McCain, titled "The Case for More Troops." Also expected Sunday, a column by George Will called "Surge, or Power Failure?" It comes out mildly against the idea, adding that a *massive* escalation might work.

The *Chicago Sun-Times* said nothing. Ditto for nearly everyone else. A *Miami Herald* editorial on Saddam's hanging closed with, "Now it is up to Iraqis and their international supporters, especially the United States, to find a way out of the despair and darkness that have been Iraq's unfortunate fate for far too many years"—but it did not say a word about the "surge."

This failure of will comes even after liberal bloggers led the way, as a call went forth last week: Henceforth ye shall purge the "surge" from your vocabularies and laptops and replace it with "escalation"—with all its echoes of Vietnam and, incidentally, accuracy regarding the current situation.

An editorial in Baltimore's *Sun* on Wednesday should have served as a template for others in the media. Here is its key passage: "A generation ago this would have been called an 'escalation,' and the problem with escalations, as President Lyndon B. Johnson learned, is that when they don't furnish the promised results the pressure to follow with further escalations is just about inescapable."

Two months ago, President Bush termed the sudden rise in U.S. fatalities in Iraq in October only a temporary blip. That month's 2006 record will soon be shattered this month. That's one "surge" that has already turned into an "escalation." Alas, by the time the cowardly or shortsighted speak out, this particular horse will be out of the barn.

Update: Two days later, I noted that *The Washington Post* finally did carry an editorial—which praised Sen. McCain and Sen. Lieberman for "courageously" pressing the "surge." *The New York Times* again failed to discuss the surge, even though it ran a lengthy editorial attack on Bush called "The Imperial Presidency 2.0." The closest it came to taking up the matter in the editorial was one snippet, where it accused the president of interpreting "his party's drubbing as a mandate to keep pursuing his fantasy of victory in Iraq." Subsequently, with Bush about to announce his plan, it expressed skepticism but said he deserved "one last opportunity" to get it right. One had to wonder: Why?

MARCH

Bush announced his surge/escalation on January 10. Now The New York Times *and many other papers, noting the lack of firm timetables and benchmarks, came out against the idea, a wee bit late. Polls showed that about 7 in 10 Americans opposed the surge. Sen. Chuck Hagel (R-Neb.), not previously known for being ahead of the so-called "liberal" media, called it the "most dangerous foreign policy blunder in the country since Vietnam." Civilian deaths in Iraq would hit a new monthly high in January, as an official tally indicated that 34,000 perished in 2006. Gen. David Petraeus took charge of U.S. forces. On February 18, The* Washington Post *began publishing its shattering probe of conditions for outpatients at Walter Reed Army Hospital. In early March, "Scooter" Libby would be convicted by a federal jury of several felony counts including perjury and obstruction of justice in the CIA leak case. Nevertheless, many pundits called it an injustice and continued to paint Valerie Plame, her husband, and/or anti-war bloggers as the real villains.*

A *Washington Post* Editorial as a *Daily Show* Routine
MARCH 11, 2007

By now, nearly four years into the Iraq war and related controversies, one is tempted to simply disregard *The Washington Post* editorial page, and some of its regular columnists, on those matters: They have been so wrong on nearly everything for so long. The paper's news pages regularly contradict and embarrass some of the opinion writers with those stubborn things called "facts," so you might wisely spend all of your time there.

But rather than have all that copy and hard work on the opinion page go to waste, I suggest that you try to imagine any Iraq-related editorial in the *Post* as a typical exchange between Jon Stewart and an out-to-lunch "correspondent" on *The Daily Show.*

Take the *Post*'s editorial last week calling the Libby case a "pointless Washington scandal." It lamented that the case was brought in the first place. Putting that editorial into a *Daily Show* routine, it might go something like this. Nearly all of the statements by correspondent Jason Jones come directly from that *Post* editorial.

JON STEWART: To discuss the Libby verdict, we have with us tonight Senior CIA Leak Correspondent Jason Jones (applause). Jason, so they finally nailed this guy, right?

JASON JONES (STANDING IN FRONT OF THE WHITE HOUSE, SPEAKING GRAVELY): The conviction of I. Lewis Libby on charges of perjury, making false statements, and obstruction of justice was grounded in strong evidence and what appeared to be careful deliberation by a jury. His lies were reprehensible.

STEWART: So a job well done, right?

JONES: Wrong, Jon. The fall of this skilled and long-respected public servant is particularly sobering because it arose from a Washington scandal remarkable for its lack of substance. It was propelled not by actual wrongdoing, but by inflated and frequently false claims.

STEWART: False claims?

JONES: Yes, Jon. Joseph Wilson, the outed CIA agent's husband, was embraced by many because he was early in publicly charging that the Bush administration had "twisted," if not invented, facts in making the case for war against Iraq.

STEWART: But wait a minute, Jason. Wasn't Wilson right about that—when, for example, many leading newspaper editorial pages, most prominently *The Washington Post*'s, were so wrong on that?

JONES: Right you are, Jon, but listen to this. Wilson also advanced yet another sensational charge: that his wife was a covert CIA operative and that senior White House officials had orchestrated the leak of her name to destroy her career and thus punish Mr. Wilson!

STEWART: But doesn't the evidence from the trial indicate that they indeed wanted to punish Wilson—and acted so recklessly that Plame's career did come to an end?

JONES (LOOKING PEEVED): But, Jon, the partisan furor over this allegation led to the appointment of special prosecutor Patrick J. Fitzgerald. The trial has provided convincing evidence that there was no conspiracy to punish Mr. Wilson by leaking Ms. Plame's identity—and no evidence that she was, in fact, covert.

STEWART: What? Jason, the trial showed that Libby and his boss, Vice President Cheney, conspired for many days in getting back at Wilson, and they even brought Ari Fleischer into it—and Fitzgerald, the CIA, and others have said there is no question that Plame was still in a classified position when she was outed.

JONES: True, Jon, but instead, like many Washington special prosecutors before him, Fitzgerald pressed on, pursuing every tangent in the case. Mr. Fitzgerald has shown again why handing a Washington political case to a federal special prosecutor is a prescription for excess. And Wilson? Ha, the former ambassador will be remembered as a blowhard.

STEWART: Jason, you are really making no sense now. What kind of a lesson will it be for future officials if you put most of the blame on the prosecutor and the victim's spouse? But at least the trial revealed a great deal about the cooked-up reasons we went to war and how desperate the administration was to cover that up.

JONES: Not really, Jon. Mr. Fitzgerald was, at least, right about one thing: The Wilson-Plame case, and Mr. Libby's conviction, tell us nothing about the war in Iraq.

STEWART: So—forget about a pardon, and go straight to the Medal of Freedom for Scooter Libby?

JONES: That's right, Jon.

STEWART: Jason Jones, ladies and gentleman (applause). We'll be back after this.

Early on, I'd written about Col. Ted Westhusing committing suicide in Iraq early in the occupation. To the disappointment of some readers, I rejected the theory that he had been killed for knowing too much about contractor ripoffs and abuse of Iraqi prisoners. Now a new article appeared, based on fresh documents on the case with General Petraeus becoming an increasingly significant figure in the history of the war.

General Petraeus and a High-Profile Suicide

MARCH 13, 2007

The scourge of suicides among American troops in Iraq is a serious, and seriously underreported, problem, as this column has observed numerous times in the past three years. One of the few high-profile cases involved a much-admired Army colonel named Ted Westhusing. A portrait of Westhusing written by T. Christian Miller for the *Los Angeles Times* in November 2005 (which I covered at the time) revealed that Westhusing, before putting a bullet through his head, had been deeply disturbed by abuses carried out by American contractors in Iraq, including allegations that they had witnessed or even participated in the murder of Iraqis.

His widow, asked by a friend what killed this West Point scholar, had replied simply: "Iraq."

Now a new article reveals—based on documents obtained under the Freedom of Information Act—that Westhusing's apparent suicide note included claims that his two commanders tolerated a mission based on "corruption, human right abuses and liars." One of those commanders: the new leader of the "surge" campaign in Iraq, Gen. David Petraeus.

Westhusing, 44, had been found dead in a trailer at a military base near the Baghdad airport in June 2005, a single gunshot wound to the head. At the time, he was the highest-ranking officer to die in Iraq. The Army concluded that he committed suicide with his service pistol. Westhusing was an unusual case: "one of the Army's leading scholars of military ethics, a full professor at West Point who volunteered to serve in Iraq to be able to better teach his students. He had a doctorate in philosophy; his dissertation was an extended meditation on the meaning of honor," Miller explained in his *L.A. Times* piece.

"So it was only natural that Westhusing acted when he learned of possible corruption by U.S. contractors in Iraq. A few weeks before he died, Westhusing received an anonymous complaint that a private security company he oversaw had cheated the U.S. government and committed human rights violations. Westhusing confronted the contractor and reported the concerns to superiors, who launched an investigation.

"In e-mails to his family, Westhusing seemed especially upset by one conclusion he had reached: that traditional military values such as duty, honor, and country had been replaced by profit motives in Iraq, where the U.S. had come to rely heavily on contractors for jobs once done by the military." His death followed quickly. "He was sick of money-grubbing contractors," one official recounted. Westhusing said that "he had not come over to Iraq for this." After a three-month inquiry, investigators declared Westhusing's death a suicide.

Now, nearly 18 months after Miller's article, *The Texas Observer* this month has published a cover story by contributor Robert Bryce titled "I Am Sullied No More." Bryce covers much of the same ground paved by Miller but adds details on the Petraeus angle.

"When he was in Iraq, Westhusing worked for one of the most famous generals in the U.S. military, David Petraeus," Bryce observes. "As the head of counterterrorism and special operations under Petraeus, Westhusing oversaw the single most important task facing the U.S. military in Iraq then and now: training the Iraqi security forces."

Bryce refers to a "two-inch stack of documents," obtained over the past 15 months under the Freedom of Information Act, that provides many details of Westhusing's suicide. The pile includes interviews with Westhusing's co-workers, diagrams of his sleeping quarters, interviews with his family members, and partially redacted reports from the Army's Criminal Investigation Command and Inspector General. I have now examined much of this, Bryce having posted hundreds of pages on the Web.

"The documents," Bryce writes, "echo the story told by Westhusing's friends. 'Something he saw [in Iraq] drove him to this,' one Army officer who was close to Westhusing said in an interview. 'The sum of what he saw going on drove him' to take his own life. 'It's because he believed in duty, honor, country that he's dead.'"

In Iraq, Westhusing worked under two generals: Maj. Gen. Joseph Fil, and Petraeus, then a lieutenant general. In a March 2005 e-mail, Petraeus told Westhusing that he had "already exceeded the very lofty expectations that all had for you."

But Bryce continues: "By late May, Westhusing was becoming despondent over what he was seeing. Steeped in—and totally believing in—the West Point credo that a cadet will 'not lie, cheat, or steal, nor tolerate those who do,' Westhusing found himself surrounded by contractors who had no interest in his ideals. He asked family members to pray for him. In a phone call with his wife, Michelle, who was back at West Point, Westhusing told her he planned to tell Petraeus that he was going to quit. She pleaded with him to just finish his tour and return home."

When his body was found on June 5, a note was found nearby addressed to Petraeus and Fil. According to Bryce, it read:

"Thanks for telling me it was a good day until I briefed you. [Redacted name]—You are only interested in your career and provide no support to your staff—no msn [mission] support and you don't care. I cannot support a msn that leads to corruption, human right abuses and liars. I am sullied—no more. I didn't volunteer to support corrupt, money grubbing contractors, nor work for commanders only interested in themselves. I came to serve honorably and feel dishonored. I trust no Iraqi. I cannot live this way. All my love to my family, my wife and my precious children. I love you and trust you only. Death before being dishonored any more.

"Trust is essential—I don't know who trust anymore [*sic*]. Why serve when you cannot accomplish the mission, when you no longer believe in the cause, when your every effort and breath to succeed meets with lies, lack of support, and selfishness? No more. Reevaluate yourselves, cdrs [commanders]. You are not what you think you are and I know it."

Twelve days after Westhusing's body was found, Army investigators talked with his widow, who told them: "The one thing I really wish is you guys to go to everyone listed in that letter and speak with them. I think Ted gave his life to let everyone know what was going on. They need to get to the bottom of it, and hope all these bad things get cleaned up."

Bryce concludes: "In September 2005, the Army's inspector general concluded an investigation into allegations raised in the anonymous letter to Westhusing shortly before his death. It found no basis for any of the issues raised. Although the report is redacted in places, it is clear that the investigation was aimed at determining whether Fil or Petraeus had ignored the corruption and human rights abuses allegedly occurring within the training program for Iraqi security personnel.

"The report, approved by the Army's vice chief of staff, four-star Gen. Richard Cody, concluded that 'commands and commanders operated in an Iraqi cultural and ethical environment often at odds with Western practices.' It said none of the unit members 'accepted institutional corruption or human rights abuses. Unit members, and specifically [redacted name] and [redacted name] took appropriate action where corruption or abuse was reported.'

"The context, placement and relative size of the redacted names strongly suggest that they refer to Petraeus and Fil.

"Last November, Fil returned to Iraq. He is now the commanding general of the Multinational Division in Baghdad and of the 1st Cavalry Division. On February 12, Petraeus took command of all U.S. forces in Iraq. He now wears four stars."

After years of remaining extremely tight-lipped (though she did pose for that unfortunate Vanity Fair *photo), Valerie Plame finally had a chance to tell her story before Congress. Apart from anything we might learn about the actual leak case, I was most interested in whether she would fully rebut and, perhaps, even silence the pundits and editorial writers who had long claimed she was not a "covert" agent, some going so far as claiming she was little more than a secretary at the Agency—or that everyone in her neighborhood knew exactly what she did for a living, so what was the big fuss?*

Press Covers Plame's Wardrobe—Ignores Cover-up

MARCH 16, 2007

In their rush to cover the long-awaited testimony of Valerie Plame, few reporters apparently bothered to stick around the Capitol Hill hearing room yesterday to witness the equally shocking testimony of a much less heralded (and not so attractive) insider named James Knodell. This left *E&P*, covering the hearing via the Web, to provide the only in-depth "mainstream" coverage of Knodell's testimony.

But now there's a chance for others to join in, as Rep. Henry A. Waxman, who called the hearings, has sent a letter to the White House demanding answers for why, despite President Bush's vows, no one there seems to have conducted any sort of in-house investigation into the outing of a valued covert CIA operative four years ago.

Knodell, director of the Office of Security at the White House—whose appearance was opposed by the Bush team until Waxman threatened a subpoena—revealed that his records showed absolutely no interest or questioning about the leak after the outing occurred in July 2003, and none since (he became chief in August 2004).

Barely a word about this appeared in the media yesterday. *The Washington Post*, however, found space for a full review of Plame's fashion sense and a Dana Milbank column in the form of a movie script, tweaking the sale of her story to the movies. We did learn from Mary Ann Akers's fashion piece, titled "Hearing Room Chic," that Plame wore Armani ("a fetching jacket and pants"). Also: Katie Holmes should be a front-runner to play her in the movie because she, too, favors Armani.

Yet Amy Goldstein's front page story on the Plame hearing today doesn't even mention Knodell. Neither did *The New York Times* article, although it found space to quote Republican critics several times and declare that Plame's appearance "seemed less a platform for legislation than for Democrats, who now control the committee, to criticize the Bush administration." It ended with a nice line about the former spy slipping out the door. Apparently the reporters did the same.

The Boston Globe at least gave Knodell one paragraph. The AP did not, and headlined its story "Plame Sheds Little Light on Leak Case."

You would think that, on the contrary, the revelations surrounding Plame's testimony would have promoted much more interest on the evidence of the cover-up that emerged just a few minutes later in the same room. In fact, Knodell's words should have provided a sickening feeling in the guts of most reporters—especially when he admitted that the only way he knew anyone was concerned about the leak was not from the White House but from the press.

For years, conservatives have charged that Plame was not "covert" and not a valuable member of the intelligence community, and therefore pooh-poohed the 2003 outing. Yesterday, not only did Plame state, under oath, that she was indeed covert—not to mention "undercover" and "classified"—but her boss, Gen. Hayden, confirmed this in no uncertain terms.

Then she testified about the extreme damage done to her colleagues and their missions due to her exposure. The few Republicans who bothered to show up for the hearing—knowing they no longer had any case—were reduced to claiming absurdly that it was all the CIA's fault for not circulating a list of covert agents so the poor fellows in the White House would only out those with unclassified jobs.

Yet the media found of no consequence that the president and his press spokesman both had lied repeatedly in claiming that an in-house probe was conducted.

One commentator on Fox News, in responding to all of this, definitively answered the long-simmering question, *Does Brit Hume have no shame?* Hume, who has frequently claimed that Plame was hardly "covert," not only refused to admit he was wrong, he (of all people) attacked her "credibility." He suggested that Plame had lied in denying that she had sent her husband on his Niger mission.

The fact that she had undermined that stubborn rightwing charge in her testimony—under oath—did not make any impression on the slack-jawed Hume. Nor did he appear outraged about the harm inflicted on American interests that Plame had outlined.

APRIL

In what would become one of the most famous quotes of the war, Sen. John McCain on March 27 declared that in Baghdad, "General Petraeus goes out there almost every day in an unarmed Humvee." Two days later, the U.S. Senate passed a war spending bill that would require U.S. troops to leave Iraq by April 2008, but the president vowed to veto it. On April 1, McCain strolled through Baghdad to show its everyday safety—accompanied by 100 soldiers, three helicopters, and two Apache gunships.

A Woman's Dentures in the Dirt

April 1, 2007

Two days ago, *The New York Times* published a plain color photograph of a set of dentures, the eleven white teeth set off by the pink plastic. You don't expect to see a row of false teeth in the International section of the *Times*—or anywhere else in the paper—but there they were, right at the top of page A10. This part seemed especially odd: They were resting on the ground next to some pebbles. What's this all about?

Returning to the front page, anyone who overlooked the accompanying story at first—its headline was rather too typical, "Iraqi Widow Saves Her Home, but Victory is Brief"—might discover that the dentures were just about all that was left behind when the widow in question was carted off to the morgue last Wednesday in Baghdad, after she "was shot dead while walking by a bakery in the local market."

Also left at the scene: a bullet casing and a pool of her blood. The false teeth, it turns out, were uppers.

And so began one of the most haunting and important stories, with pictures, of the entire war: an up-close look at what can only be called ethnic cleansing. The reporter was Edward Wong, a veteran *Times* reporter, and the photographer Ashley Gilbertson, who won the Robert Capa Gold Medal prize for pictures from Iraq. But my question today is: Where are the fallen dentures in the online version of the story? The Web article is accompanied by a slide show, which includes all of the remarkable pictures that ran with the Friday piece, plus two others, but absent one: the dentures shot.

It has been replaced by a dull picture of the bullet casing. Why? Given the incredible work by Wong and Gilbertson, and the decision of the *Times* to run it on Page 1 with three photos even before the jump, I don't want this to sound like nitpicking, but: It was the shot of the dentures that was the most disturbing of all the images; in fact, it was one of the most gut-wrenching of the past four years.

Newspapers have been criticized for running precious few photographs that reveal the true carnage of the war—and let's not forget the ban on returning coffins. But here was a picture that literally got inside the war. Few things are more personal than this piece of dental work—now all that was left of Suaada Saadoun. It was all the more haunting in print because at the top of the front page of the *Times* we could see her talking to a group of Kurdish and American soldiers, dentures presumably in place, less than a day before she was blown away in this revenge killing.

In fact, the entire *Times* package might represent the first time a reporter/photographer team chronicled one death with so much prescience (or luck, if you will): They were there to hear and picture her complaints to the authorities, then witness the men who came to evict her from her house, and, on the following day, observe the grieving relatives—and the false teeth on the ground.

After reading the following, consider Sen. John McCain on Sunday offering a cruel April Fool's joke—flying into Baghdad and a few minutes later declaring all's swell with the "surge," following the most violent week in Iraq in months. Which included the execution of Saadoun. Here's an excerpt from the Wong piece:

BAGHDAD—The two men showed up on Tuesday afternoon to evict Suaada Saadoun's family. One was carrying a shiny black pistol. Ms. Saadoun was a Sunni Arab living in a Shiite enclave of western Baghdad. A widowed mother of seven, she and her family had been chased out once before. This time, she called American and Kurdish soldiers at a base less than a mile to the east.

The men tried to drive away, but the soldiers had blocked the street. They pulled the men out of the car. "If anything happens to us, they're the ones responsible," said Ms. Saadoun, 49, a burly, boisterous woman in a black robe and lavender-blue head scarf.

The Americans shoved the men into a Humvee. Neighbors clapped and cheered as if their soccer team had just won a title.

The next morning, Ms. Saadoun was shot dead while walking by a bakery in the local market.

The final hours of Ms. Saadoun's life reveal the ferocity with which Shiite militiamen are driving Sunni Arabs from Baghdad house by house, block by block, in an effort to rid the capital of them. It is happening even as thousands of additional American troops and Iraqi soldiers have been sent to Baghdad as part of President Bush's so-called surge strategy. . . .

An American patrol rolled out to Ms. Saadoun's home at 2 P.M. More than a dozen women dressed in black sat wailing in the back yard, awaiting the arrival of Ms. Saadoun's body from the hospital. "I told you, 'Don't go out, they'll kill you,'" one daughter cried out. "I told you, my lovely mother, 'Don't go out, they'll kill you.'"

Matthew Dowd, a top Bush 2004 campaign strategist (and no relation to Maureen Dowd, he once assured me), came out against the war—he had a son who may soon be in the line of fire. The president called Dowd's reaction "emotional." Despite the surge, civilian deaths were up 13 percent across Iraq in May, according to Iraqi figures. Sen. McCain's highly guarded trip to Baghdad has earned much mockery, from both the mainstream media and Comedy Central (or is that mainstream now?).

Has "Straight Talk" by Media Derailed McCain?

APRIL 4, 2007

If Sen. John McCain's campaign for the GOP nomination gets seriously derailed by his dangerously absurd visit to a Baghdad market on Sunday, he can blame the press for that. Unwilling to play tourist during McCain's open-air stroll, reporters quickly revealed the extraordinary security that surrounded this purported "typical day" at the Shorja market. Then, over the next two days, they went back and interviewed some of the merchants, who have thoroughly repudiated the sunny accounts of the visit offered by McCain and his congressional sidekicks.

In short order, McCain went from the ridiculous to the maligned.

But the most revealing and chilling episode featured Rep. Mike Pence (R-Ind.). He was widely quoted in the initial accounts declaring that he found the Shorja bazaar "like a normal outdoor market in Indiana in the summertime." Pence later described one rug merchant who kept patting his heart and refused to take his money: "His eyes, like so many others, radiated with affection and appreciation." Pence said he was "deeply moved" by this.

Well, a National Public Radio reporter returned and found that grateful merchant—and uncovered a quite different story. The carpet seller, Ahmed al-Kurdi, recalled for NPR: "I didn't accept the money. I said to myself, 'They must be guests, so I must give them a good impression of Iraqis.' After all, we are occupied by these Americans—and they are accompanied by a lot of U.S. security."

Al-Kurdi then said that actually he favored the insurgents: "We are not against the resistance. We are with them. However, he who claims to be with the resistance must fight the occupiers, not the Iraqi people. A huge number of U.S. forces came yesterday. Why didn't they shoot at them—instead of harming us?"

So: Maybe patting the heart was a secret signal to open fire on visiting Americans?

The NPR reporter talked to another merchant who said he always keeps an employee stationed outside his shop to watch for cars carrying suicide bombers heading their way. Just like in Indiana? Well, at least Rep. Pence got a good deal on those rugs.

It turns out snipers did open fire at the market shortly after McCain and friends left. Then it emerged today in press reports that 21 workers or merchants in that same market had been found bound and executed north of Baghdad. Was this a retaliatory action or just an example of a real "typical day" in Iraq?

On Tuesday, *The New York Times* and other news outlets published the results of their own interviews with merchants at that market, almost uniformly hostile to McCain or his views. *The Washington Post* added its own quotes in the same vein today, plus some startling statistics on violence in Iraq in this supposedly improving "surge" environment.

New morgue statistics obtained by the *Post* "paint a more complicated picture and underscore the country's precarious security environment," the paper revealed. "U.S. and Iraqi forces launched the security offensive in February. In March, violent deaths dropped in Baghdad, according to Iraqi morgue and police statistics. But violence rose elsewhere in Iraq, fueled largely by suicide bombings. . . . Meanwhile, the numbers of unidentified bodies found across Baghdad are rising again, suggesting an increase in sectarian-motivated death squad killings."

A U.S. military official on Tuesday described McCain's comments about Baghdad's safety as "a bit of hyperbole. . . . Things are indeed better in Baghdad, for now," he asserted. "It's just a very fragile situation that could turn at any moment."

The *Post* pictured a merchant at the market named Hassan shutting down his shop early, worried about the threat of kidnapping. About two weeks ago, thugs entered a neighboring shop at around this time, handcuffed the owner, and stole all his money. Among the shop owners at Shoria, he was considered lucky. "They usually ask for ransom, and then behead the hostage," said Hassan.

Sen. McCain denounced a "hostile press corps." Sig Christenson of the San Antonio *(Tex.)* Express-News *told E&P from Iraq: "It seems McCain is proud of the fact that he's made five visits to Iraq since 2003. Curiously, so have I. But I'd guess that my visits have run longer and involved more danger, starting with the invasion. I'd bet that every journalist who has been here could say the same thing." U.S. deaths in Iraq had now hit 3,300. Documents were finally released relating to one of my long-term interests—the condolence or "solatia" payments in Iraq.*

"Sorry We Shot Your Kid, but Here's $500"

APRIL 14, 2007

The most revealing new information on Iraq—guaranteed to make some readers sad or angry, or both—is found not in any press dispatch but in a collection of several hundred PDFs posted on the Web this week. Here you will find, for example, that when the U.S. drops a bomb that goes awry, lands in an orchard, and does not detonate—until after a couple of kids go out to take a look—our military does not feel any moral or legal reason to compensate the family of the dead child because this is, after all, broadly speaking, a "combat situation."

Also: What price (when we do pay) do we place on the life of a 9-year-old boy, shot by one of our soldiers who mistook his book bag for a bomb satchel? Would you believe $500? And when we shoot an Iraqi journalist on a bridge, we shell out $2,500 to his widow—but why not the measly $5,000 she had requested?

This, and much more, is found in the new PDFs of Iraqi claims, which are usually denied.

Last June, *The Boston Globe* and *The New York Times* revealed that a custom known as "solatia" had now been adopted by the U.S. military—it means families receive financial compensation for physical damage or a loss of life. The *Globe* revealed that payoffs had "skyrocketed from just under $5 million in 2004 to almost $20 million last year, according to Pentagon financial data."

In a column at that time, I asked: How common is the practice? And how many unnecessary deaths do the numbers seem to suggest? It's necessary to ask because the press generally has been denied information on civilian killings and, in recent years, it has become too dangerous in much of Iraq for reporters to go out and investigate shootings or alleged atrocities.

Now we have more evidence, thanks to an American Civil Liberties Union (ACLU) request for files on payments by the military. The FOIA request produced 500 case studies to date, which deserve broad attention.

An Army spokesman told *The New York Times* that the total payments so far had reached at least $32 million. Yet this figure apparently includes only the payments made in this formal claim process that requires official approval. The many other "solatia" or "condolence payments" made informally at a unit commander's discretion are not always included.

The ACLU site, www.aclu.org, now features a searchable database of reports (the ACLU is seeking more of them in case this is just the tip of the iceberg). *The New York Times* comments today: "There is no way to know immediately whether disciplinary action or prosecution has resulted from the cases. Soldiers hand out instruction cards after mistakes are made, so Iraqis know where to file claims. . . ."

Exploring the case reports in PDF form quickly turns disturbing. They often include the scrawled claims by a victim's family member detailing a horrific accidental or deliberate killing (all names blacked out) and then a ruling by a U.S. Army captain or major with the Foreign Claims Commission.

Occasionally the officer orders a payment, although it can still make you scream, as for example: "Claimant alleges that her two brothers were returning home with groceries from their business, when U.S. troops shot and killed them, thinking they were insurgents with bombs in the bags. I recommend approving this claim in the amount of $5,000."

More often the officer denies the claim due to alleged lack of evidence, or threatening behavior by the deceased (usually just failing to stop quickly enough while driving), or the death occurring in some sort of vague combat situation. Many of the denials seem arbitrary or unfair, particularly when the only reason cited is a "combat exemption"—as in the case of the dead kid in that orchard.

Jon Tracy, a former Army captain who helped administer and make day-to-day condolence or "solatia" payment decisions in Iraq as a Judge Advocate in 2004 and 2005, tells me that every Iraqi he dealt with in Iraq "expressed shock and disbelief" when he told them he could only offer them, at most, $2,500 for a precious life lost. He observed that this "limits the unit's ability to adequately assist in the most egregious cases." Under the rules, "the full market value may be paid for a Toyota run over by a tank in the course of a non-combat related accident, but only $2,500 may be paid for the death of a child shot in the cross-fire. . . . The artificial limit leaves survivors bitter and frustrated at the U.S." In other words, it can do more harm than good.

Then there's this example from the case reports:

"Claimant's son and a friend were fishing, in a small boat, 15 kilometers north of Tikrit on the Tigris river at 2200 hours on 31 March 2005. The claimant and his son had fished the Tigris many nights recently, but the father did not join his son this night. U.S. Forces helicopters were flying overhead, like they usually did, and there were no problems.

"A U.S. Forces HMMWV ['Humvee'] patrol pulled up to the beach near where they were fishing. The patrol had spotted and destroyed a boat earlier in the evening that had an RPG in it. They set off an illumination round and then opened fire. The claimant's only son was shot and killed. His friend was injured, but managed to get the boat to the other side of the river. At the small village across the river they received medical help and were taken to the hospital. But it was too late for the claimant's son.

"The claimant and his son were huge supporters of democracy and up to this day held meetings and taught their friends about democracy. The claimant provided two witness statements, medical records, a death certificate, photographs, and a scene sketch, all of which supported his claim.

"*Opinion:* There is sufficient evidence to indicate that U.S. Forces intentionally killed the claimant's son. Unfortunately, those forces were involved in security operations at the time. Therefore, this case falls within the combat exception."

Sometimes the Army officer, perhaps feeling a bit guilty for his ruling—or the whole war—authorizes a small payment in "condolence" money, which does not require admitting any wrongdoing on our part. One of the PDFs notes that a U.S. army memo states a maximum condolence payment scale: $2,500 for death, $500 for property, $1,000 for injury.

One payment noted in a report was a little more generous, but loss of property was compensated, not loss of life. The incident involved two fishermen in Tikrit. They tried to appear non-threatening to an American helicopter crew overhead, holding up their fish "to show they meant no harm," said the report. One was killed anyway. The Army refused to pay for the killing, ruling that it was "combat activity," but approved $3,500 for a boat, net, and cell phone, which all drifted away and were stolen.

To give you more of the flavor, here are some excerpts, with a few obvious typos corrected (also true of the examples above).

Claimant filed a claim for $5,500 on 3 Sept. 2005.

Facts: Claimant alleges that a CF [coalition force] dropped a bomb in his orchard. The bomb allegedly did not explode upon impact. Claimant's son went to investigate and was killed when the UXO [unexploded explosive ordnance] detonated. Claimant's cousin was seriously injured in the explosion. A couple of hours later, CF allegedly took the body and Claimant to LSA Anaconda for medical treatment. In support of their claims, the Claimants have offered witness statements, medical records from LSA Anaconda, and police and judicial reports.

Opinion: Under AR 27-20, paragraph 10-3, Claims arising "directly or indirectly" from combat activities of the U.S. Armed Forces are not payable. AR 27-20 defines combat activities as "Activities resulting directly or indirectly from action by the enemy, or by the U.S. Armed Forces engaged in armed conflict, or in immediate preparation for impending armed conflict." Here, an airstrike clearly constitutes combat activity. While unfortunate, this claim is precluded from compensation under the combat exception.

Recommendation: The claim is denied.

April 15, 2005.
Claimant alleges that on or about 24 February 2005, he was riding in a mini-bus with his nine-year-old son on his lap when Coalition Forces fired a round into the bus. The round allegedly hit his son in the head, causing the son's death later on. xxxxx alleges that some Americans came to the hospital and apologized. He also states that one of the HMMWV's had "32" on the side. Claimant has enclosed an autopsy report.

Allow me to express my sympathy for your loss, however, in accordance with the cited references and after investigating your claim, I find that your claim is not compensable for the following reason: In your claim you failed to provide sufficient evidence that U.S. Forces and not someone else is responsible for your damages. Accordingly, your claim must be denied.

On 11 April 2005, Claimant's father was allegedly killed by CF forces near the Samarra Museum.
Claimant says that his father was deaf and would not have heard danger nearby. The claimant did not personally witness the shooting and relies solely on eye-witnesses. Eyewitnesses related that victim was shot by CF forces. The Claimant does not know if his father was shot by CF forces responding to an AIF attack, or whether CF fired directly on his father.

The claimant presented a claim in the amount of $4,000 on 21 November 2005.

Recommendation: this claim be denied.

On 11 April 2005, at about 11:30 A.M., Claimant's 8-year-old sister, xxxx, was allegedly killed by CF forces near the Al Khatib Secondary School, Samarra. xxxx says that his sister was playing near the school and was shot by CF. Deceased's death certificate . . . she was killed by gunfire. The claimant did not personally witness the shooting and relies solely on eyewitnesses. Eyewitnesses related that victim was shot by CF forces by a "random shot." During the interview, it was impossible to clarify what the claimant meant by a "random shot." A SIGACTS investigation revealed no activity or incidents in Samarra on that date.

Recommendation: Based upon the investigation by this FCC, it is reasonable to conclude that the CF activity can be characterized as combat activity. I recommend this claim be denied.

June 17, 2005.
Claimant alleges that on the above date at the above mentioned location, his brother xxxxx was traveling in his car with rugs that he was taking to a rug store to sell. He was shot by U.S. soldiers, and the rugs and cash on his possession were never recovered . . . and his body left there.

I recommend approving this claim in the amount of $3,000.00.

April 23, 2006, Samarra.
Claimant alleges that Coalition Forces fired upon his two sons as they were leaving the market. The claimant's sons waved their shirts and their underwear as a sign of peace. The claimant provided death certificates, legal expert and witness statements to substantiate the claim.

Opinion: There is not enough evidence to prove the claim.

Recommendation: The claim is denied.

A Pew Survey found that the "most knowledgeable" news consumers watch the faux-news The Daily Show *and* Colbert Report. *But the White House Correspondents Association, still reeling from Colbert's routine at last year's annual dinner, booked the creaky and apolitical Rich Little. Turns out the funniest joke was Karl Rove being seated at a* New York Times *table—where he was accosted by liberals Sheryl Crow and Laurie David. Little, with shockingly dyed hair, said at the outset that he was "not political" but rather a "nightclub performer who does a lot of dumb, stupid jokes," then proved that.*

A little more than four years after I appeared with Bill Moyers during the U.S. invasion, he took a look back on his revived PBS show.

Moyers Returns with "Devastating" Probe of Media and Iraq

April 21, 2007

The most powerful indictment of the news media for falling down in its duties in the run-up to the war in Iraq will appear on April 25, a 90-minute PBS broadcast called "Buying the War," which marks the return of *Bill Moyers Journal*. While much of the evidence of the media's role as cheerleaders for the war presented here is not new, it is skillfully assembled, with many fresh quotes from interviews (with the likes of Tim Russert and Walter Pincus) along with numerous embarrassing examples of past statements by journalists and pundits that proved grossly misleading or wrong. Several prominent media figures, prodded by Moyers, admit the media failed miserably, though few take personal responsibility.

The war continues today, now in its fifth year, with the death toll for Americans and Iraqis rising again—yet, Moyers points out, "the press has yet to come to terms with its role in enabling the Bush administration to go to war on false pretenses."

Among the few heroes of this devastating film are reporters with the Knight Ridder/McClatchy bureau in D.C. Tragically late, Walter Isaacson, who headed CNN, observes, "The people at Knight Ridder were calling the colonels and the lieutenants and the people in the CIA and finding out, you know, that the intelligence is not very good. We should've all been doing that."

At the close, Moyers mentions some of the chief proponents of the war who refused to speak to him for this program, including Thomas Friedman, Bill Kristol, Roger Ailes, Charles Krauthammer, Judith Miller, and William Safire. But Dan Rather, the former CBS anchor, admits, "I don't think there is any excuse for, you know, my performance and the performance of the press in general in the roll-up to the war. We didn't dig enough. And we shouldn't have been fooled in this way." Bob Simon, who had strong doubts about evidence for war, was asked by Moyers if he pushed any of the top brass at CBS to "dig deeper," and he replies, "No, in all honesty, with a thousand mea culpas, I don't think we followed up on this." Instead he covered the marketing of the war in a "softer" way, explaining to Moyers: "I think we all felt from the beginning that to deal with a subject as explosive as this, we should keep it, in a way, almost light—if that doesn't seem ridiculous."

Moyers replies: "Going to war, almost light."

Walter Isaacson is pushed hard by Moyers and finally admits, "We didn't question our sources enough." But why? Isaacson notes there was "almost a patriotism police" after 9/11 and when the network showed civilian casualties it would get phone calls from advertisers and the administration and "big people in corporations were calling up and saying, 'You're being anti-American here.'"

Moyers then mentions that Isaacson had sent a memo to his staff, leaked to *The Washington Post*, in which he declared, "It seems perverse to focus too much on the casualties or hardship in Afghanistan" and ordered them to balance any such images with reminders of 9/11. Moyers also asserts that editors at the *Panama City* (Fla.) *News Herald* received an order from above, "Do not use photos on Page 1A showing civilian casualties. Our sister paper has done so and received hundreds and hundreds of threatening e-mails."

Walter Pincus of *The Washington Post* explains that even at his paper, reporters "do worry about sort of getting out ahead of something." But Moyers gives credit to my old friend, Charles J. Hanley of The Associated Press, for trying, in vain, to draw more attention to United Nations inspectors failing to find WMD in early 2003.

The disgraceful press reaction to Colin Powell's presentation at the United Nations seems like something out of Monty Python, with one key British report cited by Powell being nothing more than a student's thesis, downloaded from the Web—with the student later threatening to charge U.S. officials with "plagiarism."

Phil Donahue recalls that he was told he could not feature war dissenters alone on his MSNBC talk show and always had to have "two conservatives for every liberal." Moyers resurrects a leaked NBC memo about Donahue's firing that claimed he "presents a difficult public face for NBC in a time of war. At the same time our competitors are waving the flag at every opportunity."

Moyers also throws some stats around: In the year before the invasion, William Safire (who predicted a "quick war" with Iraqis cheering their liberators) wrote "a total of 27 opinion pieces fanning the sparks of war." *The Washington Post* carried at least 140 front-page stories in that same period, helping to make the administration's case for attack. In the six months leading to the invasion, the *Post* would "editorialize in favor of the war at least 27 times."

Of the 414 Iraq stories broadcast on NBC, ABC, and CBS nightly news in the six months before the war, almost all could be traced back to sources solely in the White House, Pentagon, or State Department, Moyers tells Russert, who offers no coherent reply.

The program closes on a sad note, with Moyers pointing out that "so many of the advocates and apologists for the war are still flourishing in the media." He then runs a pre-war clip of President Bush declaring, "We cannot wait for the final proof: the smoking gun that could come in the form of a mushroom cloud." Then Moyers explains: "The man who came up with it was Michael Gerson, President Bush's top speechwriter. He has left the White House and has been hired by *The Washington Post* as a columnist."

JUNE

Testifying before Congress on April 24 about the new revelations in the cover-up of the friendly-fire killing of Pat Tillman in Afghanistan, his brother, Kevin Tillman (who served with him there), accused the Bush administration of twisting the facts of his brother's death to distract public attention from the just-emerging abuses at Abu Ghraib. The following day, Laura Bush told NBC that watching the images of death and violence in Iraq hurt the First Family deeply: "No one suffers more than their president and I do," she said. The House passed its Iraq withdrawal bill, despite the promised Bush veto—which indeed came on May 1. The Iraqi government had banned journalists from the sites of bomb blasts. More Americans died in Iraq in May (127) than any month since 2004. Tony Snow compared the future of the U.S. in Iraq to our presence in Korea— which had run 57 years, so far. In an editorial, The Washington Post endorsed a long U.S. tenure in Iraq, if not necessarily half a century. Speaking of doing hard time: The federal judge sentenced "Scooter" Libby to 30 months in jail, and talk of a Bush pardon quickly spread.

Better Late than Never: A Major Paper Calls for Pullout

JUNE 13, 2007

"I see no moral reason to wait until fall," Jim Newton, editorial-page editor at the *Los Angeles Times*, told me earlier today. "We need to evaluate in real time. That's part of the motivation for the editorial this week. Besides General Petraeus, others have a right to assess the facts as well."

Newton was referring to an editorial in his paper on Tuesday calling for peace talks and a ceasefire in Iraq. It's the kind of talk we heard often in relation to Vietnam and later conflicts but that is oddly missing in regard to Iraq. But the *Times* is taking all sorts of bold stands on the war these days. Six weeks ago, the paper advocated—hold on to your hats—that the U.S. actually start to disengage in Iraq. That editorial was titled simply, if eloquently, "Bring Them Home."

Rather than chide the vast majority of newspaper editorial pages, yet again, for continuing to endorse, or at least accept, the continuing (now expanding) U.S. mission in Iraq, I am happy to tip my hat to the only ultra-large paper that has come out for the start of an American pullout. That position, until now, has been left to papers such as *The Seattle Times, Minneapolis Star Tribune, The Orange County Register,* and *The Roanoke Times.*

What's happening at the L.A. paper, which as recently as January backed the "surge"? It's as if a little-noted earthquake struck Spring Street this spring and really shook things up.

That May editorial reflected, "This newspaper reluctantly endorsed the U.S. troop surge as the last, best hope for stabilizing conditions so that the elected Iraqi government could assume full responsibility for its affairs. But we also warned that the troops should not be used to referee a civil war. That, regrettably, is what has happened." It concluded that "the longer we delay planning for the inevitable, the worse the outcome is likely to be. The time has come to leave."

This week's editorial urged: "The United States might have liked to wait until September for Army Gen. David H. Petraeus's report on the results of the troop surge in Iraq, but that wishful timetable has been overtaken by events. President Bush must begin planning a strategic and orderly disengagement that addresses the increasingly unstable geopolitical terrain."

How did this come about? I wondered. The change took place shortly after Newton, who had been the city-county bureau chief at the paper, took charge of the editorial page, following the abrupt departure of Andres Martinez. But he said he was not really responsible for the change, except in a roundabout way. When he took over, he had called a meeting of the editorial board, "partly to educate myself where we were" on Iraq. "Members of the board suggested that we sit back and take stock of our position: Are we comfortable where we are, or should we change?"

Like other papers, the *Times* had been very critical of the conduct of the war but had refused to advocate a real change in course, and had supported the surge "as a last ditch attempt" to turn things around, as Newton puts it. But by the time he came to the editorial page, "the caveat we had put on our support for the surge, that our presence there was not to oversee a civil war," seemed to be proving prophetic.

So at the board meeting, he recalls, when "we went around the table and talked about where we were, there was a strong sense that the surge was not producing and had no realistic hope for producing what we wished for when the paper reluctantly supported it. From there we moved to a discussion of a sensible course change and what would be necessary to produce change there and, frankly, safeguard American lives." Before going to press, he showed the editorial to his publisher, who made a few suggestions that were incorporated in it.

"That first editorial was our attempt to really say in a forthright way how we should move forward," Newton says. The most recent one this week calling for peace talks and a ceasefire was "more of an attempt to apply principles we laid out in the previous one to changing facts on the ground."

Newton says the response from readers has been about 75 percent positive "from what has come to me," many calling it "an important message for an important newspaper to send." As for his own response: "I feel very strongly what we wrote in that first editorial—an honest appraisal of where we are." He said again that this appraisal could not be postponed: "There's lot of talk that we will have this national debate in the fall, but the problem is, every day that goes by, the conflict shifts and in some ways worsens."

In fact, today White House spokesman Tony Snow joined generals who had previously stated that all this talk about a "September reassessment" was no longer operative, because who could judge success of the surge by then? My feeling, in any case, has always been that there is no chance that Petraeus would ever state in September that the mission—which he is now so tightly connected with—is actually failing.

Following the example of the *L.A. Times*, perhaps other papers will urgently feel a "moral" need to reassess the facts—and "take stock" of their positions on the war.

Tony Snow claimed that, while far from the front lines, the president is "in the war every day." The revered Shiite Askariya mosque at Samarra was bombed for the second time in 16 months, setting off a new round of sectarian bloodshed and the razing of Sunni mosques. Dana Priest and Anne Hull, the same team that broke the Walter Reed scandal for The Washington Post, *returned with a follow-up on the mental health woes of returning Iraqi vets. Also at the* Post, *Bob Woodward admitted in an online chat that he should have probed WMD more intensely in the pre-war period.* Foreign Policy *magazine looked at a new "failed-states index" and revealed that Iraq ranked second, just behind the Sudan.*

A Rare Look at One Civilian Casualty

JUNE 19, 2007

The civilian death toll in Iraq is, by all accounts, frightful. Car bombs enact a terrible price, and this is widely covered by the press almost every day. But civilians who die at the hands of American troops get much less attention. There are many reasons for this. The incidents are widely scattered and usually do not involve large numbers at one time. The U.S. military rarely admits wrongdoing—in some cases, it may not even know that anyone has died. The media, amid horrible violence, have trouble investigating.

But a recent episode involving a single casualty has drawn unusual attention—only because the youth happened to be the son of a *Los Angeles Times* employee in Baghdad.

Tina Susman told the story last Tuesday in that paper. The boy was 17, but she did not name him, nor identify the father.

Susman, the paper's Baghdad bureau chief (and veteran foreign correspondent), wrote, "U.S. military officials say troops are trained to avoid civilian casualties and do not fire wildly. Iraqis, however, say the shootings happen frequently and that even if troops are firing at suspected attackers, they often do so on city streets where bystanders are likely to be hit. Rarely is it possible to confirm such incidents. In this case, the boy was the son of a *Los Angeles Times* employee, which provided reporters knowledge of the incident in time to examine it. Witness and military accounts of the shooting offered a rare look into how such killings can occur."

She revealed that since February, stringers for the newspaper across Iraq have reported at least 18 incidents of American troops firing wildly with at least 22 noncombatants killed. Surely this only scratches the surface, as Walter Pincus observed yesterday in a *Washington Post* article on the "solatia" or condolence payments that I have often written about. Thousands of such payments have been made by the U.S.

Susman noted that in most cases the wild firing occurs after an IED or car bomb goes off (as happened most tragically in Haditha).

She graphically recounted the testimony of a man named Abu Mohammed who owned a shop where the youth ran for help after getting shot. "I was hesitant to open the door because I was afraid that the American soldiers would shoot me dead," he said, recalling when the boy began beating on his door. Even as he let the boy in and helped him to the floor, he said, troops kept firing.

"They were confused and angry and suspecting anyone around," Mohammed said. "If a bird had passed by, they would have shot it." The U.S. military said troops fired in self-defense.

"It's a psychological thing. When one U.S. soldier gets killed or injured, they shoot in vengeance," Alaa Safi told Susman. Safi was the minister of civil society in the government of former Prime Minister Ibrahim Jafari, after the toppling of Saddam. He said his brother, Ahmed, was killed April 4 when U.S. troops riddled the streets of their southwestern Baghdad neighborhood with bullets after a sniper attack.

By e-mail yesterday, I asked Susman how the military had responded to her article. She replied today: "I have not had any official response from the military or otherwise here on the article, but there is no reason that they would have been expected to say anything. They do not have time to respond to every article written about U.S. troop actions in Iraq.

"I got a few e-mails from individual soldiers as well as citizens, here and in the States. Most were critical and accused us of being ultra-liberals and failing to comprehend the reality of what soldiers face." She added that one letter-writer suggested that the dead boy's father, the *L.A. Times* employee, "was at fault for not having sent his son out of the country when the war began."

Susman's article, on the contrary, was important and balanced. As Chris Hedges, the former *New York Times* war reporter, puts it this week at the Truthdig site: "The reality of the war—the fact that the occupation forces have become, along with the rampaging militias, a source of terror to most Iraqis—is not transmitted to the American public. The press chronicles the physical and emotional wounds visited on those who kill in our name. The Iraqis, those we kill, are largely nameless, faceless dead."

———————————————

JULY

A Newsweek poll found that, amazingly, 40 percent of Americans still believed that Saddam was involved with 9/11—with the number actually rising in the past two years. One in five claimed there were Iraqis among the 19 hijackers that day. Only 29 percent in a Gallup survey said the U.S. was winning the war on terrorism. Some polls showed that President Bush's approval rating had also dipped to 29 percent or below. Word of new alleged U.S. atrocities surfaced in Iraq and Afghanistan.

Many expected Bush to pardon "Scooter" Libby before he trotted off to prison, but few anticipated a commutation of his sentence before he even got there. When that happened, a firestorm erupted: Was the president now participating in a new obstruction of justice? Even more unexpectedly, Sen. Richard Lugar, the longtime Republican leader and armed forces expert, took to the floor of the Senate to suggest that he didn't need to wait until the official "surge" report in September to declare that the escalation was fruitless and U.S. troops should start to come home. Other GOP senators soon joined him, if tentatively. But others hadn't given up, blaming our current troubles in Iraq on al-Qaeda—and Iran.

Haven't We Been Through This Movie Before?

July 3, 2007

As if he hadn't done enough damage already, helping to promote the American invasion of Iraq with deeply flawed articles in *The New York Times*, Michael R. Gordon is now writing scare stories that offer ammunition for the growing chorus of neo-cons calling for a U.S. strike against Iran—his most recent effort appearing just this morning. What's most lamentable is that editors at the *Times*, who should have learned their lessons four years ago, are once again serving as enablers.

The *Times* carried Gordon's latest opus at the top of its front page today. *The Washington Post*, in contrast, carried the same claims by an American military spokesman, in an article by Joshua Partlow, on page A8. After a brief accounting of the military's assertion, Partlow devotes much of the rest of the story to a general war roundup (including news of civilians south of Baghdad killed by our bombs).

At least the *Times*, fittingly, ran today's long list of names of U.S. war dead in a box within the Gordon article.

The latest official effort to blame Iran so that perhaps we can bomb Iran revolves around new claims by Brig. Gen. Kevin J. Bergner that the deaths of five American soldiers in Karbala in January were actually plotted by Iranian militants. Gordon's breathless article first appeared on his paper's site yesterday with absolutely no caveats—revealing his true motives and standards. "In effect, American officials are charging that Iran has been engaged in a proxy war against American forces for years," Gordon declared approvingly.

Perhaps even his editors were concerned or embarrassed. The same story suddenly gained a couple of qualifiers, though not nearly enough, later yesterday (first spotted by Salon blogger Glenn Greenwald), and then got enlarged somewhat today, and with the byline of John F. Burns added to Gordon's.

The story even has a lead character reminiscent of "Curveball" and "Baseball Cap Guy" from Judy Miller's reporting on Iraq in 2003. Our new star informer is a Lebanese citizen named Ali Musa Daqdug, aka "Hamid the Mute," who supposedly (this is all coming from General Bergner) has a "24-year history in Hezbollah. The general said Mr. Daqdug had been sent by Hezbollah to Iran in 2005 with orders to work with the Quds Force, an elite unit of the Iranian Revolutionary Guards, to train 'Iraqi extremists.'"

The *Times* article contains a number of howlers delivered with all seriousness. Here's one: "General Bergner, seemingly keen to avoid a renewal of the criticism that the American command has used the allegations of Iranian interference here to lend momentum to the Bush administration's war policy, declined to draw any broader political implications. . . ."

That's topped by this, in explaining that "Hamid the Mute" had suddenly started talking: "The official said the shift had been achieved without harming Mr. Daqduq. 'We don't torture,' the official said. 'We follow scrupulously the interrogation techniques in the Army's new field manual, which forbids torture, and has the force of law.'"

And who is General Bergner? He arrived in Iraq just a few weeks ago from his previous job, as special assistant—to President Bush in the White House.

At his press conference on Monday, which supplied quotes for Gordon, he admitted he could not explain the motivation for the attack on the five U.S. soldiers; why the Iranians would feel any need to outsource to Hezbollah; or why they would risk this kind of "exposure."

The danger of the *Times* article—given the prominence attached to it—is real. For example, Sen. Joe Lieberman responded to the allegations by asserting that this means Iran "has declared war on us." He'd already been advocating some kind of U.S. strike on Iran.

You may recall that this past February, Gordon had trumpeted the charge that Iran was now supplying a new form of IED—or as the *Times* put it, the "deadliest weapon aimed at American troops" in Iraq. This charge, promoted by the U.S. military and given prominent play by the *Times*, also came at a time of rising calls for taking action against Iran. Experts subsequently disputed key parts of evidence cited by Gordon, and the charge largely subsided—until now.

Meanwhile, he has written many articles more optimistic about the "surge" than most of his colleagues in the press. They reflect the view of the surge he stated on Charlie Rose's PBS show back in January (he was chastised by his editors then for speaking his mind too freely): "So I think, you know, as a purely personal view, I think it's worth one last effort for sure to try to get this right, because my personal view is we've never really tried to win. We've simply been managing our way to defeat. And I think that if it's done right, I think that there is the chance to accomplish something."

Gordon, of course, is the same *Times* reporter who, on his own or with Miller, wrote some of the key—yet badly misleading or downright inaccurate—articles about Iraqi WMD in the run-up to the 2003 invasion. Gordon, in fact, wrote with Miller the paper's most widely criticized—even by the *Times* itself—WMD story of all, the Sept. 8, 2002, "aluminum tubes" scoop that proved so influential, especially after the administration embraced it lovingly on TV talk shows. Surely you remember "the first sign of a smoking gun . . . may be a mushroom cloud."

He also wrote, following Secretary of State Colin Powell's crucial, and appallingly wrong, speech to the United Nations in 2003 that helped sell the war, that "it will be difficult for skeptics to argue that Washington's case against Iraq is based on groundless suspicions and not intelligence information."

In a radio interview, Amy Goodman once asked Gordon if he was sorry that he'd written the aluminum tube/mushroom cloud article. He said absolutely not, and suggested she did not know that good journalism means writing what you know at the time, and then doing more reporting later. This may be true enough in most cases, but not when it comes to greasing the path to war—with your words.

With evidence of success for the "surge" still spotty—particularly in terms of reforms by the al-Maliki government—several prominent Republicans broke, tentatively, with Bush policy and a few editorial pages finally came out for a withdrawal. The Olympian of Olympia, Wash., serves an area with a heavy military presence. "The Fourth of July is a time when Americans celebrate the values that have made us a great nation," its publisher, John Winn Miller, told me. "So it seemed like an appropriate time to editorialize on what has become a national disgrace." Three days later, The New York Times finally took an historic step, in an editorial called "The Road Home," which opened: "It is time for the United States to leave Iraq, without any more delay than the Pentagon needs to organize an orderly exit." It concluded: "This country faces a choice. We can go on allowing Mr. Bush to drag out this war without end or purpose. Or we can insist that American troops are withdrawn as quickly and safely as we can manage— with as much effort as possible to stop the chaos from spreading."

On NBC's Meet the Press on July 22, David Brooks declared that 10,000 Iraqis a month would perish if the U.S. pulled out. Bob Woodward challenged him on this, asking his source. Brooks admitted: "I just picked that 10,000 out of the air."

From Hanging with George Clooney to Hanging Bad Guys in Iraq

JULY 23, 2007

My favorite "feel good," America-as-land-of-opportunity story of the month involves a man named Basam Ridha. Where else could a young exile end up appearing with George Clooney in a Hollywood movie—and then, thanks to the man in the White House, get a chance to return to his native land to serve as official hangman?

Ridha, former actor in the Clooney film *Three Kings* and on television in *24*—yes, he has a Screen Actors Guild card—now acts as an advisor to Prime Minister Nouri al-Maliki. He also appears as a spokesman for the Iraqi government on American TV, and handles all the arrangements for executions in Iraq. He's the guy who is frequently quoted when hangings there are botched. When one notorious prisoner's head got severed in the process back in January, Ridha called it an "act of God," adding, in something of an understatement, "it was not a pretty scene."

I discovered that and other interesting details in doing my own research following last weekend's piece about him by Tina Susman of the *Los Angeles Times*. That story had featured a can't-miss lede: "Basam Ridha traded the business of Hollywood for the business of hanging." She went on to call him "the go-to man for all things gallows."

Now I've found a picture of Ridha posing with George Clooney on the set of *Three Kings*. It was featured in the *Daily Reveille*, the newspaper for Lousiana State University, on April 23, 2003. The story opens: "LSU graduate Basam Ridha Al-Husaini had to flee for his life, leaving his family behind and the country he calls home. After the recent fall of Saddam Hussein's regime he will finally be able to return to Iraq after 21 years. . . . In May 1982 two of his brothers had been imprisoned by Hussein, and Al-Husaini decided to leave Iraq and come to the United States." Eventually he dropped the Al-Husaini part of his name.

Currently, Ridha is putting his engineering degree to use in carefully planning the next high-level hanging, starring "Chemical Ali." At least 100 such executions have taken place since 2005. Ridha denies any blame for the circus surrounding Saddam Hussein's passing: Surprised by the speed with which it was carried out, he was not in the room that night but far away in Dubai. After another botched execution early this year, he ordered a new gallows built.

Naturally I had to ask Susman, the *L.A. Times* bureau chief in Baghdad, how she got her story. "I'd first spoken to Basam in February over the phone for a story about an upcoming execution," she replied. "He was always happy to talk and became a great source of information whenever a hanging was in the works. Little by little I began learning about his background. When I learned that he lived in L.A. so long, it seemed a natural story for the *L.A. Times.* The Hollywood bit was icing on the cake.

"But it's the kind of story that could not have worked without the perfect subject, and he is a great subject. He's remarkably up-front about his attitudes, enjoys talking to journalists, and is one of those rare political types who says exactly what he thinks, even if he knows it might offend some people. The interview was at times entertaining, and at times, such as when he talked about the search for his brothers and the toll it had taken on his family, quite heart-wrenching. I wanted to portray him as someone who was angry and wanting revenge, but using that anger in a way he believes is somehow good for other Iraqis. It's not such an unusual attitude here."

Susman had pointed out in her story, "Ridha plays down his Hollywood experience but admits it was lucrative. He still collects residuals." He did have a speaking role in *Three Kings*, after all. Perhaps he could star in a remake of the Sergio Leone/Clint Eastwood classic, *Hang 'Em High.*

In googling for other Ridha material, I found that Laila Fadel of McClatchy Newspapers had profiled Ridha back in March. He told her, "We're not accustomed to executing; that's why we made mistakes, unlike Saddam and his people. They did not care." Last December, he informed *The New York Times* that Iraqis were lining up to slip the noose around Saddam's neck.

As recently as ten days ago he was serving as a spokesman on non-hanging matters. Fox News went to him after al-Maliki's government got passing grades on only 8 of 18 benchmarks from the U.S. Fox observed that Ridha took exception to how this was characterized. "We are making progress," he said. "A lot of people say there is pressure and we have a deadline. There is no such thing. I think for the most part it looks like a war in Washington, a media war, more than a war in Iraq.

"The question is: a failing grade as far as the Americans are concerned or as far as we are concerned, which we count the most. . . . We are going to conduct our own business, for our own country, for our own agenda, for the thing that works for us."

Ridha had also served as advisor to a previous prime minister, Ibrahim al-Jafari. *USA Today* on Feb. 12, 2006, quoted Ridha defending his boss by explaining that he would "not be able to make an overnight success of Iraq, but he has a vision."

When I asked Susman what Ridha thought of her piece, she responded: "I haven't heard from him on the story. I got one response from a reader who insinuated that Basam himself should hang for his attitudes. Funny enough, the stories I get the most reaction to are those about the oil legislation here. People are passionate about revenue-sharing agreements."

AUGUST

For years, polls had shown that large numbers of Americans continue to falsely believe that some of the 9/11 hijackers came from Iraq. In reality, the overwhelming number hailed from Saudi Arabia. Now it turned out that our ally is also home to the largest number of so-called "foreign fighters" in Iraq, despite administration efforts—aided by many in the media—to paint Iran and Syria as the main outside culprits there. The Los Angeles Times *reported that according to a senior U.S. military officer and Iraqi lawmakers, about 45 percent of all foreign militants "targeting U.S. troops and Iraqi civilians and security forces are from Saudi Arabia," including large numbers of suicide bombers.*

More allegations of abuse or killing of Iraqi civilians surfaced. A McClatchy report from Baghdad revealed that during the past year, U.S. soldiers had killed or wounded 429 Iraqi civilians at checkpoints or near patrols and convoys. The Los Angeles Times *reported on the testimony of a Marine corporal, Saul Lopezromo, at the trial of Cpl. Trent D. Thomas, charged with murdering an Iraqi near Hamandaya. Lopezromo said Marines in his unit began routinely beating Iraqis after officers ordered them to "crank up the violence level."*

Why Aren't the Media on a Suicide Watch?

AUGUST 13, 2007

Would it surprise you to learn that according to official Pentagon figures, at least 118 U.S. military personnel in Iraq have committed suicide since April 2003? That number does not include many unconfirmed reports, or those who served in the war and then killed themselves at home (a sizable, if uncharted, number). While troops who have died in "hostile action"—and those gravely injured and rehabbing at Walter Reed and other hospitals—have gained much wider media attention in recent years, the suicides (at least 3 percent of our overall Iraq death toll) remain in the shadows.

For whatever reason, I have always found soldiers who take their own lives especially tragic, though some might argue the opposite. Since the beginning of the war, I have written numerous columns on self-inflicted deaths, from average grunts to Col. Ted Westhusing (angry about contractor abuses), Alyssa Peterson (appalled by interrogation techniques), and Linda Michel (denied medication after returning home). But generally, the suicides get very little local or national attention.

In a sense, the press doesn't know what to do about them. Did they serve their country well but ultimately let it down? Or is their country fully responsible for putting them in a suicide-producing situation in the first place, and does it have blood on its hands?

One recent case illustrates some of the issues. The Pentagon revealed the death, joining more than 3,650 others, on July 5 in one of its pithy releases: "Pfc. Andrew T. Engstrom, 22, of Slaton, Texas, died July 4 in Taji, Iraq, from injuries suffered in a non-combat related incident. His death is under investigation."

Investigations can last months, and the press normally reports that the death was "non-hostile," which also covers the many killed in vehicle or gun accidents, and leaves it at that. But in this case, a reporter for *The Lubbock* (Tex.) *Avalanche-Journal*, Marlena Hartz, wrote that she had learned from one of Engstrom's friends and a family friend that his parents had been told he died from a self-inflicted gunshot wound "in the head."

A local radio station published a couple of heartbreaking photos of the young man on its Web site, captured from MySpace, along with a message his mother had posted online before his death: "My dearest son, you should know how much daddy and I are so proud of you, taking the stand like you did, when you did, living out what you dreamed of doing since you were a young child. Keep your chin up, your head down, and remember dad and I love you with our whole being. Mom."

I found his page at MySpace (he called himself Sir Knight). The "last login" came on the day he died. His lead quote reads: "These are the times that try men's souls." Biographical details included the statement "I don't have heroes." The top entry in the comments section by his MySpace friends came from a young woman who wrote on July 13: "R.I.P. Andy." His younger brother, 18, and his mother each have their own MySpace pages, which now include tributes. His mother described her "mood" in July as "depressed."

As I said: I can barely stand the tragedy in all of this, even after the mother claimed, in a phone call to me, that suicide was not certain and that the military probe may never come to a clear conclusion.

On August 5, in response to an earlier piece on this subject, I received the following e-mail: "My 26 yr old son hung himself June 21st. He was an 'outstanding' SSG with 'great leadership skills' per his Army records. Something is very wrong with the services that they receive. He had been stationed at Fort Carson. Disch[arged] on May 2 with PTSD [post-traumatic stress disorder] 50 percent disability and dead less than six weeks later, I am trying so hard to make sense of this tragedy."

This past January, Lisa Chedekel and Matthew Kauffman noted in *The Hartford Courant* that veterans' advocates found the increase of suicides in 2006 "troubling." Steve Robinson, director of government relations for Veterans for America, told them he was particularly disturbed by suicides in the war zone because combat troops are supposed to be screened for mental health issues before they join the military, and throughout their careers. "These people aren't the kind of people that you would think would take this step," he said.

Chedekel told me in an e-mail recently, "We haven't looked at 2007 suicides—and it's a tough subject to get timely statistics on. The Defense Manpower Data Center reports, which come out periodically and are broken down by casualty category, do keep a running count of self-inflicted deaths—but because some cases are listed as 'pending,' and can be moved into the 'confirmed' category months later, it's tricky to get an accurate tally by calendar year."

Not even included in these tallies are cases like the following: "Two weeks ago Iraq vet Noah Pierce shot and killed himself in a remote section of northern Minnesota. The sheriff's office revealed that he had been diagnosed with post-traumatic stress disorder and that Pierce had said, before he fled home with a few firearms, that he may be a danger to others as well as himself."

In the *Deseret* (Utah) *Morning News* last Monday, Stephen Speckman noted that the suicide rate among all veterans is now about twice the national average among non-veterans. On top of that, he added, "Among Army members, suicide rates between 2003 and 2006 for soldiers in Operation Iraqi Freedom were higher than the average Army rate, 16.1 versus 11.6 soldier suicides per year per 100,000, according to U.S. Army Medical Command spokesman Jerry Harben."

A new military report, just obtained by The Associated Press, found that

Army soldiers committed suicide last year at the highest rate in 26 years, and more than a quarter did so while serving in Iraq and Afghanistan. The report noted there were 99 confirmed suicides among active-duty soldiers during 2006, up from 88 the previous year and the highest since the 102 suicides in 1991. "Iraq was the most common deployment location for both (suicides) and attempts," the report said.

The 99 suicides included 28 soldiers deployed to the two wars and 71 who weren't. About twice as many women serving in Iraq and Afghanistan committed suicide as did women not sent to war, the report said. Failed personal relationships, legal and financial problems, and the stress of their jobs were factors. "In addition, there was a significant relationship between suicide attempts and number of days deployed" in Iraq, Afghanistan, or nearby countries where troops are participating in the war effort, it said.

As for Andy Engstrom: There is no way of knowing right now why he may have put a bullet in his head in Iraq in early July. Some victims might have killed themselves without having served multiple tours of Iraq. Engstrom had been there since last October. But there was nothing to learn from press coverage of his funeral in Slaton on July 13: There was none that I could find. Nothing at all.

These sad events are often covered extensively by local papers saluting their hometown heroes. Do the families in these cases usually request a blackout? Locally, I can understand it, but there's no excuse for the lack of national attention to the number of suicides among U.S. troops.

It was that rare "gotcha" moment where evidence went back more than a decade. C-SPAN 3 aired an interview with Dick Cheney from April 15, 1994, which disappeared into the ether until a site called Grand Theft Country copied a minute of it and posted it on YouTube in mid-August. It became wildly popular there (after I publicized it on the E&P *site) and soon turned up on* The Daily Show *and many other media outlets.*

Cheney, you'll remember, had helped direct the Gulf War for President George H. W. Bush. That effort was later criticized for not taking Baghdad, and officials like Cheney had to explain why not, for years. (Some have charged that this led to an overpowering desire to finish the job after Cheney became vice president in 2001). In the C-SPAN clip, Cheney defended the decision not to invade Iraq back then: "Once you got to Iraq and took it over, took down Saddam Hussein's government, then what are you going to put in its place? That's a very volatile part of the world, and if you take down the central government of Iraq, you could very easily end up seeing pieces of Iraq fly off: part of it, the Syrians would like to have to the west, part of it—eastern Iraq—the Iranians would like to claim, they fought over it for eight years. In the north you've got the Kurds, and if the Kurds spin loose and join with the Kurds in Turkey, then you threaten the territorial integrity of Turkey. It's a quagmire if you go that far and try to take over Iraq.

"The other thing was casualties. Everyone was impressed with the fact we were able to do our job with as few casualties as we had. But for the 146 Americans killed in action, and for their families—it wasn't a cheap war. And the question for the president, in terms of whether or not we went on to Baghdad, took additional casualties in an effort to get Saddam Hussein, was how many additional dead Americans is Saddam worth? Our judgment was, not very many, and I think we got it right."

George Bush Meets Graham Greene

AUGUST 23, 2007

Now, that's going too far. George W. Bush cited my favorite twentieth-century novel and its author—Graham Greene's prescient *The Quiet American*—in his speech on Wednesday to the Veterans of Foreign War convention. Bush drew several dubious links between the catastrophic Vietnam and Iraq conflicts. Perhaps because it's unlikely he's ever read the book, it was difficult to figure out exactly what the president meant.

Bush could have used a fact-checker as well. He describes Alden Pyle, the U.S. operative, as the "main character" in the book, when it's actually the narrator of the story, Thomas Fowler, the Saigon-based British newspaper correspondent (played by Michael Caine in the fine recent film). And, of course, "many" back in the 1970s did not say there would be "no" consequences for the Vietnamese after our pullout, as Bush alleged.

In any case, here's the Bush statement today: "In 1955, long before the United States had entered the war, Graham Greene wrote a novel called *The*

Quiet American. It was set in Saigon and the main character was a young government agent named Alden Pyle. He was a symbol of American purpose and patriotism and dangerous naivete. Another character describes Alden this way: 'I never knew a man who had better motives for all the trouble he caused.'

"After America entered the Vietnam War, Graham Greene—the Graham Greene argument gathered some steam. Matter of fact, many argued that if we pulled out, there would be no consequences for the Vietnamese people. In 1972, one anti-war senator put it this way: 'What earthly difference does it make to nomadic tribes or uneducated subsistence farmers in Vietnam or Cambodia or Laos whether they have a military dictator, a royal prince, or a socialist commissar in some distant capital that they've never seen and may never have heard of?'"

Now, what does Bush mean by all this?

My initial reaction was that Bush was equating the novelist with critics of both the Vietnam and Iraq wars who found "naive" the views of those promoting a war who had only "noble" ideals (e.g., Bush) and would succeed if the Greenes of the world just got out of the way. If this is true, Bush was trying to identify with Pyle.

Maybe someone should tell him that Pyle, in the novel, helps arrange and then defends a terror bombing that kills and maims civilians. Or perhaps Bush only saw the misbegotten 1950s movie based on the book, which shifted Pyle's guilt to the Communists.

But others have suggested that Bush meant that Greene and his ilk are the naive ones. Here's Frank James of the *Chicago Tribune* at the paper's blog The Swamp: "Bush seemed to be seizing on Greene's idea of U.S. naivete on entering the war and trying to turn it around and apply it to those now calling for a timetable for withdrawing U.S. troops from Iraq. But Greene wrote his book about the way America bumbled into Vietnam, not how it left it. By reminding people of Greene's book, Bush was inviting listeners to recall the mistakes his administration made in entering and prosecuting the Iraq War. Did he really want to do that?"

Then there was Joe Klein at *Time* magazine's Swampland blog calling *The Quiet American* a novel "whose hero is the young William Kristol . . . actually, no, the hero is an idealistic American intelligence officer named Alden Pyle, who causes great disasters in the name of a higher good. In other words, he's a premature neo-conservative. I would hope that the president will reread, or perhaps just read the book, as soon as possible because it is as good a description as there is about the futility of trying to forcibly impose Western ways on an ancient culture."

Well, you be the judge. I suppose we shouldn't joke about Graham Illusion or Graham Theft.

Greene's novel, in any case, pits the cynical, apolitical newspaperman—who has a Vietnamese girlfriend and an opium habit—against the Pyle character, who seems to be a U.S. aid official linked to the CIA (and purportedly based on the legendary Edward Lansdale). Pyle is attempting to find a "third force," a democratic alternative to the French-backed puppet government and the Communist insurgents. With brilliant writing, biting humor, and keen insight on local politics and customs (based on Greene's research there), the novel perfectly anticipates the massive U.S. urge to intervene deeply and then escalate.

Fowler, the typical newspaperman, has no use for "isms" and "ocracies," and just wants the "facts." He tells Pyle "you and your like are trying to make a war with the help of people who just aren't interested." What do they want? "They want enough rice. They don't want to be shot at. They want one day to be much the same as another. They don't want our white skins around telling them what they want."

Pyle replies: "If Indo-china goes . . ."

"I know the record. Siam goes. Malaya goes. Indonesia goes. What does 'go' mean?"

Pyle ultimately assists an urban bombing to be blamed on Vietminh insurgents, and many civilians die. Greene observes that "a woman sat on the ground with what was left of her baby in her lap; with a kind of modesty she had covered it with her straw peasant hat." Fowler asks Pyle how many such deaths he would accept in "building a national democratic front." Pyle responds: "Anyway, they died in the right cause. . . . They died for democracy."

Bush would never say something like that, but plenty of Greene's comments about Pyle would apply to him. (Phillip Noyce, director of the recent film based on the book, has said, "Bush is the ultimate Alden Pyle.") Greene's description of the character even sounds like the young Bush, with a crew cut and a "wide campus gaze." If only he were merely "reading the Sunday supplements at home and following the baseball" instead of mucking around in foreign lands.

Pyle, he writes, was "impregnably armoured by his good intentions and his ignorance. . . . Innocence is like a dumb leper who has lost his bell, wandering the world, meaning no harm. You can't blame the innocent, they are always guiltless. All you can do is control them or eliminate them. Innocence is a kind of insanity."

Long before that, Greene had opened his novel with a few lines from Byron:

> *This is the patent age of new inventions*
> *For killing bodies, and for saving souls*
> *All propagated with the best intentions.*

Or as Greene himself wrote of a character in *The Heart of the Matter*, another novel: "He entered the territory of lies without a passport for return."

SEPTEMBER

The media, during the first days of September, lavished attention, some of it skeptical, on the forthcoming report by Gen. David Petraeus to the president and Congress on the success of the "surge." Did anyone ever really expect General Petraeus to give General Petraeus a poor grade? If only the press had provided even one-tenth of that critical coverage back in January, when the most tragic turning point since the invasion of Iraq came and went with the Bush decision to escalate. As predicted, Petraeus, and then Bush, endorsed a full continuance, with a promise of token withdrawals by the end of the year (if everything kept "going well"). Not surprisingly, our old friend Michael Gordon of The New York Times *provided the key pro-surge coverage. Tom Ricks and Karen DeYoung summed it up in* The Washington Post *on September 11: "If Gen. David H. Petraeus has his way, tens of thousands of U.S. troops will be in Iraq for years to come."*

Congress responded by finally passing a tough resoluoion—condemning MoveOn.org for a newspaper ad that attacked Petraeus. Some things, indeed, never seemed to change. A new poll, sponsored by ABC News and the BBC, among others, found that 57 percent of Iraqis still supported attacks on U.S. forces in their country. And a CBS/New York Times poll found that one in three Americans, including 40 percent of Republicans, still believed that Saddam was involved in the 9/11 terrorist attacks.

"Op-Ed Soldiers" Die—as Petraeus and Bush Surge Ahead

SEPTEMBER 13, 2007

When Gen. David Petraeus appeared before the Senate Foreign Relations Committee this week to defend his call for a continuation of the "surge" for many more months, Sen. Chuck Hagel (R-Neb.) said, "By the way, I assume you read *The New York Times* piece two weeks ago—seven NCOs in Iraq, today, finishing up 15-month commitments. Are we going to dismiss those seven NCOs? Are they ignorant?"

The Op-Ed by seven active duty U.S. soldiers in Iraq questioning the war drew international attention just three weeks ago. Now two of the seven are dead. The day before Petraeus's testimony, Sgt. Omar Mora and Sgt. Yance T. Gray died in a vehicle rollover accident in western Baghdad, two of seven U.S. troops killed in the incident. The names have just been released.

The controversial *Times* column on Aug. 19 was called "The War as We Saw It," and expressed skepticism about American gains in Iraq. "To believe that Americans, with an occupying force that long ago outlived its reluctant welcome, can win over a recalcitrant local population and win this counterinsurgency is far-fetched," the group wrote.

The U.S presence "may have released Iraqis from the grip of a tyrant, but . . . it has also robbed them of their self-respect. They will soon realize that the best way to regain dignity is to call us what we are—an army of occupation—and force our withdrawal. . . . Until that happens, it would be prudent for us to increasingly let Iraqis take center stage in all matters, to come up with a nuanced policy in which we assist them from the margins but let them resolve their differences as they see fit."

It closed: "We need not talk about our morale. As committed soldiers, we will see this mission through." As it turns out, two of them did not get the chance.

Mora, 28, hailed from Texas City, Texas, and was a native of Ecuador who had just become a U.S. citizen. He was due to leave Iraq in November and leaves behind a wife and daughter. Gray, 26, had lived in Ismay, Montana, and is also survived by a wife and infant daughter.

The Daily News in Galveston interviewed Mora's mother, who confirmed he was one of the co-authors of the *Times* piece. The article today relates: "Olga Capetillo said that by the time Mora submitted the editorial, he had grown increasingly depressed. 'I told him God is going to take care of him and take him home,' she said. 'But yesterday is the darkest day for me.'"

One of the other five authors of the *Times* piece, Staff Sergeant Jeremy Murphy, an Army Ranger and reconnaissance team leader, was shot in the head while the article was being written. He was expected to survive after being flown to a military hospital in the United States.

So much for war proponent arguments that the U.S. casualty toll is "relatively low" in this conflict.

"Everybody has a right to speak out," Robert Capetillo, father of Omar Mora, told *E&P* today. "We all have a right to speak out what we feel. There are personal feelings; that is a right here we all have."

Richard Gray, father of Yance Gray, offered similar views on his son's part in the column. "I thought it was well-written and there wasn't anything in it I disagreed with, with that situation over there," he said via phone to *E&P*'s Joe Strupp from his Montana home. "He said once that they need to divide the country up into three different countries to make things work."

Gray was not surprised when he heard about his son's involvement in the column. "He thought for himself. He wouldn't just go along. The military was something he wanted to do, but he would not follow something blindly. He was taught to think for himself. . . . He was not in any way anti-military," Gray said. "But he wasn't somebody to follow along blindly."

Andrew Rosenthal, editor of the editorial page at the *Times*, told Strupp, "It was a really wonderful piece, we thought. I am proud of them. We had heard they got some grief from bosses about writing about this. But this is the twenty-first century and people communicate with each other. Not every soldier in Iraq buys this Potemkin war that they are selling."

Sen. Barbara Boxer (D-Ca.), who had also mentioned the Op-Ed in questioning Petraeus, sent President Bush a letter today, observing, "The tragic irony is that before their deaths, these two soldiers were not only trying to give us direction on how to end this war honorably, but they were also calling on us for help.

"I hope you will follow this advice and institute a new policy in which the Iraqis take center stage in defending their own country, thus avoiding the stigma of occupation that is now attached to our troops. This would allow for the immediate redeployment of the vast majority of our soldiers. . . . Mr. President, you didn't listen to Staff Sergeant Yance Gray and Sergeant Omar Mora while they were alive. I hope that you will listen to them now, as they have paid the ultimate sacrifice for our country."

OCTOBER

The Miami Herald *and* St. Petersburg Times *in editorials called for U.S. disengagement in Iraq, with the latter declaring that the "time has come to end Bush's failed Iraq war." The GOP campaign against the MoveOn.org "General Petraeus/Betray Us" ad continued, with Dick Cheney calling it an "outrage." The U.S. Senate passed a resolution hitting the group—while failing to move against the war. In a TV appearance, Thomas Ricks of* The Washington Post *said he wouldn't be surprised if "we have troops still fighting in Iraq" when the next president's term ends—his second term, that is. After years of acting as a private army in Iraq, Blackwater finally came under attack from U.S. officials, the military, and the press for its "cowboy" attitude and its attacks on Iraqi civilians. Valerie Plame Wilson, with a book just out, told the media—again—that allegations that she was not "covert" when outed by Robert Novak and the White House were false and absurd. She also criticized* The Washington Post *editorial page for asserting that her husband had done more than anyone to destroy her career, saying that when she saw the editorial she thought she was reading* Pravda.

The civilian death toll in Iraq seemed to be declining, but was it mainly because ethnic cleansing had largely been completed and millions had already fled the country? The U.S. toll was also down—but with a troubling twist.

Dying in the Dark—in the "Non-combat" Zone
OCTOBER 23, 2007

Nearly alone in the media, *E&P* for weeks had been charting a sudden increase in non-combat deaths among U.S. troops in Iraq. So it came as a surprise last week when the Pentagon announced that it would probe the perplexing trend. Lt. Gen. Carter Ham, operations director of the Joint Staff, said commanders in Iraq were concerned enough about the spike in non-combat deaths—from accidents, illness, friendly fire, or suicide—that it had asked for an assessment by an Army team.

According to Pentagon figures, 29 soldiers lost their lives in August for non-hostile reasons, and another 23 died of non-combat causes in September. Compare that with the average for the first six months of this year: fewer than nine per month. The spike has coincided with extended 15-month deployments, one senior military official admitted. The military has officially confirmed 130 suicides in Iraq since 2003, with many others under investigation.

Ham said morale remains high, but added, "I think there is a general consensus . . . that for the Army, 15 months is a long hard tour. It's hard on the soldiers and their families."

As I've noted before, the military releases little news to the press when a service member dies from a non-hostile cause, beyond saying it is "under investigation." When that probe ends, many months later, the military normally does not tell anyone but family members of the deceased. Nearly every day lately, I have combed the Web for details on new cases. Sometimes local newspapers find out about preliminary determinations—including suicides—passed along to families.

So I keep checking, for example, on October casualties Vincent Kamka, Dr. Roselle Hoffmaster, and Erik T. Garoutte. There's a new one today: a Michael D. Brown, who died in Landstuhl from an unspecified illness. I'm still trying to find out what really happened to Ciara Durkin, who gained some national attention recently when her family charged that the bullet found in her brain was fired by someone other than herself.

She may have committed suicide, but her family can't fathom that at all. Durkin was gay, always a problem in the don't-ask-don't-tell military. Back home on leave recently, she had mentioned to her family fears that she had "enemies." Not long before that, Durkin (while in Afghanistan) wrote a chilling e-mail to a friend in Massachusetts: "Ok. so today a crazy soldier pulled a 9mm on me . . . don't go telling people. . . . he's in jail and I'm doing better."

As I write this, there have been 3,834 confirmed deaths among U.S. troops in Iraq, more than 700 from non-hostile causes. The authoritative Web site on Iraq coalition casualties, www.icasualties.org, reveals that more than 7,500 of those injured in a non-hostile incident since 2003 required "medical transport." This is nearly as high as the 8,400 wounded in battle who needed to be evacuated.

But why has the press given this disturbing aspect of the war so little attention, going back to the early days of the war? Paul Rieckhoff, an Iraq vet and now leader of the Iraq and Afghanistan Veterans of America, has long shared my concerns and frustration.

Rieckhoff, author of the memoir *Chasing Ghosts*, calls this "one of the most under-reported stories of the war. I've been pitching the story to people for over two years. A lot of deaths are taking place under questionable circumstances—the number would surprise you—and no one looks at them, in theater or at home. It's a broad research project, and maybe it is not sexy, but it needs to be done."

The Veterans Administration doesn't track the deaths, Rieckhoff says. "I'd like to see a study of how many Iraq vets have died under any circumstance back in this country," he declares. "We have suicide rates tracked in the military, but once they leave it is untraced. We have argued for a national registry, if you have been in the war.

"Nobody has ever taken the step of pulling it all together. I know it would be expensive, time-consuming, and difficult for the media, but it is their responsibility. They did it with body armor, with corruption, now with Blackwater. Blackwater! I knew something was wrong with them way back when I was over there.

"You could at least do a clustering, like around Fort Bragg—look at the deaths of all veterans within a 100-mile radius. If we could fund it, we would, but our group is too small."

What is his theory about the recent spike? "We know that our people are under tremendous stress," he replies. "The operational tempo is unprecedented. I met a guy in a bar who has been there eight times. He said, 'Thank God I am young and single.' We can push them harder, but is it smart? I don't think it is smart or right."

The surge in non-hostile deaths does not mean just suicides, but accidents due to overwork. Soldiers don't have a union like police and firemen, Rieckhoff points out. Federal agencies such as the Occupational Safety and Health Administration "would have a field day with working conditions," he adds.

Why has there been so little coverage? "I know access to the battle zone is an issue," he admits. "And dealing with families is delicate, but you can still handle that sensitively." But he also cites what he calls a cultural issue: "After World War II, a lot of vets went into media and could navigate the system. Now so few

October 2007

reporters have served. Many don't know the difference between a brigade and a battalion. Also there is fear of how it is going to play in the pro- or anti-war debate. But this is not a partisan issue. Either way—get to the bottom of this.

"American people don't know a lot about these issues. People abroad ask me, are Americans stupid? I say, 'No, they just aren't told enough.'"

SOURCE NOTES
REFERENCED IN THE ARTICLES

(order follows appearance in the text)

2003

January
On the War Path
Michael Getler, "Get Ready for Some Football, and War?" *The Washington Post*, January 12, 2003.

February
Powell Conquers the Media
Bill Schneider, *CNN Live Today*, February 6, 2003.

Bob Woodward, "Analysis of Colin Powell's Speech Before the U.N.," interview by Larry King, *Larry King Live*, CNN, February 5, 2003.

George Will, "Disregarding the Deniers," *The Washington Post*, February 6, 2003.

Mark Jurkowitz, "Powell's U.N. Speech Proves Persuasive for Commentators," *The Boston Globe*, February 13, 2003.

Editorial, "A Strong Case, but for War?" *San Francisco Chronicle*, February 6, 2003.

Editorial, "U.N. Should Heed Powell," *The Denver Post*, February 6, 2003.

Editorial, "Powell Masterfully Presents Case Against Outlaw Hussein," *The Tampa Tribune*, February 6, 2003.

Editorial, "The Facts Accumulate Over Iraq," *The Oregonian*, February 6, 2003.

Editorial, "Powell Makes a Strong Case—but Not for All-Out War," *San Jose Mercury News*, February 6, 2003.

Editorial, "Our Turn: Powell's Case Persuasive that Iraq Poses a Threat," *San Antonio Express-News*, February 6, 2003.

Editorial, "Irrefutable," *The Washington Post*, February 6, 2003.

Jim Hoagland, "An Old Trooper's Smoking Gun," *The Washington Post*, February 6, 2003.

Mary McGrory, "I'm Persuaded," *The Washington Post*, February 6, 2003.

Richard Cohen, "A Winning Hand for Powell," *The Washington Post*, February 6, 2003.

Editorial, "The Case Against Iraq," *The New York Times*, February 6, 2003.

Steven R. Weisman, "Threats and Responses: Security Council; Powell, in U.N. Speech, Presents Case to Show Iraq Has Not Disarmed," *The New York Times*, February 6, 2003.

Adam Clymer, "Threats and Responses: The History; a Reprise of 1962, with Less Electricity," *The New York Times*, February 6, 2003.

Michael R. Gordon, "Threats and Responses: News Analysis; Powell's Trademark: Overwhelm Them," *The New York Times*, February 6, 2003.

Editorial, "Iraqi Proof: Only the Blind Could Ignore Powell's Evidence," *The Dallas Morning News*, February 6, 2003.

Editorial, "Powell Lays out Convincing Evidence of Iraq's Defiance," *USA Today*, February 5, 2003.

March
Rummy Meets McNamara
Julie Hinds, "War Close-up May Not Be Showing the Big Picture," Knight Ridder/Tribune News, March 26, 2003.

April
Moyers: Beginning of the End—or Just the Beginning?
Greg Mitchell, "Politics and Economy," interview by Bill Moyers, *NOW*, PBS, April 4, 2003.

May
Back in the Daze of Mission Accomplished
Chris Matthews, *Hardball*, MSNBC, May 1, 2003. [Transcript not available online.]

Elisabeth Bumiller, "Aftereffects: News Analysis; Cold Truths Behind Pomp," *The New York Times*, May 2, 2003.

Michael R. Gordon and Eric Schmitt, "Aftereffects: The New Strategy; U.S. Plans to Reduce Forces in Iraq with Help of Allies," *The New York Times*, May 3, 2003.

Dexter Filkins and Ian Fisher, "Aftereffects: A Nation's Future; U.S. Is Now in Battle for Peace After Winning the War in Iraq," *The New York Times*, May 3, 2003.

David E. Sanger, "Aftereffects: The President; Bush Declares 'One Victory in a War on Terror,'" *The New York Times*, May 3, 2003.

Editorial, "A Long Way from Victory," *The New York Times*, May 2, 2003.

Martin Deppe, Letter to the Editor, *The New York Times*, May 3, 2003.

David E. Sanger, "Aftereffects: The President; Bush Says It Will Take Time to Find Iraq's Banned Arms," *The New York Times*, May 4, 2003.

Maureen Dowd, "The Iceman Cometh," *The New York Times*, May 4, 2003.

Thomas Friedman, "Our New Baby," *The New York Times*, May 4, 2003.

The New York Times, "New American Deaths in Iraq," May 6, 2003.

September
Why We Are in Iraq
Charles J. Hanley, Associated Press, August 9, 2003.

On the Second Anniversary of 9/11
Associated Press, "Poll: 70 Percent Believe Saddam, 9-11 Link," *USA Today*, September 6, 2003.

2004

February
How We Treat the Injured
Sara Corbett, "The Permanent Scars of Iraq," *The New York Times Magazine*, February 15, 2004.

Theola Labbe, "Suicides in Iraq, Questions at Home: Pentagon Tight-Lipped as Self-Inflicted Deaths Mount in Military," *The Washington Post*, February 19, 2004.

March
Did You Hear the One About the Missing WMD?
Jennifer Frey, "George Bush, Entertainer in Chief: At Radio-TV Dinner, President Competes with Trump's Show," *The Washington Post*, March 25, 2004.

Associated Press, "Bush Pokes Fun at Himself, Staff: Mock Slide Show Featured at Dinner," MSNBC, March 25, 2004. http://www.msnbc.msn.com/id/4596717/

April
Good Morning, Vietnam
Bill O'Reilly, "Continuing Chaos in Iraq," *Talking Points*, Fox News, April 6, 2004.

Patrick Buchanan, "Is Failure Now an Option?" *The American Cause*, April 7, 2004. http://www.theamericancause.org/patisfailurenowanoption.htm

Coffin Fit
The Seattle Times, "Father Believes Son Among Dead Depicted in Controversial Coffin Photo," April 28, 2004.

May

Why Did the Press Ignore Early Report on Abu Ghraib?
Charles J. Hanley, "Former Iraqi Detainees Tell of Riots,
Punishment in the Sun, Good Americans, and Pitiless Ones,"
Associated Press, November 1, 2003.

A Rare Call for Withdrawal
Al Neuharth, "Should Cowboy Bush Ride into the Sunset?" *USA
Today*, May 15, 2004.

Rush Limbaugh, Abe Rosenthal, and Me
Abe M. Rosenthal, "Insulting the Victims," *New York Sun*, May 18,
2004.

About Times: *It Finally Accepts Blame on WMD*
Editorial, "From the Editors; The *Times* and Iraq," *The New York
Times*, May 26, 2004.

July

The Pluck of the Irish
Carole Coleman, "President George W. Bush," *Prime Time*, RTE,
June 24, 2004. http://www.rte.ie/news/2004/0624/primetime.html

Jim Dee, "Bush, E.U. Reps Meet Behind Walls of Castle," *Boston
Herald*, June 26, 2004.

Susan Falvella-Garraty, "Politicus Interruptus: Prez's Media
Handlers Complain to Embassy About RTE Interview," *The Irish
Echo*, June 30–July 6, 2004 issue.

August

Post *War Apology Falls Short*
Howard Kurtz, "The Post on WMDs: An Inside Story: Prewar
Articles Questioning Threat Often Didn't Make Front Page," *The
Washington Post*, August 12, 2004.

November

From Fallujah to Landstuhl: What About the Wounded?
Robert F. Worth, "As Fire Crackles in Fallujah, G.I.'s Look to
Rebuild a Wasteland," *The New York Times*, November 17, 2004.

Jackie Spinner, "Fallujah Battered and Mostly Quiet after the
Battle," *The Washington Post*, November 16, 2004.

Dexter Filkins, "In City's Ruins, Military Faces New Mission: Building Trust," *The New York Times*, November 16, 2004.

2005

January
Rathergate vs. Weaponsgate
Colin Powell, "Newsmaker: Colin Powell," interview by Jim Lehrer, *NewsHour with Jim Lehrer*, PBS, January 13, 2005.

Editorial, "Bulletin: No WMD Found," *The New York Times*, January 13, 2005.

Declare Victory—and Pull Out
Joseph L. Galloway, "Vote, Declare Victory, and Come Home," *The Philadelphia Inquirer*, January 5, 2005.

May
No Pat Answers in the Tillman Case
Josh White, "Tillman's Parents Are Critical of Army: Family Questions Reversal of Cause of Ranger's Death," *The Washington Post*, May 23, 2005.

Steve Coll, "Army Spun Tale Around Ill-Fated Mission," *The Washington Post*, December 6, 2004.

July
Plame Gets the "-Gate"
David Johnston and Richard Stevenson, "Rove Reportedly Held Phone Talk on CIA Officer," *The New York Times*, July 15, 2005.

Craig Crawford, "Quantum Leak," *The Huffington Post*, July 15, 2005.

Why the Pentagon Is Blocking Abu Ghraib Images
John King, Jamie McIntyre, Ed Henry, and Dana Bash, "Rumsfeld: Unreleased Images 'Cruel and Inhuman,'" CNN, May 8, 2004.

August
Cindy Sheehan and the Lost Boys
W. Leon Smith, "Bill Mitchell, Whose Son Was Killed Same Day as Cindy's, Flies to Texas from California to Offer Support: *Iconoclast* Publisher Makes Midnight Visit to Camp Casey," *The Lone Star Iconoclast*, August 10, 2005.

October
The Scooter and Judy Soap Opera: "As the Aspens Turn"
David Ignatius, "Lessons of the Miller Affair," *The Washington Post*, October 5, 2005.

Times Drops Bombshell—on Judy Miller
Don Van Natta, Jr., Adam Liptak, and Clifford J. Levy, "The Miller Case: A Notebook, a Cause, a Jail Cell, and a Deal," *The New York Times*, October 16, 2005.

Judith Miller, "A Personal Account: My Four Hours Testifying in the Federal Grand Jury Room," *The New York Times*, October 16, 2005.

Time to End Miller's High Life
Maureen Dowd, "Woman of Mass Destruction," *The New York Times*, October 22, 2005.

Byron E. "Barney" Calame, "The Miller Mess: Lingering Issues Among the Answers," *The New York Times*, October 23, 2005.

November
Murtha Speaks Out—a "Cronkite Moment"?
Rod Dreher, "Murtha Breaks," *National Review Online*, November 17, 2005.

2006

February
Oprah "Freys" George W. Bush
Eugene Robinson, "Into the Freying Pan," *The Washington Post*, January 31, 2006.

Norman Solomon, "Domestic Lying: The Question that Journalists Don't Ask Bush," *The Huffington Post*, January 29, 2006.

March
David Brooks Plays Rummy
David Brooks, "Rumsfeld's Blinkers," *The New York Times*, March 16, 2006.

David Brooks, "The Certainty Crisis: George W. Bush's Waffle-Free Directness Alarms the Fashionably Doubtful Commentariat," *London Times*, March 7, 2003.

David Brooks, "Game Over," *The Weekly Standard*, March 24, 2003.

Editorial, "Picking up the Pieces in Iraq," *International Herald Tribune*, March 20, 2006.

On Third Anniversary: Editorials Dither While Iraq Dies
Editorial, "The Stuff that Happened," *The New York Times*, March 19, 2006.

Editorial, "One Year After," *The New York Times*, March 19, 2004.

Donald Rumsfeld, "What We've Gained in Three Years in Iraq," *The Washington Post*, March 19, 2006.

Editorial, "Shock, Awe, and Humility," *Los Angeles Times*, March 19, 2006.

April
Even Stephen: Colbert Roasts President—and the Press
"White House Correspondents Dinner," C-SPAN, April 29, 2006.

May
Neil Young and the Restless
J. Freedom du Lac, "Neil Young's Anti-War Howl," *The Washington Post*, May 3, 2006.

John Gibson, "Neil Young and Pink Blame Wrong Leaders," Fox News, April 28, 2006.

A History of the "Friedman Unit"
Fairness in Accuracy and Reporting (FAIR), "Tom Friedman's Flexible Deadlines," May 16, 2006.

Thomas Friedman, "The Chant Not Heard," *The New York Times*, November 30, 2003.

Thomas Friedman, "The Last Mile," *The New York Times*, November 28, 2004.

June
Media Slow to Probe Haditha
Hamza Hendawi, "Alleged U.S. Misconduct Adds to Iraqi Woes," Associated Press, June 4, 2006.

Thomas E. Ricks, "In Haditha Killings, Details Came Slowly: Official Version Is at Odds with Evidence," *The Washington Post*, June 4, 2006.

John F. Burns, "Getting Used to War as Hell," *The New York Times*, June 4, 2006.

Mark Mazzetti, "War's Risks Include Toll on Training Values," *The New York Times*, June 4, 2006.

Dead and Loving It: Media Air Graphic Images of Zarqawi
New York Post, "Gotcha!—How America Killed a Master Terrorist," June 9, 2006.

Philip Kennicott, "A Chilling Portrait, Unsuitably Framed," *The Washington Post*, June 9, 2006.

David Zurawik and Nick Madigan, "TV Stations, Web Sites Exercise Little Restraint," *The Sun* (of Baltimore), June 9, 2006.

The Cost of Killing Civilians
Bryan Bender, "Condolence Payments to Iraqis Soar," *The Boston Globe*, June 8, 2006.

Bruce Springsteen vs. Ann Coulter
Bruce Springsteen, "The Boss' New Tune," interview by Soledad O'Brien, CNN, June 23, 2006.

September
A Comma or a Coma?
George W. Bush, "The Situation Room: Exclusive Interview with President Bush," interview by Wolf Blitzer, CNN, September 20, 2006.

October
Will the Media Finally Count the Dead?
Malcolm Ritter, "Study: 655,000 Iraqis Died Due to War," Associated Press, October 10, 2006.

Mara Liasson and Lynn Neary, "Bush: North Korea Faces 'Serious Repercussions,'" NPR, October 11, 2006. http://www.npr.org/templates/story/story.php?storyId=6247253

David Brown, "Study Claims Iraq's 'Excess' Death Toll Has Reached 655,000," *The Washington Post*, October 11, 2006.

Bush Among Friends
U.S. News & World Report, "Transcript: The President's Interview with Print Media Columnists," October 25, 2006. http://www.usnews.com/usnews/news/articles/061025/25bushtranscript.htm

November
She Killed Herself—After Objecting to Torture Techniques
Larry Hendricks, "Flagstaff Soldier Killed Self After Protest," *The Arizona Daily Sun*, November 2, 2006.

Kayla and Alyssa: Why One Survived
Kayla Williams, "President Bush Declassifies Sections of National Intelligence Estimate; Condoleezza Rice Takes on Bill Clinton; Rewriting Rules on Torture," interview by Soledad O'Brien, *Paula Zahn Now*, CNN, September 26, 2006.

Kayla Williams, interview, CNN, October 8, 2005. [Transcript not available online.]

She Outlived Iraq—Then Killed Herself at Home
Kate Gurnett, "A Casualty Far from the Battlefield," *Times Union* (Albany), November 13, 2006.

December
The Last Soldier to Die for a Mistake
Christian Davenport and Joshua Partlow, "Like the Nation, Military Families Divided on Iraq," *The Washington Post*, December 10, 2006.

Media Leave Audience Hanging
Bill Carter, "How Much Should Be Shown of a Hanging? Network Executives Wonder and Wait," *The New York Times*, December 30, 2006.

Editorial, "The Rush to Hang Saddam Hussein," *The New York Times*, December 29, 2006.

Bill Carter, "Hard Choices Over Video of Execution," *The New York Times*, January 1, 2007.

2007

January
Surge Protectors
Editorial, "The Ugly Death of Saddam Hussein," *The New York Times*, January 4, 2007.

Charles Krauthammer, "The Hanging: Beyond Travesty," *The Washington Post*, January 5, 2007.

Editorial, "A 'Surge' in Iraq?" *The Washington Post*, January 7, 2007.

Editorial, "The Imperial Presidency 2.0," *The New York Times*, January 7, 2007.

March
A Washington Post *Editorial as a* Daily Show *Routine*
Editorial, "The Libby Verdict: The Serious Consequences of a Pointless Washington Scandal," *The Washington Post*, March 7, 2007.

General Petraeus and a High-Profile Suicide
T. Christian Miller, "The Conflict in Iraq; A Journey that Ended in Anguish," *Los Angeles Times*, November 27, 2005.

Robert Bryce, "I Am Sullied—No More," *The Texas Observer*, March 9, 2007.

Press Covers Plame's Wardrobe—Ignores Cover-up
Mary Ann Akers, "Hearing Room Chic," *The Washington Post*, March 16, 2007.

Mark Leibovich and Neil A. Lewis, " 'Purely Political Motives' in Outing, Ex-Agent Says," *The New York Times*, March 17, 2007.

April
A Woman's Dentures in the Dirt
Edward Wong, "Iraqi Widow Saves Her Home, but Victory Is Brief," *The New York Times*, March 30, 2007.

Has "Straight Talk" by Media Derailed McCain?
Sudarshan Raghavan, "Sum of Death Statistics: A Perilous Iraq," *The Washington Post*, April 4, 2007.

"Sorry We Shot Your Kid, but Here's $500"
Bryan Bender, "Condolence Payments to Iraqis Soar," *The Boston Globe*, June 8, 2006.

Paul Von Zeilbauer, "The Reach of War; Civilian Claims on U.S. Suggest the Toll of War," *The New York Times*, April 12, 2007.

Moyers Returns with "Devastating" Probe
Bill Moyers, "Buying the War," *Bill Moyers Journal*, PBS, April 25, 2007.

June
Better Late than Never: A Major Paper Calls for Pullout
Editorial, "Bring Them Home," *Los Angeles Times*, May 6, 2007.

A Rare Look at One Civilian Casualty
Tina Susman, "Civilian Casualties Rise in Iraq," *Los Angeles Times*, June 18, 2007.

July
Haven't We Been Through This Movie Before?
John F. Burns and Michael R. Gordon, "U.S. Says Iran Helped
Iraqis Kill Five G.I.'s," *The New York Times*, July 3, 2007.

From Hanging with George Clooney to Hanging Bad Guys in Iraq
Tina Susman, "The Conflict in Iraq: From Auditions to
Executions," *Los Angeles Times*, July 22, 2007.

Rebecca Markway, "Alumnus Selected to Help Rebuild Iraqi
Homeland," *Daily Reveille*, April 23, 2003.

August
Why Aren't the Media on a Suicide Watch?
Marlena Hartz, "Death of Slaton Soldier in Iraq Draws Scrutiny,"
The Lubbock Avalanche-Journal, July 6, 2007.

Lisa Chekedel and Matthew Kauffman, "Army's Suicide Struggles
Continue," *The Hartford Courant*, January 31, 2007.

Stephen Speckman, "VA Offers New Suicide-Prevention Hotline,"
Deseret Morning News, August 6, 2007.

George Bush Meets Graham Greene
"President Bush Attends Veterans of Foreign Wars National
Convention, Discusses War on Terror," Office of the White
House Press Secretary, August 22, 2007.
http://www.whitehouse.gov/news/releases/2007/08/
20070822-3.html

September
"Op-Ed Soldiers" Die—As Petraeus and Bush Surge Ahead
Buddhika Jayamaya, Wesley D. Smith, Jeremy Roebuck, Omar
Mora, Edward Sandmeier, Yance T. Gray, and Jeremy A. Murphy,
"The War as We Saw It," *The New York Times*, August 19, 2007.

ABOUT THE AUTHOR AND CONTRIBUTORS

Greg Mitchell is the editor of *Editor & Publisher*, the journal of the newspaper business that has won several major awards for its coverage of Iraq and the media. He has written eight books, including *Hiroshima in America* (with Robert Jay Lifton), *The Campaign of the Century: Upton Sinclair's Race for Governor of California and the Birth of Media Politics* (winner of the Goldsmith Book Prize), and *Tricky Dick and the Pink Lady: Richard Nixon vs. Helen Gahagan Douglas*. Articles have appeared in dozens of leading newspapers and magazines. He lives in the New York City area.

Joseph L. Galloway is one of the most respected war correspondents of our time and currently writes a syndicated column on military affairs. He co-authored the bestselling *We Were Soldiers Once . . . and Young* and *We Are Soldiers Still*. He was awarded a Bronze Star for valor in Vietnam.

Bruce Springsteen has won fifteen Grammy Awards and an Oscar. He has sold over 60 million albums in the United States, and was inducted into the Rock and Roll Hall of Fame and the Songwriters Hall of Fame in 1999.

INDEX